The Institute of Chartered Accountants in England and Wales

LAW

For exams in 2014

Study Manual

www.icaew.com

ICAEW

Law
The Institute of Chartered Accountants in England and Wales

ISBN: 978-0-85760-818-5

Previous ISBN: 978-0-85760-454-5

First edition 2007
Seventh edition 2013

British Library Cataloguing-in-Publication Data
A catalogue record for this book is available from the British Library

Printed in the United Kingdom by Polestar Wheatons

Polestar Wheatons
Hennock Road
Marsh Barton
Exeter
EX2 8RP

Your learning materials are printed on paper obtained from traceable,
sustainable sources.

Welcome to ICAEW

I am delighted that you have chosen to study for the ICAEW Certificate in Finance, Accounting and Business (ICAEW CFAB), or our world-leading chartered accountancy qualification, the ACA.

ICAEW CFAB provides key practical skills and essential knowledge for today's competitive business world. It is a stand-alone qualification that consists of the Certificate Level of the ACA qualification, so it can also be a stepping stone to achieving the ACA.

The ACA is one of the most advanced learning and professional development programmes available. Its integrated components provide an in-depth understanding across accountancy, finance and business. Combined, they help build the technical knowledge, professional skills and practical experience needed to become an ICAEW Chartered Accountant.

Accountants have been providing financial information to organisations for hundreds of years. Today, organisations of every size around the world depend on the skill and expertise of chartered accountants. They are respected for their understanding of complex financial information, and trusted for their strategic business advice.

As part of a worldwide network of over 19,000 students, you will have access to a range of resources and support as you progress through the ACA. Take a look at the key resources available to you on page ix.

I wish you the very best of luck with your studies; we are with you every step of the way.

Michael Izza
Chief Executive
ICAEW

Contents

1 Introduction

ACA Overview

The ICAEW chartered accountancy qualification, the ACA, is one of the most advanced learning and professional development programmes available. Its integrated components provide you with an in-depth understanding across accountancy, finance and business. Combined, they help build the technical knowledge, professional skills and practical experience needed to become an ICAEW Chartered Accountant.

Each component is designed to complement each other, which means that students put theory into practice and can understand and apply what they learn to their day-to-day work. The components are:

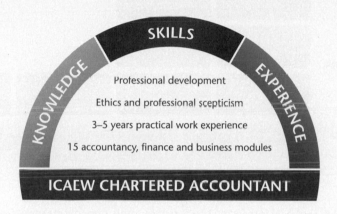

Professional development

ICAEW Chartered Accountants are known for their professionalism and expertise. Professional development will prepare you to successfully handle a variety of different situations that you'll encounter throughout your career.

The ACA qualification improves your ability and performance in seven key areas:

* adding value
* communication
* consideration
* decision making
* problem solving
* team working
* technical competence.

Ethics and professional scepticism

Ethics is more than just knowing the rules around confidentiality, integrity, objectivity and independence.

It's about identifying ethical dilemmas, understanding the implications and behaving appropriately. We integrate ethics throughout the ACA qualification to develop your ethical capabilities – so you'll always know how to make the right decisions and justify them.

3-5 years practical work experience

Practical work experience is done as part of a training agreement with one of our 2,850 authorised training employers around the world. You need to complete 450 days, which normally takes between three and five years. The knowledge, skills and experience you gain as part of your training agreement are invaluable, giving you the opportunity to put what you're learning into practice.

15 accountancy, finance and business modules

You will gain in-depth knowledge across a broad range of topics in accountancy, finance and business. The modules are designed to fit with your practical experience, so you constantly progress through the qualification.

There are 15 modules over three levels. These can be taken in any order with the exception of the Case Study which has to be attempted last. You must pass every exam (or receive credit) – there are no options. This ensures that once qualified, all ICAEW Chartered Accountants have a consistent level of knowledge, skills and experience.

Certificate Level

There are six modules that will introduce the fundamentals of accountancy, finance and business.

They each have a 1.5 hour computer-based assessment which can be sat at any time. You may be eligible for credit for some modules if you have studied accounting, finance, law or business at degree level or through another professional qualification.

These six modules are also available as a stand-alone certificate, the ICAEW Certificate in Finance, Accounting and Business (ICAEW CFAB). If you are studying for this certificate, you will only complete the first six modules. On successful completion, the ICAEW CFAB can be used as a stepping stone to studying for the ACA.

Professional Level

The next six modules build on the fundamentals and test your understanding and ability to use technical knowledge in real-life scenarios. Each module has a 2.5–3 hour exam, which are available to sit four times per year. These modules are flexible and can be taken in any order. The Business Planning: Taxation and Business Strategy modules in particular will help you to progress to the Advanced Level.

Advanced Level

The Advanced Level module of Corporate Reporting requires you to apply the technical knowledge you have built at Professional Level, along with analytical techniques and professional skills, to resolve compliance and business issues that arise in the context of the preparation and evaluation of corporate reports and from providing audit services. At the Strategic Business Management module, you will need to demonstrate quantitative and qualitative skills to make realistic business recommendations in complex scenarios. You will also need to demonstrate business awareness at strategic, operating and transactional levels. These modules have a 3.5 hour exam and are available to sit twice a year.

The Case Study will require you to provide advice in respect of complex business issues, and will assess your ability to analyse financial and non-financial data, exercise professional and ethical judgement, and develop conclusions and recommendations. The Case Study is a 4 hour exam and is available to sit twice a year.

The preceding diagram illustrates how the knowledge of law principles gives a platform from which a progression of skills and accounting expertise is developed.

The Advanced Level exams are fully open book, so they replicate a real-life scenario where all the resources are at your fingertips.

For more information on the ACA qualification exam structure and syllabus, visit icaew.com/students

2 Law

2.1 Module aim

To provide students with an understanding of the principles of English law.

On completion of this module, students will be able to:

- explain the nature of contractual agreements, the agency relationship and the consequences of negligence

- understand the legal implications of incorporation, including the roles of shareholders and directors, and the main implications of insolvency law

- identify instances of criminal behaviour that may be encountered by professional accountants

- identify other key areas in which the law affects the role and work of the professional accountant.

2.2 Specification grid

This grid shows the relative weightings of subjects within this module and should guide the relative study time spent on each. Over time the marks available in the assessment will equate to the weightings below, while slight variations may occur in individual assessments to enable suitably rigorous questions to be set.

Syllabus area	Weighting (%)
1 The impact of civil law on business and professional services	35
2 Company and insolvency law	40
3 The impact of criminal law on business and professional services	10
4 The impact of law in the professional context	15
	100

3 Key Resources

Student support team

Our student support team are here to help you as much as possible, providing full support throughout your studies.

T +44 (0)1908 248 250

F +44 (0)1908 248 069

E studentsupport@icaew.com

Student website

The student area of our website provides you with information on exam applications, deadlines, results and regulations as well as applying for credit for prior learning (CPL)/exemptions. The study resources section includes advice from the examiners, module syllabi, past papers and sample papers, webinars and study guides. The study guides are designed to help put the learning for each module into context and highlight the practical significance of what you'll learn. They also include the syllabus, technical knowledge grids and learning outcomes for each module, enabling you to gain an overview of how your learning links to the qualification. Visit icaew.com/students for these resources and more.

Online student community

The online student community is a forum to ask questions, gain study and exam

advice from fellow ACA and CFAB students and access our free webinars. There are also

regular Ask a Tutor sessions to help you with key technical topics and exam papers. Access the community at icaew.com/studentcommunity

Tuition

The ICAEW Partner in Learning scheme recognises tuition providers who comply with our core principles of quality course delivery. If you are receiving structured tuition with an ICAEW Partner in Learning, make sure you know how and when you can contact your tutors for extra help. If you are not receiving structured tuition and are interested in classroom, online or distance learning tuition, take a look at our recognised Partner in Learning tuition providers in your area, on our website icaew.com/students

Faculties and Special Interest Groups

Faculties and special interest groups support and develop members and students in areas of work and industry sectors that are of particular interest. There are seven faculties which provide knowledge, events and essential technical resources including the Law faculty. Our 12 groups provide practical support, information and representation within a range of industry sectors including Charity and Voluntary, Entertainment and Media, Farming and Rural Business, Forensic, Healthcare, Insolvency, Valuation, Tourism and Hospitality, and more. Students can register free of charge for provisional membership of one special interest group and receive a monthly complimentary e-newsletter from one faculty of their choice. To find out more and to access a range of free resources, visit icaew.com/students

The Library & Information service (LIS)

The Library & Information service (LIS) is ICAEW's world-leading accountancy and business library. You have access to a range of resources free of charge via the library website, including the catalogue, LibCat. Visit icaew.com/library for more details.

CHAPTER 1

Contract formation

Learning objectives

- Define a contract ☐

- Identify the essential elements of a contract ☐

- Be aware of factors which might affect the validity of a contract and their consequences ☐

- Understand and apply the rules relating to offer, acceptance and the intention to create legal relations ☐

- Understand and apply the rules relating to consideration ☐

- Understand that contract terms may be express or implied into the contract. ☐

The specific syllabus reference for this chapter is 1a.

Syllabus links

As seen above, the issue of contract formation could be relevant in many different areas of the syllabus, for example accounting and auditing, employment, business and financial management.

Contracts are also important in assurance; for instance, a key contract is the engagement letter between the client and the assurance provider.

Examination context

Contract is an important part of the syllabus. Typically seven out of fifty questions relate to contract law. Understanding the basic precepts relating to contract is vital.

You are likely to be presented with scenarios and may have to conclude whether a valid contract has been formed. Many cases are referred to in this and later chapters. They will not be examined directly, but illustrate points of law that could be.

In the assessment, candidates may be required to:

- Recognise when a legally binding contract exists between two parties

- Understand how a contract may be enforced

1 The validity of a contract

Section overview

- **A valid contract is a legally binding agreement**, between two parties, which agreement may be evidenced by writing, words or action.

- Three essential elements must be present, namely

  - Agreement
  - An intention to create legal relations
  - Consideration.

It is almost invariably the case that the two parties to a contract bring with them differing levels of **bargaining power**. A contract may be made between a large retail company and an individual for example. In such cases, the agreement is likely to be in the form of a **standard form contract**, prepared by the dominant party and which the other party has no choice but to take or leave.

Generally speaking the law will not wish to restrict or interfere with the ability of contractual parties to decide whether or not to enter into a contract and, if so, upon what terms ('**freedom of contract**'). However, it will often intervene where one party seeks an unfair advantage as a result of his superior bargaining position.

Such intervention will be made by the courts or by legislation. Thus, for example, the Sale of Goods Act implies terms into a contract which impose obligations on the business seller as to the quality and fitness for purpose of the goods he sells. Likewise the Consumer Credit Act affords the consumer protection where he enters into credit agreements. In respect of exclusion clauses, in which typically the stronger party seeks to avoid liability, the Unfair Contract Terms Act (discussed in Chapter 2) may result in such a clause being void outright or void if the court considers it to be unreasonable.

You should be aware that the European Commission put forward a draft regulation for a new Common European Sales Law (CESL) in 2011. This was intended to be implemented at the end of 2012, but continuing opposition from the UK government and others means that it now seems unlikely to become law in the near future. The CESL aims to promote trade between member states, by creating a harmonised contract law which is designed to apply to cross-border contracts for the sale of goods, digital content and related services. It will apply only where the parties choose to adopt it.

In order to be valid, three essential elements of a contract must be shown to be present. These are dealt with in detail in sections 2 – 4 below. Suffice it to say here that those elements are

- Agreement between the parties
- An intention to create legal relations
- Consideration

1.1 Void and voidable contracts

Even if these essential elements can be shown, a contract may nonetheless be rendered **void** or **voidable** by one or more of the following vitiating factors:

	Rule (in broad terms)	Effect of rule not being followed
Lack of capacity	An individual must be of sound mind and aged eighteen or over	Voidable at the option of the person without capacity
Absence of free will	A party should not be made to enter into a contract other than by his own free will, ie not by **duress** or **undue influence**	Voidable
Illegality	A contract should not be illegal or offend public policy	Void

	Rule (in broad terms)	Effect of rule not being followed
Mistake	You should be aware that if one or both parties alleges that they were mistaken in some way, this may affect the validity of the contract. However, the law is as complex as the facts of each case are varied and you do not need to know the law for the purposes of your studies.	
Misrepresentation	If A makes a pre-contractual statement of fact that is intended to and does cause B to enter into the contract but turns out to be untrue (**misrepresentation**) the other party may choose to avoid the contract	Voidable

The consequences of a contract being rendered void or voidable are as follows:

Void	A **void contract** is not a contract at all. The parties are not bound by it and if they transfer property under it they can generally recover their goods even from a third party.
Voidable	A **voidable contract** is a contract which one party may set aside. Property transferred before avoidance is usually irrecoverable from a third party.

1.2 Unenforceable contracts

Even if a contract satisfies the above requirements and is valid, it may still be **unenforceable**. This means that if either party fails to perform his part of the contract, the other party cannot compel him to do so.

A contract will be unenforceable where it is not in the correct **form**. Generally speaking a contract may be made orally or in writing and an oral agreement will be just as binding as a written contract. However in certain cases the law provides that an oral contract will not be sufficient, for example agreements for the transfer of land and consumer credit agreements (that are regulated by the Consumer Credit Act 1974 (as amended by the Consumer Credit Act 2006)) must be in writing. Note that, increasingly, contracts are made electronically and an electronic signature can be used as evidence of the validity of a contract in the same way as a written signature (s. 7 Electronic Communications Act 2000).

Another example with which you should be familiar is a **guarantee**. This is where a guarantor promises to pay a creditor the sum of the debtor's debts, in the event that the debtor fails to pay them himself. The agreement itself need not be in writing but the terms must be evidenced in writing before any action is brought. The written evidence should be signed (or acknowledged in some way) by the guarantor.

Golden Ocean Group Ltd v Salgaocar Mining Industries PVT 2011

The facts: Brokers for Golden Ocean and SMI exchanged a number of emails in which the terms of a charterparty by SMI's Singaporean chartering arm, Trustworth, were negotiated, but they were never formalised into a written agreement. Emails early in the exchange had stated that the charter would be 'fully guaranteed' by SMI. When Trustworth refused to take delivery, Golden Ocean sued SMI on the guarantee.

The decision: The Court of Appeal recognised that contracts are often negotiated informally by email (particularly in the shipping industry) and held that a single document was not necessary. Nor was it material that no documents had been signed in the traditional way. The typed name of the broker for SMI in the final email had clearly signified his agreement to all negotiated terms and constituted a valid signature.

Interactive question 1: Essentials of a valid contract   [Difficulty level: Easy]

What will be the consequences of the following in relation to a purported contract between two parties?

		Void	Voidable	Unenforceable
A	There is clear agreement between the parties on all terms and they intend to create a legally binding agreement but there is no consideration.	☐	☐	☐
B	One of the parties is aged 17	☐	☐	☐
C	The contract is an agreement to defraud HM Revenue & Customs.	☐	☐	☐
D	The contract is made orally and provides for Graham to pay Harry the debt owed to Harry by Imran.	☐	☐	☐

See **Answer** at the end of this chapter.

2 Offer and acceptance

Section overview

- As noted above, the first essential element in the formation of a valid and binding contract is agreement. This is usually analysed and understood in terms of 'offer' and 'acceptance'.

- It is a matter of interpretation whether something amounts to an offer.

- There are a number of rules which determine whether an offer has been validly accepted.

2.1 What constitutes an offer?

An **offer** is a **definite promise to be bound on specific terms**. It is made by an **offeror**.

It is a matter of interpretation as to whether something is sufficiently definite to comprise an offer capable of acceptance. **A statement that is vague** and that cannot be rendered certain by reference to previous dealings or custom cannot be an offer. Only an offer in the proper sense may be accepted so as to form a binding contract. A **statement which sets out possible terms of a contract** is not an offer unless this is **clearly indicated**, although if, in the course of negotiations for a sale, the vendor states the price at which he will sell, that statement may be an offer which can be accepted.

An offer must be something more than a supply of information or a statement of intention. For example, advertising that an auction will take place is a **statement of intention**, not an offer to sell. Potential buyers may not sue the auctioneer if the auction does not take place. Likewise, saying that you might be interested in buying your neighbour's car is a statement of intention not an offer to buy.

It is also important to distinguish between an offer and a mere **invitation to treat**. Where a party is initiating negotiations, he is said to make an invitation to treat. An invitation to treat cannot be accepted to form a binding contract, it is simply an indication that a person is prepared to receive offers with a view to entering into a binding contract.

That indication is evidenced in the following situations.

- **Advertisements** (in a newspaper, for example)

- **Goods displayed for sale in a shop window or on self-service shelves.** (If it were the case that a customer accepted an offer to sell by removing goods from the shelf, he could not then change his mind and put them back as this would constitute breach of contract.)

- **Circulation of a price list**

Worked example: Offer or invitation to treat

Ken offered to sell Leah a flick knife for £20. He also advertised the flick knives in the local newspaper and put one on display in his shop window with a price tag on it. Will he be liable to prosecution for 'offering for sale' an offensive weapon?

He will be guilty of the offence with regard to his offer to Leah. However, the advertisement and shop window display are not offers but invitations to treat and do not render him guilty of this offence.

An offer does not have to be made to a particular person. It may be made to a **class of persons** or to the **world at large**.

Carlill v Carbolic Smoke Ball Co 1893

The facts: The manufacturers of a medicinal carbolic smoke ball published an advertisement by which they undertook to pay '£100 reward ... to any person who contracts ... influenza ... after having used the smoke ball three times daily for two weeks'. The advertisement added that £1,000 had been deposited at a bank 'showing our sincerity in this matter'. Carlill read the advertisement, purchased the smoke ball and used it as directed. She contracted influenza and claimed her £100 reward.

In their defence the manufacturers argued against this.

- The offer was so vague that it could not form the basis of a contract, as no time limit was specified.
- It was not an offer which could be accepted since it was offered to the whole world.

Decision: It was a valid offer capable of acceptance. It was not vague but clear that the smoke ball must protect the user during the period of use. Further, it was accepted that an offer could be made to the world at large (by analogy with reward cases where it was accepted that a notice offering a reward could be accepted by anybody).

You should note that Carlill is an unusual case in that advertisements are not usually regarded as offers. However, it established the principle that an offer can be made to the world at large and is generally seen as a landmark case. You should be familiar with it.

Worked example: Negotiations in respect of a contract

It is often unclear at what point, if at all, actions or statements during negotiations constitute an offer capable of acceptance. This was the case in *Gibson v Manchester City Council 1979*.

Gibson lived in a council house in Manchester and received a brochure from the council seeking to determine whether council tenants would be interested in buying their council houses. Interested parties were advised to return the form attached to the brochure, which Gibson did. As a result, the council sent him a letter saying that the council may be prepared to sell him the house for £2,180. The letter enclosed an application form to purchase the house which Gibson filled out and returned.

After Gibson had sent his application, the council changed hands and the new council reversed the policy on selling council houses. Only in cases where there had been an exchange of contracts were the sales completed. Gibson sued the council, claiming that the letter he had been sent by the former council was an offer which he had accepted at the time when he made his formal application.

The House of Lords concluded that no binding contract had been formed because the council's letter was not a formal offer but was still part of the negotiations taking place surrounding the potential sale. The letter was not unequivocal and it was still at a level of negotiation about a potential sale at a potential price.

Note that, in contrast, Gibson's formal application could have been seen to be an offer capable of acceptance. However, there would still not have been a contract, as the council had not accepted this offer by the time that the council's policy on selling houses had changed.

Interactive question 2: Offer or invitation to treat [Difficulty level: Easy]

Bianca sees the following notice in a newspaper:

'20 orthopaedic beds, £100 each'

How would you describe this notice in terms of contract law?

☐ Offer   ☐ Supply of information

☐ Invitation to treat   ☐ Advertisement

See **Answer** at the end of this chapter.

2.2 Termination of offer

In the absence of an acceptance, an offer may be terminated in any of the following ways:

Method of termination	Consequence
Rejection	Rejection by the offeree terminates the offer
Counter-offer	A **counter-offer** is when the offeree proposes new or amended terms, thereby terminating the original offer (since acceptance must amount to an unqualified agreement to all the terms of the offer). The counter-offer is then open to the offeror to accept or reject.
	Hyde v Wrench 1840
	The facts: D offered to sell property to C for £1,000. Two days later, C made a counter-offer of £950 which D rejected. C then informed D that he accepted the original offer of £1,000.
	Decision: The original offer of £1,000 had been terminated by the counter-offer of £950.
	If the offeree's response is actually a **request for information**, the offer is not affected.
	Stevenson v McLean 1880
	The facts: D offered to sell iron at '40s net cash per ton, open till Monday'. C enquired whether he would agree to delivery spread over two months. D did not reply and (within the stated time limit) C accepted the original offer. Meanwhile D had sold the iron to a third party.
	Decision: There was a contract since C had merely enquired as to a variation of terms and had not rejected the offer or made a counter-offer.
Lapse of time	An offer may be expressed to last for a **specified time**. If, however, there is no express time limit set, it expires after a **reasonable time**.
	Ramsgate Victoria Hotel Co v Montefiore 1866
	The facts: D applied to the company in June for shares and paid a deposit. At the end of November the company sent him an acceptance by issue of a letter of allotment and requested payment of the balance due. D contended that his offer had expired and could no longer be accepted.
	Decision: The offer was for a reasonable time only and five months was much more than that. The offer had lapsed.

Method of termination	Consequence
Revocation by the offeror	The offeror may **revoke** his offer at any time before acceptance either expressly or by implication. Even if he undertakes that his offer shall remain open for acceptance for a specified time he may nonetheless revoke it within that time, unless he has bound himself to keep it open by a separate contract.
	Revocation initially takes effect when it is **communicated to** or **received by** the offeree. (Note that the postal rule discussed below applies only to acceptance and **not** to revocation of an offer.)
Failure of a pre-condition	An offer may be 'conditional' in that it is dependent on some event occurring or there being a change of circumstances. If that event or change of circumstances does not occur, the offer is not capable of acceptance.

Worked example: Request for information about an offer

Oscar has horses to sell and offers two each to Abby and Ben for £4,000, stating that the offer will be open until Monday. Abby asks Oscar whether she could have one now and the other in a month's time. Oscar does not reply, so on Sunday, Abby accepts his original offer. Ben replies on Saturday saying that he will take them for £3,500. Oscar does not reply, so on Saturday Ben accepts his original offer.

If Abby's enquiry whether she could have the horse now and the other later had been a counter-offer, then she could not have accepted the original offer, as a counter-offer would have terminated it. However, in this case, Abby has simply requested more details of the terms of the offer and can still accept the original offer to form a contract.

Ben's reply amounts to a counter-offer which has the effect of terminating Oscar's original offer. Ben's purported acceptance of the purchase at £4,000 is therefore not effective and there is no contract.

2.3 Acceptance

The offeree's response must amount to an **unqualified agreement to all the terms of the offer** in order to constitute a valid acceptance. Acceptance may be made by **express words** to that effect by the offeree or his authorised agent, or it can be **inferred from conduct**.

Brogden v Metropolitan Railway Co 1877

The facts: For many years C supplied coal to D. D's agent sent a draft agreement to C for consideration and the parties applied the terms of the draft agreement to their dealings, but they never signed a final version. C later denied that there was any agreement between them.

Decision: The conduct of the parties was only explicable on the assumption that they both agreed to the terms of the draft.

There must be some **act** on the part of the offeree to indicate his acceptance. An offeror cannot dictate that his offer shall be deemed to have been accepted unless the offeree actually rejects or accepts it.

Felthouse v Bindley 1862

The facts: C wrote to his nephew offering to buy the nephew's horse, adding 'If I hear no more about him, I consider the horse mine'. The nephew intended to accept his uncle's offer but did not reply.

Decision: C had no title to the horse as the nephew's silence could not constitute acceptance.

Similarly in Carlill's case (above), once Carlill began using the influenza product, this was a positive act that constituted acceptance of the offer.

Worked example: Offer and acceptance

In January Elle offered to buy Jane's boat for £3,000.

*Elle's offer of £3,000 is an **offer**. Many offers are in fact made by prospective buyers rather than by sellers.*

Jane immediately wrote a letter to Elle saying 'For a quick sale I would accept £3,500. If not interested please let me know as soon as possible.'

*Jane's letter forms a **counter-offer**, which has the effect of terminating Elle's offer. Elle may now accept or reject this counter-offer.*

Elle did not see the letter until March when she returned from a business trip.

*There is nothing to indicate that Jane's (counter-) offer is not still open in March. An offer may be expressed to last for a **specified time**. It then expires at the end of that time. If, however, there is no express time limit set, it expires after a **reasonable time**. It would not appear that the offer would have lapsed by March.*

She then replied. 'I accept your offer. I trust that if I pay £3,000 now, you can wait until June for the remaining £500.'

*Elle's reply, using the words 'I accept your offer,' **appears conclusive. However, it is not**. The enquiry as to variation of terms does not constitute acceptance and is more than a request for information. Elle's reply is probably best analysed as being a **new counter-offer** including terms as to deferred payment.*

On receiving the letter, Jane attached a 'sold' sign on the boat but forgot to reply to Elle.

***By affixing a 'sold' sign**, it appears that Jane accepts the revised terms as to dates for payment of the £3,500. However, the court would need to decide whether, in all the circumstances, acceptance can be deemed to have been communicated (we will look at communication in the next section).*

Interactive question 3: Offer and acceptance   [Difficulty level: Easy]

On 1 October, Adam posts a letter to Belinda offering to sell his fridge. On 2 October, Belinda receives Adam's letter. On 3 October, Adam changes his mind and posts a letter to Belinda saying that the fridge is no longer for sale. Later that day, Belinda telephones Adam and accepts his offer.

Which **one** of the following best describes the state of the contract between Adam and Belinda for the sale of Adam's fridge?

A   It is valid because acceptance took place before Belinda received Adam's revocation.
B   It is invalid because Adam posted his revocation before Belinda accepted.
C   It is valid because Adam cannot revoke the offer once Belinda has received it.

See **Answer** at the end of this chapter.

2.4   Communication of acceptance

The general rule is that acceptance **must be communicated** to the offeror and the acceptance is not effective (and hence there is no agreement) until this has been done. However, it is always open to the offeror to waive this requirement either expressly or by implication. Thus, in Carlill's case it was held that it was sufficient for the claimant to act on the offer without notifying her acceptance of it. The need for acceptance to be communicated was impliedly waived.

The offeror may require that communication of acceptance is made by **some prescribed method**, in which case the offeree should communicate by that method or (unless the wording is very specific) by some other method which is no less expeditious or effective.

Where **no mode of communication is prescribed** by the offeror, the offeree can choose any **reasonable** method (a reply by letter to an offer by email, for example, might not be acceptable). Note that where acceptance is made **by post**, communication will be effective the moment the acceptance is posted even if it is delayed or lost altogether in the post, subject to the following:

- If the delay is attributable to the offeree's negligence, for example by stating the address incorrectly, it will not be the case that posting amounts to acceptance.

- Use of the post must have been **within the contemplation of the parties**, which intention can be deduced from the circumstances and need not be express.

This is often referred to as 'the postal rule' (and applies only to acceptance, **not** revocation). The postal rule will not operate where the offeror requires acceptance '**by notice in writing**' as the words 'notice in writing' must mean notice actually received by the offeror. Nor does the rule apply to instantaneous methods of communication.

The law is unclear as to when an acceptance sent by e-mail becomes effective. It is not possible to say that the communication of acceptance is instantaneous, rather it is likely to be linked to when the offeror actually saw the e-mail or when he should have read it or might have been expected to read it. Given the legal uncertainty as to the time of acceptance by e-mail, it is advisable for the terms of an offer which is made online to make express provision as to the means and timing of acceptance.

Interactive question 4: Formation of contract   [Difficulty level: Exam standard]

Frank writes to Xiao-Xiao on 1 July offering to sell him his sailing dinghy for £1,200. On 10 July, having received no reply, he decides to withdraw this offer and sends a second letter. On 10 July, Xiao-Xiao receives the original letter and posts a reply to Frank accepting the offer. Frank never receives Xiao-Xiao's letter and sells the boat to Mel on 13 July.

Indicate whether or not each of the following statements is true or false.

A	Frank's original letter constitutes an offer, which Xiao-Xiao is entitled to accept or reject	☐ True	☐ False
B	Xiao-Xiao's reply constitutes a valid acceptance	☐ True	☐ False
C	Frank is legally entitled to sell the boat to Mel on 13 July since he revoked his offer	☐ True	☐ False

See **Answer** at the end of this chapter.

Acceptance will only be effective to create agreement where the offeree is **aware of the offer**. Thus, if A offers a reward to anyone who finds and returns his property and B, unaware of A's offer, returns the property, B cannot have 'accepted' A's offer since he was unaware of it and there is no agreement.

2.5 Agreement without offer and acceptance

As mentioned above, agreement is normally understood in terms of an offer made by one party being accepted by the other party. However, in some cases this may not be appropriate but an agreement might still be said to exist between the parties. The courts may consider the words and actions of the parties and construct a contract. The following case illustrates this principle:

Clarke v Dunraven 1897

The facts: C and D entered a regatta. Each undertook to obey the club's rules, including an obligation to pay for all damage caused by fouling. D's yacht fouled C's yacht, which sank. C sued for damages. D argued that his only liability was under the Merchant Shipping Act 1862 and was therefore set at £8 per ton.

Decision: A contract had been created between the parties when they entered their yachts for the regatta and accepted the club's rules. C was entitled to recover the full cost of the damage.

3 Intention to create legal relations

Section overview

- The intention to create legal relations is the second essential element of a valid contract. It may be completely obvious but, if not, one of two rebuttable presumptions may be applied.

The nature of the relationship between the parties	Presumption
Social, domestic and family	It is presumed that social, domestic and family arrangements are **not** intended to be legally binding unless there is **clear evidence** which points **to the contrary**. All circumstances will be taken into account, including whether husband and wife were separated at the time of contract, the nature of the relationship between the parties and the type of contract. For example, if the parties are a husband and wife living apart or if the contract relates to property matters, the presumption is more likely to be rebutted.
Commercial	It is presumed that there **is** an intention to enter into legal relations unless this is expressly disclaimed or the circumstances give a clear contrary indication. It is not easy to rebut this presumption. In *Edwards v Skyways Ltd 1964*, where D promised to make an *ex gratia* payment to its employee, the argument that the words '*ex gratia*' showed that there was no intention to create legal relations failed.

Care needs to be taken during the negotiation stage as to whether a contract is intended. Use of the words '**subject to contract**' amounts to a strong presumption that **no** immediately binding contract is intended.

RTS Flexible Systems Ltd v Molkerei Alois Muller GmbH 2010

The facts: A letter of intent set out a draft contract which was not to become effective until signed and executed by the parties. The contract was not signed but the parties proceeded with the project of installing two production lines in the claimant's factory.

The decision: The Supreme Court held, first, that it was unrealistic to conclude that major works would have been carried out in the absence of a contract and, secondly, that there was evidence of an agreement and an intent to create legal relations in this case. The court made it clear that it would not always be the case, in circumstances where works commence before a contract is finalised, that the contract that exists between the parties contains the same terms as those in the negotiated contract. That would be a question of fact in all the circumstances.

Similarly, calling an agreement 'a personal agreement until a fully legalised agreement, drawn up by a solicitor and embodying all the considerations herewith stated, is signed', was held to be a binding agreement, notwithstanding that it was obviously intended to be replaced by a more formal contract at a later date (*Branca v Cobarro 1947*).

4 Consideration

Section overview

- Consideration is the third essential element of a contract. Put simply, it is what each party gives or agrees to give to the other, usually payment or a promise to do something in return.

In more legal language, consideration has been defined as follows:

'A valuable consideration in the sense of the law may consist either in some right, interest, profit or benefit accruing to one party, or some forbearance, detriment, loss or responsibility given, suffered or undertaken by the other,' (*Currie v Misa 1875*) and

'An act or forbearance of one party, or the promise thereof, is the price for which the promise of the other is bought, and the promise thus given for value is enforceable' *(Dunlop v Selfridge 1915)*.

There are three types of consideration

- Executed (valid)
- Executory (valid)
- Past (generally invalid)

4.1 Valid consideration

Type of consideration	Meaning
Executed	**A performed, or executed, act in return for a promise**. For example, payment for goods at the time those goods are delivered.
Executory	**A promise given for a promise**. The consideration in support of each promise is the other promise, not a performed act. For example, a promise to pay for goods which are to be delivered and paid for at a later date.

4.2 Invalid consideration

Past consideration is something which has already been done at the time the promise is made, for example where works are carried out and then a promise is made to pay for them:

Re McArdle 1951

The facts: Under a will the testator's children were entitled to a house after their mother's death. During the mother's lifetime, one of the children and his wife lived in the house with the mother. The wife made improvements to the house. The children later agreed in writing to repay the wife 'in consideration of your carrying out certain alterations and improvements', but they refused to do so when the mother died.

Decision: The work on the house had all been completed before the promise was made. The improvements were therefore past consideration and so the promise was not binding.

However, if it could be said that there was an **implied promise** before the works were carried out that they would be paid for at a later date, then they will constitute valid consideration. Whether there was such an implied promise will be a question of fact but it will need to be shown that the works were requested by the promisor and that the parties must have understood and assumed that they would be paid for. If such a promise is implied, then the amount to be paid will be determined by reference to the actual promise made after the works are completed.

Worked example: Essentials of a contract

A and B are negotiating to enter into a contract with the intention to enter into legal relations with one another.

They have been negotiating for some time. When A says, 'I will sell you twenty barrels of oil for £20 each, take it or leave it', B says, 'Done'. Here they have achieved a second essential as A has made an offer and B has accepted it, creating an agreement.

The third essential element is consideration, which both parties giving (or promising to give) something of value to the contract. In this case, A has promised 20 barrels of oil and B has promised £400, so this essential element is also present.

4.3 Adequacy and sufficiency of consideration

The court will also seek to ensure that a particular act or promise can actually amount to valid consideration. Learn these rules:

- **Consideration need not be adequate** (that is, equal in value to the consideration received in return). There is no remedy at law for someone who simply makes a poor bargain.

- **Consideration must be sufficient**. It must have some identifiable value in order to be capable in law of being regarded as valid consideration.

It is presumed that each party is capable of serving his own interests, and the courts will not seek to weigh up the comparative value (or adequacy) of the promises or acts exchanged.

Thomas v Thomas 1842

The facts: By his will C's husband expressed the wish that his widow should have the use of his house during her life. After death, his executors (the defendants), allowed her to do so (a) in accordance with her husband's wishes and (b) in return for her undertaking to pay a rent of £1 per annum. They later said that their promise to let her occupy the house was not supported by consideration.

Decision: Compliance with the husband's wishes did not constitute valid consideration (since no economic value attached to it), but the nominal rent was sufficient consideration (even though it could hardly be said to be adequate).

In order to be sufficient (however inadequate or tenuous), the consideration must contain some element that can be seen as the price of the other party's promise. If all that is offered is something that the promisee was bound to do anyway, then there is unlikely to be sufficient consideration. This can be the case where the promisee is obliged to do something by law or under an existing contract, either with the promisor or a third party. You should familiarise yourself with the following:

Performance of existing statutory duty	**Not** consideration **unless** it can be shown that some extra service **over and above** the scope of the statutory duty is also being offered. For example, if someone agrees to pay another a sum of money for appearing in a court, when that other person has been subpoenaed to attend in any event, there is no consideration to support the promise to pay.
Performance of existing contractual duty owed to the promisor	**Not** consideration **unless** it can be shown that the promisee is actually giving or doing something **over and above** the scope of the contractual obligation. The facts need to be examined closely in each case to see whether what is being done or offered **is** actually over and above the existing contractual (or statutory) duty and also to ensure that the case is not actually one of duress. It may be enough where the promisor obtains some **extra practical benefit**:

Williams v Roffey Bros & Nicholls (Contractors) Ltd 1990

The facts: D subcontracted part of its work refurbishing a block of flats to C for £20,000. During the works C found itself in financial difficulties and D promised to pay an extra £10,300 to ensure that the work was completed on time, but later refused to pay all of the extra amount.

Decision: D's argument that there was no consideration for the promise to pay £10,300 failed. It was significant that D's promise was not made as a result of C's duress or fraud. It was considered important that D derived the added practical benefit of not having to engage somebody else to complete the work and also of avoiding a penalty clause for late performance in his own contract.

Where the question concerns the waiver of all or part of a debt, the waiver needs to be supported by consideration and the decision in Williams v Roffey Bros is not likely to be applied (see section 4.4 below).

Performance of existing contractual duty owed to a third party	This can amount to valid consideration. Thus in *Scotson v Pegg 1861*, C contracted with X to deliver cargo as X directed. X directed C to deliver it to D. D contracted with C to unload the cargo if C delivered it to D (which he was already bound to do under his contract with X). It was held that C's obligation owed to X to deliver the cargo to D was sufficient consideration for D's promise.
Forbearance or waiver of existing rights	Forbearance or the promise of it may be sufficient consideration if it has some value, or amounts to giving up something of value. For example, A might agree to forego his right to take action against B in return for B's promise to A.

Worked example: Consideration

A crew of 30 men contracts to sail a ship from Lands End to John O'Groats for £2,000 each. During the voyage, two crew members desert and the captain promises an additional £500 to the remaining 28 if they will complete the voyage short-handed. Can this promise be enforced?

Solution

No. The 28 crew members are already contractually bound to complete the voyage and they would be expected to deal with normal emergencies arising en route. The fact that they have to cover two missing crew members does not amount to something over and above what they are bound to do anyway.

If, on the other hand, many more had deserted, so as to make the continuation of the voyage exceptionally hazardous, then their agreement to complete for an extra £500 each would amount to valid consideration. (Note that the position might be different in each case if it were a case of the remaining crew members refusing to go further without extra payment.)

4.4 Waiver of existing debt

If X owes Y £100 but Y agrees to accept a lesser sum, say £80, in full settlement of Y's claim, that is a promise by Y to waive his entitlement to the balance of £20. The promise, like any other, should be supported by consideration. The case below is important:

Foakes v Beer 1884

The facts: D had obtained judgment against C. Judgment debts bear interest from the date of the judgment. By a written agreement D agreed to accept payment by instalments, no mention being made of the interest. Once C had paid the amount of the debt in full, D claimed interest, claiming that the agreement was not supported by consideration.

Decision: D was entitled to the debt with interest. No consideration had been given by C for waiver of any part of her rights against him.

However, in the following cases the waiver will be binding:

- **Alternative consideration.** If X offers and Y accepts anything to which Y is not already entitled, the extra thing is sufficient consideration for the waiver, for example **goods** instead of cash, or **payment in advance** of the due date.

- **Bargain between the creditors.** If X arranges with creditors that they will each accept part payment in full entitlement, that is a bargain between the creditors. Even though X has given no consideration, the creditors are bound individually to the agreed terms.

- **Third party part payment.** If a third party (Z) offers part payment and Y agrees to release X from Y's claim to the balance, Y has received consideration, in the form of the offer from Z, against whom he had no previous claim and that is sufficient.

Worked example: Waiver of entitlement to debt

A owes B, C and D £100 each. Each of the creditors agrees to accept £90 in full satisfaction of the debt. A also owes X £200. T offers to pay X £150 on the condition that X discharges A from the £200 debt. Can creditors B, C and D take action against A for the remaining £30? Can X take action against A for the debt of £200 or any part of it?

The answer is no in each case. The arrangement between the creditors will bind each of them as the law effectively imports a consideration to support the creditors' agreement (although the exact legal reasoning for this is far from clear). X cannot sue A for the original debt as he has now received consideration from T, against whom he had no previous claim. Like the creditors' agreement, this instance is another exception to the rule in *Foakes v Beer*.

Interactive question 5: Consideration [Difficulty level: Exam standard]

Alice owns a classic car. Alice and Barry are negotiating a deal for Barry to clean the outside of Alice's car for her before Saturday, when she is lending her car to Claudia for her wedding. Alice will pay £10 and allow him to borrow the car on Sunday when Claudia is finished with it.

On Thursday Alice gets mud in the car and therefore when Barry comes on Thursday to clean the car, she asks him to clean the inside as well.

Barry cleans the car and asks for £15 to cover the fact that he cleaned the inside as well as the outside. Alice refuses to pay Barry extra. She also discovers that she does not have £10 to pay him, only £5. She offers him £5 and a week's loan of the car in full settlement.

Indicate whether or not each of the following statements is true or false.

A	Alice's consideration of £10 and a loan of her car is valid consideration for Barry's promise to clean her car.	☐	True	☐	False
B	By the time he raises the issue with Alice, the fact that Barry has cleaned the inside of the car is past consideration and therefore he cannot demand additional payment for it.	☐	True	☐	False
C	Alice has offered Barry additional consideration (extended loan of the car) for his waiver of the other £5 and therefore, on acceptance by Barry, the waiver will be binding.	☐	True	☐	False

See **Answer** at the end of this chapter.

5 The terms of the contract

Section overview

- As a general rule, the parties to a contract may expressly include in the agreement whatever **terms** they choose. This is part of the principle of **freedom of contract**.

- Terms may also be implied into the contract by the courts, by statute or by custom.

5.1 Express terms

In a wholly **oral contract**, the court must ascertain, as a question of fact, what was expressly agreed by the parties.

In a written contract, as a general rule, the terms expressed therein will be treated as the contract. However, the following should be taken into account:

- Terms must be **substantially complete** on the face of it or capable of being clarified. The parties are entitled to leave a term to be determined at a later date, (for example a price can be left to be determined by an agreed arbitrator). However, if a term is left outstanding and there is no provision for its clarification, there will be no contract.

  Scammell v Ouston 1941

  D ordered a motor-van from C 'on the understanding that the balance of the purchase price can be had on hire-purchase terms over a period of two years'. The hire-purchase terms were never supplied and so no agreement could be identified.

  However if a term is vague but also meaningless and unnecessary (such as 'the usual conditions of acceptance apply') it can be disregarded.

- A **statement of fact made before the contract** which induces a party to enter into the contract may **become a term** of the contract. The court will consider all the circumstances to determine whether it became a term or was simply a representation.

  Thus if the person making the statement had **special knowledge** of the subject, it is more likely the statement will be treated as a term of the contract. Likewise the courts will asses the significance of **how much time passed** between the representation and the making of the contract and why the contract **omitted to incorporate** the statement. (If the statement is not treated as a term of the contract, remedies might lie in misrepresentation but not for breach of contract.)

- **Oral evidence** will not usually be admitted to add to, vary or contradict written terms, unless it can be shown that the document was not intended to comprise all the agreed terms.

  SS Ardennes (Cargo Owners) v SS Ardennes (Owners) 1951

  D contracted to take C's cargo of oranges to London 'by any route, directly or indirectly'. D's agent gave a verbal undertaking that the vessel would sail direct from Spain to London. In fact the ship went via Antwerp so that the oranges arrived late and a favourable market was missed. It was held that the verbal undertaking amounted to a warranty and was admissible as oral evidence to override the written term in the bill of lading.

In a contract entered into online, the general terms and conditions are normally in a standard form and the other party is required to scroll through them and click 'accept' before making the contract.

Parties to an international contract are well advised to include an express clause which specifies which country's law will apply to any dispute arising under its terms (usually called a 'choice of law' or 'governing law' clause). In the absence of such a provision, the relevant law will be determined in accordance with the Contracts (Applicable Law) Act 1990 (as amended, in particular to take account of European regulation 'Rome I' in 2008). (A governing clause may also provide for non-contractual disputes, although this is less straightforward.)

5.2 Implied terms

Additional terms of a contract may be **implied** by law. Such implied terms will be deemed to form part of the contract even though they are not expressly mentioned. In some cases they will add to the express terms, in others they may override express terms. Terms can be implied in the following ways:

• **By reference to custom**	But not if that would produce an inconsistency with the express terms
• **By statute**	For example by the Supply of Goods and Services Act 1982 which implies terms that work and materials should be of satisfactory quality. Such implied terms often override any express terms that do not offer as much protection to the weaker party.

- **By the courts**

(1) Necessary to give business efficacy

Terms may be implied if the court concludes that the parties **must have intended** those terms to apply to the contract in order to give **business efficacy** to the contract.

The Moorcock 1889

The facts: The owners of a wharf agreed that a ship should be moored alongside to unload its cargo. It was well known that at low water the ship would ground on the mud at the bottom. At ebb tide the ship settled on a ridge concealed beneath the mud and suffered damage.

Decision: It was an implied term that the ground alongside the wharf was safe at low tide, since both parties knew that the ship must rest on it.

(2) Implicit in the nature of the contract itself

The court may also imply a term, not based on the presumed intention of the parties, but because it is considered to be implicitly required by the nature of the contract used. Such an implied term may form a precedent for future contracts of the same type and parties will be advised to express clear wording if such an implied term is not required.

Liverpool City Council v Irwin 1977

The facts: A tenant in a tower block with no formal tenancy agreement withheld rent, alleging that the owner of the block had breached implied terms because (among other things) the lifts did not work and the stairs were unlit.

Decision: It was held that since tenants could only occupy the building with access to stairs and/or lifts, the agreement between the parties implicitly required implied obligations on the owner's part to maintain the common parts of the building.

5.3 Battle of the forms

Disputes sometimes arise because each party is accustomed to doing business on its own standard terms and argues that they apply to the contract, rather than the other party's terms. Great care should be taken during the negotiation stage to clarify which standard (or other) terms will apply. Where it is not clear, the contract must be considered objectively, but taking into account what has actually happened (the 'factual matrix').

GHSP Inc v A B Electronic Ltd 2010

The facts: The claimant, a manufacturer of control systems for motor vehicles, purchased pedal sensors from the defendant which were defective and caused substantial losses. Both parties argued that their standard terms applied to the contract. The defendant's standard terms excluded liability for consequential loss or damage and limited liability to carrying out works of repair.

The decision: The contract was not governed by either set of standard terms, as it was clear that neither party had accepted the other party's terms. The court held that the contract was governed by the terms implied by the Sale of Goods Act 1979.

6 Privity of contract

Section overview

- As a general rule, only a person who is a party to a contract has enforceable rights or obligations under it. This is the doctrine of privity of contract.
- The Contracts (Rights of Third Parties) Act 1999 has had a fundamental effect on the doctrine.

The law requires that consideration must move from the promisee and **only a party to a contract can enforce it**. No-one may be entitled to or bound by the terms of a contract to which he is not a party.

Where A promises B that (for a consideration provided by B) A will confer a benefit on C, then C cannot as a general rule enforce A's promise since C has given no consideration for it.

There are a number of equitable and statutory exceptions to the privity of contract rule, for example a person injured in a road accident may claim against the motorist's insurers under the Road Traffic Act 1972. However the two principal exceptions of which you should be aware are as follows:

- Where an **agent** enters into a contract with a third party on behalf of his principal, the resulting contract is actually enforceable by and between the principal and the third party. The agent cannot enforce it.

- The **Contracts (Rights of Third Parties) Act 1999** provides that a third party may enforce a term of the contract provided:

  - The contract expressly provides that he may; or

  - The term confers a benefit on him, unless it appears that the contracting parties did not intend him to have the right to enforce it.

  The third party must be expressly identified in the contract by name, class or description, but need not be in existence when the contract is made (for example, an unborn child or a future spouse). The Act enables a third party to take advantage of exclusion clauses as well as to enforce 'positive' rights. The Act does not apply to employment contracts, so, for example, a customer of an employer cannot use this Act to enforce a term of a contract of employment against an employee.

Interactive question 6: Essentials of a valid contract [Difficulty level: Exam standard]

You have been asked to act as legal advisor to Catherine, advising her whether or not a contract exists between her and David after the following course of events.

On Monday, David advertised a table and chairs for sale for £100 in the local newspaper. Catherine saw the advertisement and telephoned David offering him £75. David offered to sell the table and chairs to Catherine for £80. She accepted. Two days later, Catherine rang David and said that she would give him £85 if he delivered the table and chairs as well. David refused. Catherine said that if she had to collect the table and chairs herself she would only give David £75. During the course of their negotiations, Catherine and David have discovered that they know each other through the local gardening club.

Indicate whether each of the following statements is true or false.

A	As Catherine and David are acquaintances, they cannot form a binding contract.	☐	True	☐	False
B	Catherine and David have not formed a valid contract as they have been unable to come to an agreement about price.	☐	True	☐	False
C	Delivery is capable of constituting sufficient consideration for an increase in contract price.	☐	True	☐	False
D	If David accepts Catherine's final suggestion, there will be a binding contract between them at a price of £75.	☐	True	☐	False

See **Answer** at the end of this chapter.

Summary and Self-test

Summary

A valid contract is a legally binding agreement, formed by the mutual consent of two parties

The **three essential elements** of a contract are **offer and acceptance**, **consideration** and **intention to enter into legal relations**.

There are a number of factors which may affect the validity of a contract. For a contract to be binding it must also satisfy various tests relating to **certainty**, **legality**, **form** and the **genuineness of consent** of the parties

A contract contains **express** terms and additional terms may be **implied** by custom, statue or the courts
- Business efficacy
- Necessarily incidental

Generally speaking it can only be enforced by the parties to it. Exceptions
- Agency
- Contracts (Rights of Third Parties) Act 1999

A contract which is not valid may be:
- Void (neither party is bound)
- Voidable (the contract is binding unless and until one party chooses to avoid it)
- Unenforceable (the contract is valid but its terms cannot be enforced in a legal sense (although it may be ratifies)

Essential element	Components	Definition	Rules	Exceptions
Agreement	Offer	'A definite promise to be bound on specific terms'	Cannot be vague	
			Does not have to be made to particular person	
			Must be distinguished from invitation to treat	
			May be express words, action of inferred from action, but not silence	
	Acceptance	'A positive act by a person to whom an offer has been made which, if unconditional, brings a binding contract into effect'	Must be unconditional acceptance of terms (ie not counter-offer or request for information)	
			Must be communicated to the offeror	Unless: (1) Offeror waives the need (2) Under postal rule, a posted letter does not arrive acceptance remains valid
			Offer can only be accepted when it remains open – it may lapse in the following situations: (1) Rejection or counter-offer (2) Lapse of time (3) Revocation (4) Failure of condition	
Intention		'An agreement will only become legally binding if the parties intend that this will be so'	In the absence of express intention, the courts apply 'rebuttable presumptions:' (1) Family or social agreements not intended to be binding (2) Commercial agreements intended to be binding	No exceptions – but remember the presumptions are rebuttable – if you can prove otherwise, the courts will apply what you can prove
Consideration		'A valuable consideration in the sense of the law may consist either in some right, interest, profit or benefit accruing to one party, or some forbearance detriment, loss or responsibility given, suffered or undertaken by the other'	Must not be past	Implied promise to pay for a service
			Need not be adequate	
	Executed or Executory		Must be sufficient	
			Waiver of rights under a contract must be matched by consideration from the other party	(1) Alternative consideration given (goods, early settlement) (2) Third party pays part – rest is cancelled
			Consideration must move from the promisee (privity of contract), only then have the rights in the contract	(1) Contracts (Rights of Third Parties) Act (2) Agency

Self-test

Answer the following questions.

1 Which one of the contracts below is a standard form contract?

A A document put forward for the customer's signature by a supplier of goods in which pre-printed contractual terms are set out

B A document signed by both parties to a contract in which contractual terms as negotiated between them are set down

C An oral agreement to enter into relations on the basis of terms as agreed following negotiations between the parties

D An oral agreement between two parties who have negotiated terms regarding the standards of performance to be met by each party in the main contract

2 A new Common European Sales Law has been proposed and will be mandatory in all cross-border contracts..

True ☐

False ☐

3 A valid contract is a legally binding agreement. The three essential elements of a contract are
(1) .... (2) .... and (3) ....

4 A voidable contract is not a contract at all.

True ☐

False ☐

5 Match the term to its definition.

(a) Voidable

(b) Unenforceable

(c) Void

(1) The contract is valid but the parties cannot be held to its terms

(2) Neither party is bound

(3) The contract is binding unless and until one party chooses to avoid it

6 How is the circulation of a price list categorised in the law of contract?

Offer	Tender
Invitation to treat	Auction

7 **Fill in the blanks** in the statements below, using the words in the box.

- As a general rule, acceptance must be (1) .... to the (2) .... and is not effective until this has been done.

- An (3) .... is a definite promise to be bound on specific terms, and must be distinguished from a supply of (4) .... and from an (5) ....

- A counter-offer counts as (6) .... of the original offer.

• Information	• Offer	• Invitation to treat
• Rejection	• Communicated	• Offeror

8   Advertising an auction is an offer to sell.

True ☐

False ☐

9   Give three examples of situations likely to be invitations to treat.

....

....

....

10   As a general rule, silence cannot constitute acceptance.

True ☐

False ☐

11   Define the postal rule.

12   Give four instances when an offer is terminated.

13   Distinguish between executed and executory consideration.

14   Past consideration, as a general rule, is not sufficient to make a promise binding.

True ☐

False ☐

15   Consideration need not be (1) .... but it must be (2)
....

16   A promise of additional reward for existing duties is not generally binding.

True ☐

False ☐

17   In the context of contractual considerations, payment of a lesser sum cannot be satisfaction for the whole sum unless something is added to it, such as earlier payment, or payment by a different method.

True ☐

False ☐

18   What is the name of the express clause typically incorporated into an international contract and which specifies which country's law will apply to any dispute under it?

....

Now go back to the Learning Objectives in the Introduction. If you are satisfied you have achieved these objectives, please tick them off.

Answers to Interactive questions

Answer to Interactive question 1

A   Void
B   Voidable
C   Void
D   Unenforceable

Answer to Interactive question 2

An advertisement is an invitation to treat, ie an invitation to a reader to make an offer which the advertiser can either accept or reject.

Answer to Interactive question 3

A   It is valid because acceptance took place before the revocation was received. Revocation must be received to be effective. It is not effective on posting (unlike an acceptance).

Answer to Interactive question 4

A   True. Frank's letter constitutes an offer.

B   True. The acceptance by Xiao-Xiao takes effect when posted on 10 July. The revocation letter posted 10 July will arrive too late to prevent acceptance on 10 July. Therefore a contract is formed on 10 July.

C   False. Frank's sale of the dinghy to Mel is in breach of his contract with Xiao-Xiao.

Answer to Interactive question 5

A   True. Consideration does not have to be adequate but must be sufficient. In other words, it must have identifiable value. In this case, Alice is offering both £10 and the loan of her car, both of which have identifiable value and thus constitute valid consideration.

B   True on the face of it, since anything that has been done before a promise in return is given is past consideration. However, if it can be argued that the parties must have assumed that there would be payment for this extra work, then it may be valid consideration.

C   True. Alice cannot afford to pay Barry the £10 she agreed and asks him to waive his right to it. This request is accompanied by additional and alternative valuable consideration (the extension of the loan period to a week) and if he accepts those terms, the waiver is binding.

Answer to Interactive question 6

A   False. The presumption that friends do not intend to form contractual agreements is rebuttable and is rebutted in this case – their acquaintance was not recognised or relevant at the time of making the contract.

B   False. David's original advert is an invitation to treat so cannot be accepted as an offer. Catherine's offer of £75 is rejected by David so no contract is formed at this point. However, David then makes an offer of £80 which is accepted by Catherine, at which point a contract is made. The further offer of £85 is rejected but this does not affect the agreement already reached.

C   True. Delivery is clearly valuable to Catherine, as she implies by her offer of an extra £5 for delivery.

D   False. Catherine is asking David to waive his rights under the contract but there is no consideration to support this waiver and it would not be binding on David.

1   A

2   False. The proposed Common European Sales Law is intended to be voluntary and apply to sales of goods, digital content and related services only.

3   Offer and acceptance, consideration, intention to create legal relations

4   False

5   Voidable (3)

    Unenforceable (1)

    Void (2)

6   Invitation to treat

7   (1) communicated (2) offeror (3) offer (4) information (5) invitation to treat (6) rejection

8   False. It is merely a statement of intention.

9   Advertisements

    Exhibition of goods for sale

    Circulation of a price list

10 True

11 The postal rule states that, where the use of the post is within the contemplation of both the parties, the acceptance is complete and effective as soon as a letter is posted, even though it may be delayed or even lost altogether in the post.

12 Rejection

    Lapse of time

    Revocation by the offeror

    Failure of a condition to which the offer was subject

    Counter-offer

13 Executed consideration is an act in return for a promise, such as paying for goods when the shopkeeper hands them over. Executory consideration is a promise given for a promise, such as promising to pay for goods that the shopkeeper puts on order for you.

14 True

15 (1) adequate (2) sufficient

16 True

17 True

18 Governing law clause or
    Choice of law clause

CHAPTER 2

Termination of contract

Introduction

Examination context

Topic List

1   Discharge of the contract

2   Remedies

3   Exclusion clauses in contracts

Summary and Self-test

Answers to Interactive questions

Answers to Self-test

Learning objectives

- Understand the various ways in which a contract may be discharged ☐

- Recognise when a contract can be said to have been frustrated and understand the consequences of frustration ☐

- Define breach of contract and recognise when it arises ☐

- Understand and apply the rules relating to damages ☐

- Be aware of alternative contractual remedies and the circumstances in which they might be awarded ☐

- Recognise an exclusion clause and understand how it might be affected by the Unfair Contract Terms Act ☐

Specific syllabus references for this chapter are: 1a, b.

Syllabus links

You will have learnt about liabilities and provisions in your accounting paper. It is helpful to see how, in practice, such liabilities of companies might arise.

Examination context

You should expect several questions on contract termination. They are likely to be a mixture of application 'scenario' questions and definition questions.

In the assessment, candidates may be required to:

- Identify the circumstances under which a contract can be terminated
- Identify possible remedies for breach of contract
- Recognise an exclusion clause and assess whether it is effective

1 Discharge of the contract

Section overview

- A contract is usually discharged by performance of the parties' obligations contained in the contract.

- Events may take place which make performance of the contract impossible or meaningless, thereby discharging the contract by frustration.

- In the absence of frustration (or other lawful excuse), non-performance will constitute breach of the contract.

1.1 Performance

Performance is the normal method of discharge of a contract: each party fulfils or performs his contractual obligations and the agreement is then ended. Although it is commonly said that **complete and exact performance** of all the contract terms is required to discharge the contract, in fact the courts will apply an important qualification to this rule. This is that so long as there is **substantial** performance of a party's contractual obligations, that will be a sufficient discharge, although the other party will be entitled to seek redress for that part of the performance that did not completely and exactly match the contract terms.

While partial performance cannot discharge the contract as a whole, most contracts are treated as **'severable'** which means that they consist of a number of obligations and can be 'severed' or discharged through performance of only part of those obligations, leaving the remaining obligations to be performed. For example, employment contracts usually provide for payment each week or month and building contracts usually provide for payment at various stages of the contractor's progress. Each of these payment dates or stages represents a point at which the contract can be severed or, effectively, divided into smaller contracts.

If one party prevents performance, the offer of performance by the other party is sufficient discharge of his obligations and he will be entitled to sue for damages for breach of contract, or alternatively bring a **quantum meruit** (literally 'as much as he deserved') action to claim for the amount of work already completed.

> *Planché v Colburn 1831*
>
> *The facts:* C had agreed to write a book on costumes and armour for D's 'Juvenile Library' series. He was to receive £100 on completion. He did some research and wrote part of the book. D then abandoned the series.
>
> *Decision:* C was entitled to 50 guineas as reasonable remuneration on a *quantum meruit* basis.

Interactive question 1: Discharge by performance   **[Difficulty level: Easy]**

Carol employs Lawrence as an interior designer and decorator to do some work on her apartment. The contract price is £15,000. Lawrence completes the work within the allotted time. When inspecting the work, Carol notices that a lampshade she specified has not been supplied, that the door handles are of the wrong design and that two of the new bathroom tiles are cracked. She tells Lawrence the job is incomplete and refuses to pay. Advise Lawrence.

☐ Lawrence is not entitled to payment since he has not performed his obligations completely and exactly.

☐ Lawrence is entitled to receive the full contract price since he has substantially performed his part of the contract.

☐ Lawrence is entitled to receive the contract price less a reasonable deduction for the defects and omissions.

See **Answer** at the end of this chapter.

ICAEW

1.2 Discharge by frustration

If it is **impossible** to perform the contract when it is made, there is usually no contract at all. In respect of impossibility arising after the contract has been made, the parties are free to negotiate escape clauses or *force majeure* clauses (for example in respect of adverse weather or strike action in a building contract) which will prevail if the anticipated impossibility arises.

However if, after the contract is made, performance or further performance of the contract is rendered impossible or totally futile by some extraneous cause, for which neither party is responsible (and for which the contract makes no provision), then the contract will be treated as discharged by **frustration**. A contract will not be discharged where another mode of performance is still possible, even if that way is more expensive and/or more difficult.

The following are examples of events or changes in circumstances where contracts have been frustrated:

	Example
Destruction of the subject matter	A hall was let to a musician for a series of concerts but before the date of the first concert, the hall was accidentally destroyed by fire (*Taylor v Caldwell 1863*).
Personal incapacity to perform a contract of personal service	A drummer was contracted to perform seven nights a week in a pop group. Due to ill-health the drummer was only able to perform four nights a week (*Condor v Barron Knights 1966*).
Government intervention	Where an outbreak of war or new legislation rendered further performance of the contract illegal.
Non-occurrence of an event which is the sole purpose of the contract	A room was let for the sole purpose of overlooking the coronation procession of a King, whose illness caused the procession to be postponed (*Krell v Henry 1903*). (Note that the contract would not have been frustrated if the room had been let for several days or for some other purpose also).

The Law Reform (Frustrated Contracts) Act 1943

In most cases, the rights and liabilities of parties to a contract discharged by frustration are regulated by the Law Reform (Frustrated Contracts) Act 1943, although any express provision to the contrary will prevail. The consequences of frustration under the Act are as follows:

- Any **money paid** under the contract before the frustrating event is to be repaid.

- Any **sums due** for payment under the contract cease to be payable.

- If a person has to repay money, or if he must forego a payment that should have been made before the frustrating event, then if the court considers it just in all the circumstances of the case, he may be able to retain or recover (as the case may be) **expenses incurred**, provided they were incurred **in the performance of the contract** and before the contract was frustrated.

- If either party has obtained a **valuable benefit** (other than payment of money) under the contract before it is discharged, the court may in its discretion order him to pay to the other party all or such part of that value as it considers just, having regard to all the circumstances of the case.

    BP Exploration Co (Libya) Ltd v Hunt (No. 2) 1982

    The facts: Hunt owned an oil concession in Libya. BP was contracted to explore and exploit the potential oil fields in return for a share of the concession if successful. BP's investigation revealed a large oil field and pipelines were laid. The Libyan Government then cancelled the concession, thus frustrating the contract.

    Decision: The court held that Hunt had received a valuable benefit of around $85m in terms of the increased value of his concession as a result of discovering oil. The court awarded a 'just sum' of around $35m to represent this valuable benefit. It took into account all the circumstances, namely the value of the oil already removed, the potential claim for compensation against the Libyan Government and the allocation of risk expressed in the contract.

Interactive question 2: Frustration of contract   [Difficulty level: Easy]

Which of the following is *not* a correct statement of the law relating to frustration of contract?

A   Parties are discharged from their contract if altered circumstances render the contract
    fundamentally different in nature from what was originally agreed.   ☐

B   Parties are discharged if an event, for which neither party is responsible, occurs which
    renders performance impossible or futile.   ☐

C   Parties who contract that something should be done are discharged if performance
    becomes substantially more expensive or onerous.   ☐

D   Parties who contract that something should be done are discharged if their assumption
    that certain conditions (which are fundamental to the contract), would continue, proves
    to be totally false.   ☐

See **Answer** at the end of this chapter.

1.3   Breach of contract

Where a party does not perform his contractual obligation sufficiently, he is said to be in **breach of
contract**, unless the contract has been discharged by frustration or he has some other **lawful excuse**. A
lawful excuse may apply in the following circumstances:

*   Where he has tendered performance but this has been **rejected.**
*   Where the **other party** has made it **impossible** for him to perform.
*   Where the parties have by **agreement** permitted **non-performance**.

All breaches of contract entitle the injured party to seek damages. If the breach is **very serious**, the
injured party is entitled to treat the contract as at an end (thus discharging his own obligations) in
addition to seeking damages. Alternatively, he may elect to affirm the contract. This kind of serious
breach (sometimes called 'repudiatory breach') arises in the following circumstances:

*   Where the **breach is of a term** which the parties regard as a **fundamentally important term** or
    where the breach has the effect of **depriving the injured party of substantially the whole
    benefit** of the contract. Sometimes the test applied is whether the breach can be said to 'go to the
    root of the contract'.

*   Where one party renounces his contractual obligations explicitly or implicitly in advance by
    showing that he has no intention of performing them. This kind of breach before performance is
    due is also known as '**anticipatory breach**'.

    Hochster v De La Tour 1853

    The facts: D engaged C as a courier to accompany him on a European tour commencing on 1
    June. On 11 May D wrote to C to say that he no longer required his services. On 22 May C
    commenced legal proceedings for anticipatory breach of contract. D objected that there was
    no actionable breach until 1 June.

    Decision: C was entitled to sue as soon as the anticipatory breach occurred on 11 May.

Where the breach is sufficiently serious, the injured party may choose (at the time of the breach) either
to:

*   Treat the contract as discharged immediately and sue for damages
*   Allow the contract to continue until there is an actual breach and take action at that time

If the innocent party elects to treat the contract as still in force, he may continue with his preparations
for performance and **recover the agreed price** for his services. The duty to mitigate his losses (see
section 2.1 below) does not arise until he accepts the breach, but he will need to show that the losses
have been caused by the actual breach.

If the innocent party **elects to treat the contract as discharged**, he must **notify the other party** of his decision. This may be by way of refusal to accept further performance or refusal to perform his own obligations. In this situation, the following applies:

- He is not discharged from the contractual obligations which were due at the time of termination, but he is discharged from his future or continuing contractual obligations and cannot be sued on them.

- He need not accept nor pay for further performance.

- He may be able to refuse to pay for partial or defective performance already received, unless the contract is severable.

- He can reclaim money already paid in respect of defective performance.

- He can still claim damages from the defaulter.

2 Remedies

Section overview

- Contractual disputes may be resolved by civil litigation in the courts or by other means.

- Damages are the main remedy awarded by the courts for breach of contract and are designed to compensate the claimant by putting him in the position he would have been in, if the contract had been performed.

- In some cases, a more appropriate remedy might be awarded, such as specific performance or an injunction.

In this section, you will learn about the remedies available in the courts in an action for breach of contract. However, you should be aware that the majority of contractual disputes will not reach the courts and may be resolved by negotiation, arbitration or some other means such as mediation, adjudication or expert determination. These alternatives to litigation are usually referred to as 'alternative dispute resolution' (or 'ADR') and are actively encouraged by the courts, even once court proceedings have been commenced.

2.1 Damages

In a claim for damages the first issue is **remoteness of damage**. Here the courts consider how far down the sequence of cause and effect the consequences of breach should be traced before they should be ignored.

Under the rule in *Hadley v Baxendale* (see below) damages may only be awarded in respect of those losses which may fairly and reasonably be considered as, either:

- Arising naturally (ie according to the usual course of things) from such breach of contract, or

- Such as may reasonably be supposed to have been in the contemplation of both parties, at the time of making the contract, as the probable result of the breach.

> *Hadley v Baxendale 1854*
>
> *The facts:* C owned a mill at Gloucester. When the main crank shaft had broken, C made a contract with D for the transport of the broken shaft to Greenwich to serve as a pattern for making a new shaft. Owing to D's neglect, delivery was delayed and the mill was out of action for a longer period. D did not know that the mill would be idle during this interval, simply that he had to transport a broken millshaft. C claimed for loss of profits of the mill during the period of delay.
>
> *Decision:* Although D's failure to perform the contract promptly was the direct cause of the stoppage of the mill for an unnecessarily long time, the claim must fail since it was not a natural consequence of delay in transport of a broken shaft, that the mill would be out of action (the miller might have a spare for example) and D did not know that that would be the result.

If the defendant can show that the 'chain of causation' was broken and that the claimant had, in fact, caused the loss, the defendant will not be liable. This is a question of fact, but if the claimant is unaware of the breach, it is likely that only recklessness on his part would break the chain of causation (*Borealis AB v Geogas Trading SA 2010*).

If the losses are **exceptional or abnormal** and **not reasonably foreseeable**, the defendant will be liable only if he knew (at the time of the contract) of the special circumstances from which the abnormal consequence of breach could arise.

> *Victoria Laundry (Windsor) v Newman Industries 1949*
>
> *The facts:* D contracted to sell a large boiler to C 'for immediate use' in their business of launderers and dyers but were late delivering it. D was aware of the nature of C's business and had been informed that C was most anxious to put the boiler into use in the shortest possible space of time. C claimed damages for normal loss of profits for the period of delay and for loss of abnormal profits from losing 'highly lucrative' dyeing contracts which would have been undertaken, if the boiler had been delivered on time.
>
> *Decision:* Damages for loss of normal profits were recoverable since, in the circumstances, failure to deliver major industrial equipment ordered for immediate use would be expected to prevent operation of the plant. The claim for loss of special profits failed because D had no knowledge of the dyeing contracts.

Interactive question 3: Remoteness of damage   [Difficulty level: Exam standard]

Louise runs a homemade cake business. Cook & Co contract to sell her a large industrial oven to enable her to expand her business by enabling her to increase cake production. Louise tells Cook & Co that she has also been awarded a contract to bake 100 jacket potatoes daily during November and December for a local street fair in the run up to Christmas and so needs the oven by 31 October. Cook & Co agree to deliver the oven by 28 October. Unknown to Cook & Co, Louise has also agreed to allow Bob the Baker to use the oven on Fridays (her day off) so that he can meet his extra customer demands over the weekends.

Owing to a dispute between the manufacturer and Cook & Co, the oven is not delivered to Louise until 12 November. Louise is therefore unable to fulfil the jacket potatoes contract and also is unable to increase cake production as planned. She has also lost the hire payment agreed by Bob in respect of two Fridays.

Which one of the following statements best describes the legal position of Cook & Co?

A   Cook & Co could not be expected to know that Louise would not have access to a replacement oven and will not have to pay damages as a consequence ☐

B   Cook & Co were aware of the jacket potatoes contract and so are liable for that loss but not for Louise's other losses as they were not known ☐

C   Cook & Co is liable for all Louise's losses since they were all in the course of her business ☐

D   Cook & Co are not liable for the loss due to the agreement with Bob but will be liable in respect of the other losses. ☐

See **Answer** at the end of this chapter.

The second issue to be considered is how much money (what '**measure of damages**') is needed to put the claimant in the position he would have achieved if the contract had been performed. This is sometimes referred to as protecting the **expectation interest** of the claimant. A claimant may alternatively seek to have his **reliance interest** protected; this refers to the position he would have been in had he not relied on the contract. In such cases, he is claiming for wasted expenditure and the onus is on the defendant to show that the expenditure would not have been recovered if the contract had been performed.

Anglia Television Ltd v Reed 1972

The facts: C engaged an actor to appear in a film they were making for television. He pulled out at the last moment and the project was abandoned. C claimed the preparatory expenditure, such as hiring other actors and researching suitable locations.

Decision: Damages were awarded as claimed. It is impossible to tell whether an unmade film will be a success or a failure and, had C claimed for loss of profits, they would not have succeeded.

In a recent case, the court confirmed that a claim for wasted expenditure was also subject to the general principle that an award of damages should not put a claimant in a better position than he would have been in if the contract had been performed. Reliance damages will not be awarded regardless of the anticipated profit to be made by the claimant, but would only be awarded where his gross profits were likely to exceed his expenditure (*Omak Maritime Ltd v Mamola Challenger Shipping Co 2010*).

Generally speaking, damages will only be awarded for **actual financial loss**. In vary rare cases, damages have been recovered for **mental distress** where that is the main result of the breach. It is uncertain how far the courts will develop this concept.

Jarvis v Swan Tours 1973

The facts: C entered into a contract for holiday accommodation at a winter sports centre. What was provided was significantly inferior to the description given in D's brochure. Damages on the basis of financial loss only were assessed at £32.

Decision: The damages should be increased to £125 to compensate for disappointment and distress because the principal purpose of the contract was the giving of pleasure.

Mitigation of loss

In assessing the amount of damages, it is assumed that the claimant will take all reasonable steps to reduce or **mitigate** his loss. He is not required, however, to take discreditable or risky measures as these are not 'reasonable'. The burden of proof is on the defendant to show that the claimant failed to take a reasonable opportunity of mitigation.

Payzu Ltd v Saunders 1919

The facts: The parties had entered into a contract for the supply of goods to be delivered and paid for by instalments. When C failed to pay for the first instalment on the due date, D declined to make further deliveries unless C paid cash in advance with their orders. C refused to accept delivery on those terms. The price of the goods rose, and they sued for breach of contract.

Decision: D had no right to repudiate the original contract, and was therefore liable in damages. However, C should have mitigated their loss by accepting D's offer of delivery against cash payment. Damages were limited to the amount of their assumed loss, had C paid in advance, ie interest over the period of pre-payment. The judge commented that 'in commercial contracts, it is generally reasonable to accept an offer from the party in default'.

Interactive question 4: Measure of damages [Difficulty level: Exam standard]

Chana agrees to buy a car from Mike's Motors for £6,000. Mike had paid £5,500 for the car. On the agreed day, Chana arrives at the dealers but refuses to accept or pay for the car. In the meantime, the car's market value has risen to £7,000. The following week Mike sells the car for £7,500. Mike claims against Chana for damages. What sum is Mike likely to be awarded?

Nothing ☐   £6,000 ☐

£5,500 ☐   £7,000 ☐

See **Answer** at the end of this chapter.

2.2 Liquidated damages and penalty clauses

To avoid later complicated calculations of loss, or disputes over damages payable, the parties may include up-front in their contract a fixed sum or a formula for determining the damages payable for breach (**liquidated damages**).

Such a clause will be effective provided it is considered to be a genuine attempt to pre-estimate the likely loss. This will be a question of fact. If the sum is arbitrary or excessive, it will be construed as a **penalty clause** and will not be enforceable.

Ford Motor Co (England) Ltd v Armstrong 1915

The facts: D had undertaken not to sell C's cars below list price, not to sell Ford cars to other dealers and not to exhibit any Ford cars without permission. A £250 penalty was payable for each breach as being the agreed loss which C would sustain.

Decision: Since the same sum was payable for different kinds of loss and was considered to be arbitrary and excessive, it was not a genuine pre-estimate of loss. It was therefore in the nature of a penalty and unenforceable.

In *Hall v Van Der Heiden 2010,* on the other hand, a provision for liquidated damages of £700 per week was enforceable where a contractor failed to complete refurbishment works to the claimant's flat. The sum was considered to be a genuine pre-estimate of loss, which took into account the cost of alternative accommodation and could not be described as a penalty.

Worked example: Liquidated damages

Edith and Furaha are negotiating the terms of a contract whereby Furaha is fitting out Edith's shop. Edith is due to open on 1 June and she has calculated that, if the shop opens late, she will lose £400 a day. She therefore wants to include a clause in the contract stating that if Furaha overruns, she will pay Edith damages of £400 per day. As this is a genuine pre-estimate of loss, it is likely that this would be construed as an enforceable provision for liquidated damages.

2.3 Specific performance

The court may, in its discretion, make an order for specific performance. This is an equitable remedy which orders the defendant to perform his part of the contract instead of letting him 'buy himself out of it' by paying damages for breach.

It will only be awarded where damages are not an adequate remedy. For example, an order is likely to be made for specific performance of a contract for the sale of land, since the claimant may need the land for a particular purpose and would not be adequately compensated by damages for the loss of his bargain.

Specific performance will **not** be granted if it would require **supervision** of the performance (for example a building contract) or if it is a contract for personal service (such as an employment contract).

2.4 Injunction

There are three types of injunction that can be granted in the court's discretion:

- A **mandatory injunction** which is restorative in its effect. It directs the defendant to take **positive** steps to undo something he has already done in breach of contract, for example to demolish a building that he has erected in breach of contract. This is a relatively rare remedy and will only be granted where it will produce a fair result in all the circumstances.

- A **prohibitory injunction** which requires the defendant to observe a **negative** promise in a contract.

  Note that where a person enters into a contract to perform personal services for A and not to perform them for B, an injunction may be given to enforce the negative promise, even though an order of specific performance for the positive promise would be refused.

- An **asset-freezing injunction** prevents the defendant from dealing with assets where the claimant can convince the court that he has a good case and that there is a danger of the defendant's assets being exported or dissipated.

Worked example: Injunctions

Sophia agreed to sing at Andrew's theatre for six months and not to sing at Tim's theatre during that period. After a few weeks, Sophia began to give three matinee performances each week at Tim's theatre. Andrew wants to sue her for breach of contract.

Andrew would be entitled to damages. In addition he should consider seeking a prohibitory injunction, restricting Sophia from performing at Tim's theatre, ie enforcing her promise not to do so.

(Note that had the contract stipulated that Sophia should only work for Andrew and not for anybody else in any capacity whatsoever, an injunction would not be granted, even of the negative promise, because that would result in her being compelled to work for him or otherwise abandon her livelihood and starve.)

3 Exclusion clauses in contracts

Section overview

- An exclusion clause in a contract is one which purports to restrict or exclude liability for breach of contract or negligence.

- An exclusion clause must have been properly incorporated in the contract if it is to be effective.

- It will be interpreted strictly against the party seeking to rely on it.

- An exclusion clause in a standard form or consumer contract may be rendered void or subject to a test of reasonableness by the Unfair Contract Terms Act 1977.

It is often the case that when a party sues the other for breach of contract, the defaulting party will claim that his liability for breach has been restricted or excluded altogether by an **exclusion clause** contained in the contract. Such clauses are very common in standard form contracts. (A standard form contract is a contract that has been prepared by one of the parties on its written standard terms of business, rather than one where the terms have been individually negotiated and agreed by the parties.)

3.1 Incorporation and interpretation

In order to be a **properly incorporated** term of the contract, the clause or document containing the exclusion of liability must be an **integral part** of the contract. If it is actually in the nature of an unsigned receipt for payment or otherwise given after the contract is made, then it is not regarded as part of the contract and will not be effective.

Olley v Marlborough Court 1949

The facts: A husband and wife arrived at a hotel and paid for a room in advance. On reaching their bedroom they saw a notice on the wall by which the hotel disclaimed liability for loss of valuables unless handed to the management for safe keeping. A thief obtained the key and stole the wife's furs from the bedroom.

Decision: The hotel could not rely on the notice disclaiming liability since the contract had been made when they checked in and the disclaimer was too late.

Provided the document is an integral part of the contract, then, generally speaking, the following rules will apply:

- If the document is **signed**, it will be regarded as binding, even if the person has not read the term and even if the term is in 'small print' (provided no misleading explanation has been given of the term's effect).

- If the document is **not signed**, then it must be shown that the person whose rights it restricts was made **sufficiently aware** of it at the time of making the contract. In particular, **onerous terms** must be sufficiently highlighted.

Interactive question 5: Exclusion clause   [Difficulty level: Easy]

Natasha hires a car from a car rental company. On arrival at their office she is given a form, which includes terms and conditions in small print on the back, and asked to sign it. She does so and pays the hire charge. When she gets into the car, she happens to look in the glove compartment and sees a document headed 'Limitation of Liability'. This states that the hire company will not be liable for any injury caused by a defect in the car unless this is as a result of the company's negligence. While Natasha is driving on the motorway, the airbag inflates and causes her to crash. She is badly injured. Which of the following is correct?

☐ Natasha's claim will be valid as she signed the form containing terms and conditions.

☐ The claim will be invalid because the liability notice was in the car.

☐ It is unclear whether the claim will be valid because the notice in the car may have been reinforcing the terms and conditions Natasha signed.

See **Answer** at the end of this chapter.

Once an exclusion clause can be shown to be an incorporated term, the courts will **interpret** any ambiguity in the clause **against the person who relies on the exclusion.**

Basically, the clause must cover the breach complained of. For example, a clause excluding liability for 'damage caused by fire' might be interpreted to mean only accidental fire and not fire caused by the person's negligence.

The following case illustrates the point:

Photo Productions v Securicor Transport 1980

The facts: D agreed to guard C's factory under a contract by which D was excluded from liability for damage caused by any of their employees. One of the guards deliberately started a small fire which destroyed the factory and contents. It was contended that D had entirely failed to perform their contract and so they could not rely on any exclusion clause in the contract.

Decision: There is no principle that total failure to perform a contract deprives the party at fault of any exclusion from liability provided by the contract. In this case the exclusion clause was drawn widely enough to cover the damage which had happened.

3.2 The Unfair Contract Terms Act

The Unfair Contract Terms Act 1977 (UCTA) makes legislative provision for exclusion clauses in certain contracts, sometimes rendering them void altogether and sometimes rendering them void if they fail to satisfy a test of reasonableness.

Some types of contract (for example insurance and land transfer contracts) are excluded but, generally speaking, UCTA is concerned with business liability only and applies to clauses inserted into agreements by **commercial concerns or businesses**. In principle private persons may restrict liability as much as they wish.

The main provisions of UCTA can be summarised as follows:

- Any clause or notice that attempts to exclude or restrict liability for **death or personal injury** arising from negligence is **void**.

- Any clause that attempts to restrict liability for **other loss or damage arising from negligence** is void unless it can be shown to be **reasonable**.

- In contracts of sale or hire purchase, a clause that purports to exclude or limit liability for breach of the undertakings as to **title** of the seller or owner, implied by the Sale of Goods Act 1979, is **void**.

- In a contract for sale or hire purchase or for the supply of goods and services **with a consumer**, a clause that purports to exclude or limit liability for breach of the conditions relating to **description, quality, fitness and sample** implied by the Sale of Goods Act 1979 is **void** (in such a contract between businesses, the reasonableness test will apply).

- Any clause that attempts to limit liability for breach of contract, where the contract is based on standard terms or conditions, and/or where the party against whom the exclusion clause is being used is a **consumer**, is void unless it can be shown to be **reasonable**. (In respect of contracts between businesses, note that such exclusion clauses in 'bespoke contracts' (ie ones where the key terms are individually negotiated and drawn up by the parties) will be enforced as written, provided they are properly incorporated.)

UCTA defines a **consumer** as someone who neither makes (nor holds himself out as making) the contract in the course of a business, where the other party does make the contract in the course of a business. Note that UCTA does not just operate to protect consumers; businesses may also benefit from its provisions.

Where the statutory test of reasonableness applies, the term must be **fair and reasonable having regard to all the circumstances** which were, or which ought to have been, known to the parties when the contract was made. The burden of proving reasonableness lies on the person seeking to rely on the clause. Statutory guidelines have been included in the Act to assist the determination of reasonableness. By way of example, reasonableness will depend on factors such as the relative strength of the parties' bargaining positions, whether any inducement was offered and whether the innocent party knew or should have known of the term. In addition, the courts have considered other matters to be significant, such as whether insurance was in place or available to the party relying on the clause and whether any misrepresentations were made. Where the parties are of equal bargaining strength, the courts will be reluctant to hold the exclusion clause to be unfair or unreasonable and invalid.

The Unfair Terms in Consumer Contracts Regulations 1999 provide further statutory control in respect of consumer contracts and, in particular, terms which have not been individually negotiated. They provide that an 'unfair term' may be declared to be void. Unlike UCTA, the Regulations only protect individuals, not companies. You will not be examined on the Regulations.

Summary

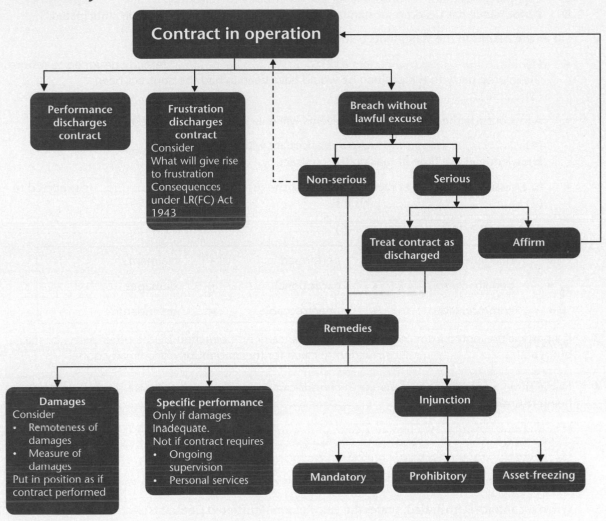

Self-test

Answer the following questions.

1 Which of the following is **not** a lawful excuse not to perform contractual obligations?

   A The contract has been discharged though frustration.
   B The parties have by agreement permitted non-performance.
   C One party has made it impossible for the other party to perform.
   D Performance has become substantially more expensive than was originally anticipated.

2 **Fill in the blanks** in the statements below, using the words in the box.

   - (1) .... are a (2) .... remedy designed to restore the injured party to the position he would have been in had the contract been (3) ....

   - A loss outside the natural course of events will only be compensated if the

     (4) .... circumstances are within the (5) ....'s knowledge at the time of making the contract.

   - In assessing the extent of recoverable losses, the (6) .... is expected to (7) .... his loss.

   - A contractual term designed as a (8) .... is (9) ....

• mitigate	• performed	• claimant
• penalty clause	• exceptional	• damages
• common law	• unenforceable	• defendant

3 If a party is prevented from completing performance of his obligation by the other party, he may bring a .... action to claim for the amount of work already done.

4 Name three types of event or change in current circumstances which will give rise to a contract being frustrated.

   (1) ....
   (2) ....
   (3) ....

5 When a contract is frustrated, under the Law Reform (Frustrated Contracts) Act 1943, any monies paid to the other party prior to frustration can be recovered but expenses incurred by that other party cannot be recovered or offset.

   ☐ True

   ☐ False

6 A claimant must do all that he can to reduce the amount of the loss he suffers.

   ☐ True

   ☐ False

7 When anticipatory breach occurs, the injured party has two options. These are to:

   (1) ....
   (2) ....

8 Name two types of Alternative Dispute Resolution (other than negotiation).

....

....

9 What is the rule set out in *Hadley v Baxendale* concerning remoteness of damage?

10 The amount awarded as damages is what is needed to put the claimant in the position he would have achieved if the contract had been performed. What interest is being protected here?

☐ Expectation

☐ Reliance

11 A court will never enforce a liquidated damages clause, as any attempt to prevent the injured party from pursuing a remedy through the courts is void.

☐ True

☐ False

12 Will a clause in a standard form contract which excludes or restricts liability for the following be rendered void or subject to the reasonableness test under UCTA?

	Void	Test
A For death or personal injury in a non-consumer contract	☐	☐
B For other loss or damage arising from breach of contract or negligence in a consumer contract	☐	☐
C For breach of the implied condition relating to fitness in a consumer contract	☐	☐

13 The following definition of a consumer is contained in UCTA. Fill in the gaps.

(a) He neither makes the contract in course of (1) .... nor holds himself out as doing so

(b) The other (2) .... does make the contract in course of (3) ....

Now, go back to the Learning Objectives in the Introduction. If you are satisfied you have achieved these objectives, please tick them off.

Answer to Interactive question 1

Lawrence is entitled to receive the contract price less a reasonable deduction for defects and omissions.

Answer to Interactive question 2

C   Greater expense or difficulty than anticipated does not result in frustration.

Answer to Interactive question 3

D   Cook & Co were aware of the nature of her business and therefore will be liable to pay damages for her loss of normal profits arising from her inability to increase cake production between 28 October and 12 November. The losses on the baked potatoes contract are also recoverable from 1 – 12 November since, although they cannot be said to arise from the ordinary course of her business, Louise made Cook & Co aware of the contract. The agreement to let Bob hire the oven was not in the ordinary course of her business and the special circumstances were not known to Cook & Co, so they would not be liable for the loss of special profits on this contract.

Answer to Interactive question 4

Nothing. Mike has completely mitigated his loss by the subsequent sale.

Answer to Interactive question 5

There must be prior notice of the presence of an exclusion clause. The answer here will depend on whether this exclusion was included in the original terms and conditions (and therefore merely reinforced by the later document) or not.

Answers to Self-test

1   D   An increase in cost does not lawfully excuse non-performance of a contract.

2   (1)   damages   (2)   common law   (3)   performed
     (4)   exceptional   (5)   defendant   (6)   claimant
     (7)   mitigate   (8)   penalty clause (9) unenforceable

3   Quantum meruit

4   Destruction of the subject matter

     Personal incapacity to perform a contract of personal service

     Government intervention

     Non-occurrence of an event which is the sole purpose of the contract

5   False. Expenses incurred in the performance of the contract prior to frustration may be recovered or offset in the court's discretion.

6   False. He is only required to take all **reasonable** steps to mitigate his loss.

7   (1)   Treat the contract as discharged forthwith

     (2)   Allow the contract to continue unless and until there is an actual breach

8   Mediation; Arbitration; Adjudication; Expert determination

9   Recoverable damages should be:

     (i)   Such as arise naturally from the breach; or

     (ii)   Which the parties may reasonably be supposed to have contemplated, in making the contract, as the probable result of the breach of it.

10   Expectation

11   False. Provided the amount is a genuine pre-estimate of loss, it will be enforceable.

12   A   Void

     B   Subject to the reasonableness test

     C   Void

13   (1)   A business
     (2)   Party
     (3)   A business

CHAPTER 3

Agency

Introduction

Examination context

Topic List

Introduction

Learning objectives

- Understand the nature of agency and its implications

- Examine the methods by which an agency is created

- Study the duties and rights of agents

- Recognise the authority an agent has to enter contracts and instances where they may be liable under them

Specific syllabus references for this chapter are: 1c, d, e.

Syllabus links

As outlined above, agency is the basis of partnership which we will go on to look at later in this syllabus.

Examination context

This is an important area for your exam. The sample paper contained five questions on agency law. It is likely to be examined in the context of partnerships.

In the assessment, candidates may be required to:

- Identify the methods by which agency can be created

- Identify the rights and duties of agents

- Recognise the authority an agent has to enter into contracts on behalf of a principal, including actual and ostensible authority

1 Agency and agents

Section overview

- Agency is a very important feature of modern commercial life and describes the relationship that exists where one party, the agent, acts on behalf of another, the principal.

- We are concerned with the law of agency in so far as it relates to the agent purporting to enter into a contract with a third party, on behalf of the principal.

- The basic principles of agency are relevant to the actions and liabilities of (among others) partners and company directors.

Where an agency relationships exists, the agent, by entering into a contract, establishes privity of contract between the principal and the third party. The contract is thus enforceable both by and against the principal and third party. Generally speaking, the agent effectively drops out of the picture and has no rights or liabilities in respect of it, provided he has acted within his authority. It is as if the principal had made the contract himself in the first place. The questions of authority and liability are addressed in sections 4 and 5 below.

Section 2 describes the various ways in which an agency relationship may come into existence. The question sometimes arises whether someone has acted as an **agent** or as an **independent contractor** in his own right. For example, there are conflicting views (and much will depend on the circumstances) in the case of a dealer who sells goods to a finance company which then lets them on hire-purchase: to what extent is the dealer the agent of the finance company? (The test of whether someone is an employee or independent contractor in relation to employment law is considered in Chapter 11.) Similarly, there may be ambiguity over which party is the principal, for example in the case of someone employed by an insurance company to solicit business: is he always the agent of the insurance company or can he sometimes be said to be the agent of the insured?

In practice, there are many examples of agency relationships to which you are probably accustomed, such as estate agents and travel agents. For the purposes of this course, you should appreciate, in particular, how a director may be held to be an agent of the company and bind the company by his acts and also how a partner is an agent of the partnership and may bind the firm by his acts. Directors' authority is discussed in more detail in Chapter 6 and partnerships in Chapter 9.

C H A P T E R

3

2 Creation of agency

Section overview

- The agency relationship is created either by mutual consent or by operation of law or by ratification.

- Express agency is created when the principal expressly appoints someone as his agent, but an agency relationship can also be implied by the conduct of the parties.

- The law may deem that an 'agency of necessity' is created in particular circumstances.

- The law may provide that an ostensible or apparent agency relationship is created if the principal holds out to a third party that the agent's authority is greater than it actually is.

- Agency can be created retrospectively, through ratification of the contract.

The agent does not form contracts with third parties on his own behalf and so it is not necessary that he has full contractual capacity. The **principal**, however, **must have full contractual capacity**.

2.1 Agency by consent

Consent may be express or implied. An agency can be expressly created either orally or in writing. There is only one exception to this, which is that if the agent is to execute a deed on the principal's behalf (for example a conveyance of land or a lease exceeding three years) then the agency must be created by deed. Essentially this means that the agent is given a power of attorney. In **commercial transactions** it is usual (but not essential) to appoint an agent **in writing**, so that the terms and extent of the relationship are set down to avoid misunderstanding.

Worked example: Express agency by consent

Peter asks Alan to take Peter's car to be repaired. Peter and Alan thereby expressly agree that Alan is to be Peter's agent in making a contract between Peter and Thomas, the car mechanic.

2.2 Agency by estoppel (or 'holding out')

Agency by estoppel arises by operation of law and is no less effective than an agency expressly created. It arises in the following situation:

- When the words or **conduct of the principal** give to a **third party** the **impression** that the person who purports to contract with the third party **is the agent** of the principal, and

- The **third party**, as a result, **acts upon this**.

The principal is 'estopped', or prevented, from denying the existence of the agency.

Agency by estoppel can only arise where the **conduct** of the **apparent principal** creates it. Agency does not arise by estoppel if it is the 'agent' who holds himself out as agent, not the 'principal'.

Worked example: Apparent authority

Paul leads Tina to believe that Adam is Paul's agent. Tina deals with Adam on that basis. In this case, Paul is bound by the contract with Tina which Adam has made on his behalf. This situation may have arisen in the following circumstances.

- When Adam, who dealt with Tina as Paul's authorised agent, continues to do so after his authority as agent of Paul has been terminated, but Tina is unaware of it.

- When Adam, to Paul's knowledge, enters into transactions with Tina as if Adam were Paul's agent and Paul fails to inform Tina that Adam is not Paul's agent.

2.3 Agency of necessity

An **agency of necessity** is another way in which an agency can arise by operation of law. Its origins can be found in mercantile law, and in shipping law in particular. It may arise where a person is faced with an emergency in which the property or interests of another person are in imminent jeopardy and, in order to preserve that property or those interests, it becomes necessary to act for that person without his authority. An agency of necessity probably only applies where there is already some **existing contractual relationship** between the parties, as the law is highly unlikely to allow a person to be bound by the act of a complete stranger.

An agent who seeks to bind a principal on the grounds of an agency of necessity will need to show that:

- The agent had **no practical way of contacting** the principal in order to obtain the principal's instructions

- His actions arose from some **pressing need for action** (usually an emergency of some kind, involving perishable goods or starving animals, for example)

- He acted in **good faith** in the interests of the principal rather than in his own interests, and

- His action was **reasonable and prudent in the circumstances**.

An illustrative case is *Sachs v Miklos 1948:*

The facts: D agreed to store C's furniture. After a considerable time had elapsed D needed the storage space for his own use. Unable to trace C, he sold the furniture and C sued him for conversion. D pleaded agency of necessity in making the sale.

Decision: There was no agency of necessity since no emergency had arisen and D had sold the furniture for his own convenience. If D's house had been destroyed by fire and the furniture left in the open, then he would then be justified in selling it.

It is fair to say that modern day telecommunications may prevent an agent of necessity from arising very often.

2.4 Ratification

In certain circumstances the relationship of principal and agent can be created or extended with **retrospective effect**, that is, once the contract has been entered into by the agent and third party. Ratification **only validates past acts** of the purported agent. It gives no authority for the future.

Thus, where A makes a contract on behalf of P at a time when A has no authority from P, P may later ratify the contract. This will have the retrospective effect of establishing an agency as at the time the contract was made. All parties are then in the same position as if the principal had been the original contracting party, ie the principal may sue or be sued by the third party and the agent no longer has any liability.

The principal may only ratify if the following conditions are satisfied:

- The **principal must have been in existence** at the time of the agent's act.

- The **principal must have the legal capacity** to make the contract himself, **both** at the time the act was carried out **and** at the time of the purported ratification.

- The agent must, at the time of making the contract, either **name or sufficiently identify** the principal on whose behalf he is making the contract.

The principal must ratify the contract within **a reasonable time** and a ratification of **part** of the contract will operate as a ratification of the **entire** contract (ie the principal cannot just select such parts of the contract as he considers to be to his advantage). In order to ratify the contract, the principal must communicate **a sufficiently clear intention of ratifying**, either by express words or by conduct, such as refusing to return goods purchased for him by an agent who lacked authority. Mere passive inactivity will not amount to ratification.

Worked example: Conditions of ratification

David is Esther's friend. He is negotiating with Farouk to buy some goods, and, as he knows the prices and credit terms that Farouk is offering are good, he thinks that Esther would like to buy some of Farouk's goods too. Unfortunately, Esther is not answering her phone, so he cannot confirm with her that she authorises him to go ahead and buy the goods on her behalf.

It may be possible for David to go ahead and make the purchase on behalf of Esther and get her to ratify the contract with Farouk once he can make contact with her. In order to do this, he must be sure that the conditions of ratification will be met:

The principal must exist at the time of the contract.	Clearly Esther does exist.
The principal must have legal capacity.	There is no indication to the contrary.
The agent must name or sufficiently identify the principal.	There appears to be no reason why David wouldn't tell Farouk that he is acting on behalf of Esther.

Therefore, David can go ahead and make the contract with Farouk for Esther to ratify later, if Farouk is happy to contract with Esther. If Esther does not want the goods, she will not ratify the contract.

Interactive question 1: Creation of agency   [Difficulty level: Easy]

A valid agency relationship can be created by:

		Yes	No
A	Law, if it is a necessity	☐	☐
B	Ratification	☐	☐
C	Consent between the parties	☐	☐
D	The agent holding himself out as an agent	☐	☐

See **Answer** at the end of this chapter.

3 Duties and rights of an agent

Section overview

- The agent owes a number of duties to the principal.
- The agent also has a number of rights.

The courts have always sought to ensure that a person does not abuse the confidence of another for whom he is acting.

'The position of principal and agent gives rise to particular and onerous duties on the part of the agent, and the high standard of conduct required from him springs from the **fiduciary relationship** between his employer and himself. His position is confidential; it readily lends itself to abuse. A strict and salutary rule is required to meet the special situation.' (*Armstrong v Jackson 1917*)

When an agent agrees to perform services for his principal for reward there is a contract between them. However, even if the agent undertakes his duties without reward (but provided there is some consideration to make the contract valid), he has obligations to his principal.

The law implies the following duties into any contract of agency:

Duties	Explanation
Accountability	An agent must provide full information to his principal of his agency transactions and account to him for all monies arising from them.
	If he accepts from the other party any commission or reward as an inducement to make the contract with him, it is considered to be a bribe and the contract is fraudulent. The principal who discovers that his agent has accepted a bribe may **dismiss** the agent and **recover the amount** of the bribe from him.
	Boston Deep Sea Fishing & Ice Co v Ansell 1888
	The facts: A, who was managing director of the claimant company, accepted commissions from suppliers on orders which he placed with them for goods supplied to the company. He was dismissed and the company sued to recover from him the commissions.
	Decision: The company was justified in dismissing A and he must account to it for the commissions.
No conflict of interest	The agent owes to his principal a duty not to put himself in a situation where his own interests conflict with those of the principal.

Duties	Explanation
Performance	The agent who agrees to act as agent for reward has a contractual obligation to perform his agreed task. (An unpaid agent is not bound to carry out his agreed duties unless there is other consideration.) Any agent may refuse to perform an illegal act.
Obedience	The agent must act strictly in accordance with his principal's instructions insofar as these are lawful and reasonable. Even if he believes disobedience to be in his principal's best interests, he may not disobey instructions (unless he is asked to commit an illegal or unreasonable act).
Skill	An agent undertakes to maintain the standard of skill and care to be expected of a person in his profession.
Personal performance	The agent is usually selected because of his personal qualities and owes a duty to perform his task himself and not to delegate it to another. (However he may delegate in certain circumstances, for example a solicitor acting for a client would be obliged to instruct a stockbroker to buy or sell listed securities on the Stock Exchange.)
Confidence	The agent must keep in confidence what he knows of his principal's affairs even after the agency relationship has ceased.

Conversely, an agent has the following **rights** (or duties owed by the principal):

Rights of the agent	Explanation
Indemnity	The agent is entitled to be repaid his expenses and to be indemnified by his principal against losses and liabilities, provided his acts are done properly within the limits of his authority. He may recover expenses properly paid even if he was not legally bound to pay; for example, a solicitor who pays counsel's fees (which the counsel cannot recover at law) may reclaim this expense from his client.
Remuneration	The agent is also entitled to be paid any agreed remuneration for his services by his principal. The entitlement to remuneration may have been expressly agreed or may be inferred from the circumstances, for example by reference to trade or professional practice. If it is agreed that the agent is to be remunerated but the amount has not been fixed, the agent is entitled to a reasonable amount.
Lien	The agent has the right to exercise a lien over property owned by the principal, i.e. a right to retain and hold goods pending payment of sums owed to him.

Interactive question 2: Duties of a principal

[Difficulty level: Easy]

There is a degree of overlap between the *rights* of an agent and the *duties* of a principal. Are the following duties of a principal or of an agent?

	Agent	Principal
A A duty not to retain benefit from the agency relationship	☐	☐
B A duty to pay agreed remuneration, even if no benefit has been derived from his acts	☐	☐
C A duty of confidence	☐	☐

See **Answer** at the end of this chapter.

4 Authority of the agent

Section overview

- An agent's authority may be
  - Expressly given
  - Impliedly given
  - Ostensible or apparent on the basis of the principal's conduct.

The **contract** made by the agent is **binding** on the principal and the other party **only if** the **agent was acting within the limits of his authority** from his principal. In analysing the limits of an agent's authority, three distinct sources of authority can be identified:

- Actual express authority
- Actual implied authority
- Ostensible or apparent authority

4.1 Actual express authority

This is authority explicitly given by the principal to the agent to make a particular contract.

Worked example: Express authority

Graham wants Hope to act as his agent to buy some goods from Imran. He sends her the following note:

'Please act as my agent to buy 12 wheelbarrows from Imran. You are only entitled to buy wheelbarrows and the most I want to pay is £600 in total.'

Hope therefore has express authority to buy some wheelbarrows for Graham. However, the limits of this authority are that she must buy them from Imran, she can only buy 12 and she must not pay more than £600.

The extent of the agent's express authority will depend on the construction of the words used on his appointment. If the appointment is in writing, then the document will need to be examined. If it is oral, then the scope of the agent's authority will be a matter of evidence.

4.2 Actual implied authority

Authority may also be **implied** from the nature of the agent's activities or from what is usual in the circumstances, save in so far as such implied authority would be contrary to authority expressly given.

Thus an agent also has actual implied authority:

- To do all things that are **incidental** to the actions expressly authorised
- To do all things that are **usual** by virtue of the agent's office.

Third parties are entitled to assume that the agent has implied usual authority unless they know to the contrary. So, for example, an agent appointed to sell a car will also have **implied incidental authority** to advertise the car for sale. Partners will have **implied usual authority** to do the usual things partners might do, for example, rent office premises, buy office paper or employ secretaries.

Watteau v Fenwick 1893

The facts: P owned a hotel and employed the previous owner, A, to manage it. Against P's express instructions, A bought cigars on credit from T. T sued P on the contract and P argued that he was not bound by the contract, since A had no actual authority to make it.

Decision: It was within the usual authority of a manager of a hotel to buy cigars on credit and P was bound by the contract (although T did not even know that A was the agent of P) since the restriction on his usual authority had not been communicated.

Note that incidental authority and usual authority are **implied** because they are not **expressly** stated but they are still part of an agent's **actual** authority.

Worked example: Actual authority

A principal employs a stockbroker to sell 100 shares at £10 each. This is the scope of the actual express authority conferred. In addition, the broker shall (unless otherwise agreed) have **actual implied authority** to do whatever is incidental to that sale and also to do anything that is usual in practice for a broker selling shares for a client to do. Any person who deals with the broker is entitled to assume (unless informed to the contrary) that the broker has the usual authority of a broker by his client. The two forms of authority are co-extensive.

4.3 Ostensible or apparent authority

The ostensible (or apparent) authority of an agent is that which his principal represents to other persons (with whom the agent deals) that he has given to the agent. As a result, an agent with limited actual authority can be held in practice to have a more extensive authority. A partner has considerable but limited implied authority merely by virtue of being a partner. If, however, the other partners allow him to exercise a greater authority than is implied, they represent that he has that greater authority and they are bound by the contracts which he makes within the limits of this ostensible authority.

Ostensible authority (unlike implied authority) is not restricted to what is usual and incidental. The principal may expressly or by inference from his conduct confer on the agent any amount of ostensible or apparent authority.

Worked example: Ostensible authority

Janelle is in partnership with Kit and Lemar to provide plumbing services. As outlined above, Janelle has implied authority to do the usual things that partners in a plumbing service do, by virtue of being a partner, and she binds Kit and Lemar by her actions. In addition Janelle has advertised and carried out electrical work in the name of the partnership and Kit and Lemar have not prevented her from doing so. This means that Janelle has ostensible authority to carry out electrical work on behalf of the partnership, even though the partnership is limited to plumbing. Thus, when Janelle wires something wrongly and causes a personal injury to a client, that client will have a claim against all three partners, not just Janelle.

(The way partners' acts bind their partnership is considered more fully in Chapter 9.)

It is not necessary that the agency agreement be in the form of a contract.

Freeman & Lockyer v Buckhurst Park Properties (Mangal) Ltd 1964

The facts: K and H carried on business as property developers. H lived abroad and the business of the company was left entirely under the control of K. As a director, K had no actual or apparent authority to enter into contracts as agent of the company and he was never formally approved as managing director. However, H and the other two directors allowed him to act as if he were MD, contracting on the company's behalf. The claimants sued the company for work done on K's instructions.

Decision: Although there had been no actual delegation and authorisation, the company had, by its directors' acquiescence, led the claimants to believe that K was the MD and, as such, an authorised agent and the claimants had relied on it. The company was bound by the contract made by K under the principle of 'holding out' (or 'estoppel'). The company was estopped from denying (that is, not permitted to deny) that K was its agent. Although K had no actual authority to bind the company, he had ostensible, or apparent, authority to do so.

It can be seen that it is the conduct of the principal which creates ostensible authority; an agent cannot claim apparent authority or hold himself out to have it. It does not matter whether there is a pre-existing agency relationship or not.

The representation must be **made to the third party** and it must be shown that the **third party relied on the representation**. If there is no causal link between the third party's loss and his reliance upon the representation, the third party will not be able to hold the principal liable.

Where a principal has represented to a third party that an agent has authority to act but subsequently revokes the agent's authority, he will not escape liability. The principal should inform third parties who have previously dealt with the agent of the change in circumstances. This is particularly relevant to partnerships and the position when a partner leaves a partnership.

Interactive question 3: Authority   [Difficulty level: Exam standard]

Michelle works in Nathan's building firm. She is employed in the purchases department. Nathan does not have approved suppliers, but Michelle is required by internal policy to get Nathan's approval for all orders. Nathan has been invited to Oliver's timber yard as Oliver is keen to get Nathan as a customer. However, Nathan is busy and doesn't want to go, so he sends Michelle in his place, telling Nathan that 'she deals with buying anyway'.

While Michelle was at Oliver's timber yard, she noticed a very good price on some timber. Knowing that Nathan needed some timber soon for an existing project, she decided to buy it for Nathan. Oliver was delighted, and set up a credit account for the timber in Nathan's name.

Indicate whether the following statements are true or false in respect of Michelle's authority to make this contract on behalf of Nathan.

		True	False
A	Michelle has no authority to make this contract on Nathan's behalf.	☐	☐
B	Michelle has express authority to make this contract on Nathan's behalf.	☐	☐
C	Michelle has implied authority to make this contract on Nathan's behalf.	☐	☐
D	Michelle has ostensible authority to make this contract on Nathan's behalf.	☐	☐

See **Answer** at the end of this chapter.

5 Liability of the parties

Section overview

- As mentioned earlier, generally speaking, a contract entered into by an agent and a third party binds the principal and the third party but not the agent, who effectively drops out of the picture.

- There are, however, instances where this general rule will not apply and these are noted in this section.

5.1 Where the agent has authority and is known to be an agent

Where the agent is known to be acting as an agent and he has authority from his principal, the principal and third party may sue and be sued on the contract and the agent has no rights and liabilities on the contract, **unless** it appears that the **parties intended otherwise**. Such an intention may be express or inferred from the circumstances (for example how the agent is named in and how he signs any documentation).

Note that **where the agent does not name the principal**, it is more likely that he will be considered to be a contracting party. However, even here, if it is clear that the parties intended that he should act only as agent, then he will drop out of the picture.

There are particular circumstances where the agent might incur personal liability:

- Under rules of trade usage

- Where he adds his name as party to a negotiable instrument (depending on the facts)

- Where he makes a contract under seal, unless he does so as trustee for the principal or unless the law provides otherwise (for example, in the case of powers of attorney).

5.2 Where the agent has authority, but is not known to be an agent

In these cases, where a principal becomes known at a later date:

- Either the agent or the principal may sue on the contract (but the agent's rights are subordinate to the principal's) and

- Either the agent or the principal may be sued on the contract (but the third party must choose which one).

These rules will only apply where the agent's authority existed at the time of making the contract **and** the contract cannot be said to have been intended to operate only between the contracting parties (on the basis of their express or implied intentions).

5.3 Where the agent has no authority

If the agent has no authority, **the principal cannot sue or be sued** on the contract unless he chooses to ratify it.

If the agent, knowing that he has no authority, makes a representation to the contrary and causes loss to the third party, he may be liable for the **tort of deceit**.

If he genuinely believes that he has authority, but is in fact mistaken, he may nonetheless be liable for **breach of warranty of authority**. This applies not just to contracts but to any business transaction where a party wrongly represents to the other that he has authority from some other person, thereby inducing the other party to enter into the contract.

Summary

```
P                                          P
|  \                                       |  \
|    \  Privity                            |    \
|      \  (Contract enforceable by P + TP) |      \  Unless P ratifies
| Authority \                              | No Authority \
|            \                             |               \
↓              \                           ↓                \
A ── Contracts ──→ TP                      A ── Contracts ──→ TP
                                                  Privity
```

		Agency by necessity	**Ratification by P**
Agency by consent (usually express, oral or written) or implied	**Agency by estoppel (or 'holding out' by P)**	• P uncontactable • emergency • A acts for P in good faith • reasonable and prudent action	• P existed • P had capability (time of contract and ratification) • P named or identifiable

↑ ↑ ↑ ↑

Agency created, giving agent authority

Actual　　　　　　　　　　**Ostensible/apparent (TP acts on representation by P)**

Express　　　　　　**(Implied) incidental (Implied) usual**

	Implied rights and duties
Rights	• Indemnity • Remuneration ('reasonable' if unspecified) • Lien
Duties	• Account for benefits (no bribes) • Avoid conflict • Perform task, not delegate • Obedience • Skill and care • Respect confidences

Self-test

Answer the following questions.

1 **Fill in the blanks** using the words in the boxes below.

.... is the........................... which exists between two ....
persons, the ....and the agent, in which the function of the agent is to form a
.... between his .... and a ....

(1) relationship	(4) principal	(6) principal
(2) third party	(5) legal	(7) agency
(3) contract		

2 Identify the four ways in which an agency can arise.

- ....

- ....

- ....

- ....

3 Which of the following is not a necessary condition of agency of necessity?

(a) Agent has no practical way of contacting principal
(b) A pressing need for action exists
(c) The agent must have the principal's permission
(d) The agent must act in good faith in the interests of the principal
(e) The action must be reasonable and prudent in the circumstances

4 A principal may, in certain circumstances, ratify the acts of the agent, which has retrospective effect.

True ☐
False ☐

5 What is the best definition of ostensible authority?

(a) The authority which the principal represents to other persons he has given to the agent.
(b) The authority implied to other persons by the agent's actions.

6 An agent may disobey the instructions of the principal if he believes disobedience to be in the best interests of the principal.

True ☐
False ☐

7 Name the three types of authority which an agent might have.

- ....

- ....

- ....

8 Provided an agent has authority and is known to be an agent, he can never have any personal liability under the contract and only the principal can be liable.

True ☐
False ☐

Now, go back to the Learning Objectives in the Introduction. If you are satisfied you have achieved these objectives, please tick them off.

Answer to Interactive question 1

A   Yes

B   Yes

C   Yes

D   No

Answer to Interactive question 2

A   Agent
B   Principal
C   Agent

Answer to Interactive question 3

A   False

B   False

C   True. As Michelle is employed in the purchasing department, she has implied authority to enter into contracts on Nathan's behalf.

D   True. Nathan has told Oliver that Michelle 'deals with buying' so he is entitled to assume that she has the authority to enter into this contract on Nathan's behalf.

1 7, 1, 5, 4 (6), 3, 6 (4), 2

2 • Agency by consent
   • Agency by estoppel
   • Agency of necessity
   • Ratification

3 (c)

4 True

5 (a)

6 False

7 • Actual express authority
   • Actual implied authority (incidental and usual)
   • Ostensible or apparent authority

8 False. Generally speaking, the contract is only enforceable by the principal and the third party but this rule is subject to a contrary intention being express or implied.

CHAPTER 4

Negligence

Introduction

Examination context

Topic List

1   The law of tort

2   The tort of negligence

3   Professional advice and negligent misstatement

4   Defences and damages

5   Vicarious liability

Summary and Self-test

Answers to Interactive questions

Answers to Self-test

Learning objectives

- Understand the nature of the law of tort ☐

- Understand and recognise what needs to be proved if an action for negligence is to be successful ☐

- Be familiar with the considerations relevant to negligence in the context of professional advice ☐

- Know the remedy available for a successful claim of negligence and when a claim might be defended successfully ☐

- Understand and recognise instances of vicarious liability ☐

Specific syllabus references for this chapter are: 1f, g.

Syllabus links

Some of the issues relating to employees in this chapter will be looked at in more detail later in this Study Manual when it focuses on employment law.

Negligent misstatement will be a relevant factor when looking at the risks an assurance firm faces and the quality processes put into place to combat them in your Audit and Assurance Paper.

Examination context

Being an important practical issue for accountants, you might expect around five questions relating to negligence and vicarious liability in your exam.

In the assessment, candidates may be required to:

- Identify instances and consequences of negligence (particularly negligent misstatement) in a given scenario

- Identify issues and consequences of vicarious liability in a given scenario

1 The law of tort

Section overview

- The law of tort includes negligence, which is considered in detail in this chapter.
- In a situation involving a breach of contract or crime, the law of tort may also be relevant.

1.1 Tort

The law of tort is a vast subject dealing with various wrongs done to an individual. The law protects certain personal interests and where these are infringed, the law might offer redress, typically in the form of damages or (in exceptional cases) an injunction.

Thus where personal security is infringed, for example, the torts of assault or false imprisonment might apply and where a person's property is infringed or damaged, the torts of trespass or nuisance might apply.

In tort, no previous transaction or contractual relationship need exist. Indeed it is quite likely that the parties involved will be complete strangers. Where the parties are in a contractual relationship and there has been both a breach of contract and a tort committed, the claimant may prefer to proceed in contract rather than tort (or *vice versa*) for reasons associated with the measure of damages or limitation periods. The measure of damages in contract will be such amount as would put the claimant in the position he would have been in had the contract been performed, whereas in tort, the award will reflect the position he would have been in had the tortious act not taken place. Broadly speaking, the limitation period (during which an injured party must take proceedings) is six years from a breach of contract or six years from the damage caused by the tortious act being suffered (or three years in the case of personal injury).

> *Robinson v P E Jones (Contractors) Ltd 2011*
>
> *The facts:* Defects in two chimney flues were discovered 12 years after the contractor built a house for Robinson. Since a contractual claim was statute-barred, Robinson sued the contractor in tort.
>
> *Decision (Court of Appeal):* Where a contractual duty of care is owed, it does not necessarily follow that a duty of care is owed in tort also. Whether or not a tortious liability arose in this case depended on the facts and the relationship between the parties, but was excluded in any event by a clause in the contract which restricted liability to that set out in the National House-Building Council standard agreement.
> This clause satisfied the reasonableness test in UCTA and excluded any potential tortious liability for economic loss. The following example illustrates how the same event can easily give rise to more than one legal liability.

Worked example: Tort, crime and contract breach

David is a hired chauffeur working for Estelle. He drives while drunk, crashes the car and runs over Ewan, seriously injuring him and injuring Estelle slightly.

This road accident may lead to proceedings for both **crime** (drink driving) and **tort** (injury to Ewan) and even in **contract** (breach of terms with Estelle).

Bad professional advice may give rise to liability both in **tort** and in **contract**. We discuss the law of tort in relation to professional advisers in section 3 of this chapter.

1.2 Elements of a tort

Generally speaking, a tort consists of an act or omission by the defendant, which act or omission is responsible for causing injury or damage to the claimant. The damage must normally be due to the fault of the defendant and it must be caused to an interest of the claimant that the law seeks to protect, ie the damage must be a type of harm which the courts will recognise as giving rise to a legal liability. The claimant will only be able to recover for damage or loss that is not considered to be too remote.

2 The tort of negligence

Section overview

- The terms 'negligence' and 'negligent' may refer to the careless way in which an act is carried out, or to the tort which arises when a person is in breach of a legal duty of care that he owes to another, thereby causing that person harm or loss.

- **Negligence** is the most important modern tort. To succeed in an action for negligence, the burden of proof is on the claimant to prove, on **a balance of probabilities**, that:

    - The defendant owed **a duty of care** to the claimant to avoid causing injury, damage or loss
    - There was **a breach of that duty** by the defendant
    - *In consequence* the claimant suffered **injury, damage or loss**.

2.1 Duty of care

It is not possible to give a clear statement of the law as to when a duty of care exists for the purposes of negligence, since the law has evolved over many years as it has had to be applied to extremely varied situations and many factors have influenced the courts' decisions. However, you should be aware of the landmark case, in which the House of Lords ruled that a person might owe a duty of care to another with whom he had no contractual relationship. Up to this point it was felt that to allow a party to recover for his loss arising out of a breach of contract between two other parties (and to which he was not a party) would be to undermine the doctrine of privity of contract.

> *Donoghue v Stevenson* 1932
>
> *The facts*: A purchased a bottle of ginger beer for consumption by B. B drank part of the contents, which contained the remains of a decomposed snail, and became ill. The manufacturer argued that as there was no contract between himself and B, he owed her no duty of care and so was not liable.
>
> *Decision*: The House of Lords laid down the general principle that every person owes a duty of care to his 'neighbour', to 'persons so closely and directly affected by my act that I ought reasonably to have them in contemplation as being so affected'.

This so-called 'neighbour principle' has been developed further and the law is extremely complex in this area. However, the principle is still relevant and an awareness of the reasoning of this case and its application is perhaps fundamental to an understanding of the tort of negligence.

For many years, this was the test applied where physical damage was the loss sustained, but where economic or financial loss was suffered, no remedy was given unless that loss was directly consequential on physical loss or unless there was also contractual liability, fraud or deceit. In 1964, however, the House of Lords refined the neighbourhood principle by requiring that a 'special relationship' (but not necessarily a contract) was needed to found an action in negligence where the claimant suffered **pure economic loss** arising out of **negligent misstatement**. This area of negligence is dealt with more fully in section 3 below.

At the present time, it is perhaps fair to say that whether or not a duty of care exists will be assessed on the basis of some or all of the following four tests. These were formulated by the House of Lords in *The Nicholas H* (*Marc Rich & Co v Bishops Rock Marine*) *1995* case.

Test		Meaning
1	Reasonably foreseeable	Was the damage reasonably foreseeable by the defendant as damage to the claimant at the time of the negligent act or omission?
2	Proximity	Is there sufficient proximity, or neighbourhood, between the parties?
3	Fair, just and reasonable	Is it fair, just and reasonable that the law should impose a duty on the defendant on the facts of the case?
4	Public policy	Is there a matter of public policy that requires that no duty of care should exist? (By way of example, the Court of Appeal has held (in 2011) that a duty should not be owed by a surveyor to a buy-to-let investor, when carrying out a rental valuation for a lender, on the grounds that such an investor (unlike a simple residential purchaser) is more likely to obtain an independent valuation.)

In applying these tests, the court is essentially looking at the relationship between the claimant and the defendant in the context of the damage suffered. *The Nicholas H* case was concerned with economic loss, but the court held that the requirements would be equally applicable in cases of physical damage to property.

Interactive question 1: Duty of care   **[Difficulty level: Exam standard]**

Which of the following tests will be considered in assessing whether a duty of care exists?

1   Whether there is a sufficient relationship of proximity between defendant and claimant
2   Whether the damage was reasonably foreseeable as a result of the defendant's carelessness
3   Whether the claimant acted in good faith and without carelessness
4   Whether it is just and reasonable for the law to impose liability

A   1 and 2 only
B   3 and 4 only
C   1, 2 and 3 only
D   1, 2 and 4 only

See **Answer** at the end of this chapter.

2.2 Breach of duty of care

The second element that must be proven by a claimant in an action for negligence is that there was a breach of the duty of care by the defendant.

Whether or not there has been a breach of duty is a question of fact. In certain circumstances where the reason for the damage is not known, but it can fairly be said that it would not have occurred without the defendant's lack of care, the claimant can argue **res ipsa loquitur** ('the facts speak for themselves') and the court will infer that the defendant was in breach of the duty of care. It will be necessary for the claimant to show that the thing which caused the damage was under the management and control of the defendant. In such cases, it will then be for the defendant to prove that the cause of the injury was **not** his negligence.

The standard of care needed to satisfy the duty of care is a question of law. Broadly speaking, it is the standard of 'a reasonable man, guided upon those considerations which ordinarily regulate the conduct of human affairs' (*Blyth v Birmingham Waterworks Co 1856*).

The following principles have been established by case law:

Principle	Explanation
Particular skill	If the defendant professes a **particular skill**, the standard is that of a reasonable person with that skill, ie a reasonable accountant or reasonable electrician.

Principle	Explanation
Lack of skill	**Peculiarities or disabilities** of the defendant are not relevant, so the standard for a learner driver is that of a reasonable driver and for a trainee accountant, that of a reasonable accountant.
No hindsight	The test is one of **knowledge and general practice existing at the time**, not hindsight or subsequent change of practice. *Roe v Minister of Health* 1954 *The facts*: A doctor gave a patient an injection taking normal precautions at that time. The drug became contaminated in a way that was not understood at the time and the patient was paralysed. *Held*: The proper test was normal practice based on the state of medical knowledge at the time. The doctor was not at fault in failing to anticipate later developments.
Body of opinion	In broad terms, a claim against a professional person will fail if he or she can point to a **body of professional opinion that supports the approach taken** and which the court considers to be reasonable.
Advantage and risk	In deciding what is reasonable care, the balance must be struck between **advantage and risk**. (For example, a driver of a fire engine may exceed the normal speed on his way to the fire but not on the way back.)
Emergency	If a defendant acts negligently in an **emergency situation**, this will be taken into account – the test is that of a reasonable man in the defendant's situation.
Vulnerability	If A owes a duty of care to B and A knows that B is **unusually vulnerable**, a higher standard of care is expected. *Paris v Stepney Borough Council* 1951 *The facts:* C was blind in one eye and was employed by D on vehicle maintenance. It was not the normal practice to issue protective goggles since the risk of eye injury was small. A chip of metal flew into C's eye and blinded him. *Decision:* There was a higher standard of care owed to C because an injury to his remaining good eye would blind him.

2.3 Loss caused by the breach

The third element that the claimant must demonstrate is that he suffered injury or loss and that this was as a result of the breach. A person will only be compensated if he has suffered actual loss, injury, damage or harm **as a consequence** of another's actions. As a general rule, loss is represented by personal injury or damage to property, or financial loss directly connected to such injury (for example, loss of earnings) or property damage. Such *consequential* economic loss, that is related in this way, is more readily recoverable than *pure* economic loss.

Spartan Steel Alloys v Martin Co Contractors 1973

The facts: C was halfway through smelting a steel ingot when a cable was damaged by D, causing C's electricity supply to be cut off.

Decision: C was entitled to claim damages for the damaged ingot, as it had been damaged by D's act and for the loss of profit consequential upon the ingot being in production at the time. However, they were not entitled to claim for loss of profits generally due to the disruption caused to the factory, as there was no actual damage to the factory. The court held that the loss should lie where it fell and it was more appropriate for factories to take out insurance against interrupted production.

However, in the later case of *Junior Books v Veitchi Co. Ltd 1982*, some doubt was expressed in the House of Lords as to whether this decision was still good law (although it was not overruled). In that case, pure economic loss was recoverable on the basis that there was sufficient proximity between a sub-contractor and an owner of a building to give rise to a duty of care in tort, despite there being no contract.

Subsequent cases have sought to emphasise the limited application of this case, however, and it remains a difficult area of law. The courts' reluctance to permit recovery of pure economic loss is largely due to the difficulties and cost in insuring against liability that would be likely to arise as a result and also concern that the floodgates would be opened to large numbers of claims for potentially enormous sums.

Whether or not the damage was caused by the defendant's breach is a question of fact. Put simply, the question is 'would the damage have occurred **but for** the defendant's act or omission?' If it can be shown that actually the damage was caused by something or someone else, then there will be no liability on the defendant's part. If something happened after the defendant's breach that caused or contributed to the damage, then the defendant's liability will cease at that point.

Even where the claimant is able to show that the loss was suffered as a result of the defendant's breach of duty, the court will not allow him to recover for loss that is considered too remote, or too far down the chain of causation. This is a question of law and is part of the assessment of a damages award made by a court. It is considered in section 4 below.

3 Professional advice and negligent misstatement

Section overview

- Negligent misstatement is one aspect of the tort of negligence.

- It tends to be considered separately, partly because liability stems from words rather than acts and partly because the damage suffered is financial rather than physical.

- It is obviously also of particular relevance to you as an accountant, as you will be giving professional advice in most aspects of your work.

Where an adviser (such as an accountant, banker, solicitor or surveyor) makes a statement in some **professional or expert capacity**, where it is likely that others would rely on what he said, then he may owe a duty of care in addition to his contractual commitments. This means a potential liability in tort if his statement, or advice, turns out to be negligently made.

As noted earlier, pure economic or financial loss (in the absence of physical damage) used not to be recoverable unless there was a liability in contract or evidence of fraud or deceit. The neighbour principle laid down in *Donoghue v Stevenson* was restricted to tortious acts or omissions that resulted in physical damage.

The turning point came in 1963 when the landmark case, outlined below, marked a new judicial approach to cases involving negligent misstatement.

> *Hedley Byrne & Co Ltd v Heller and Partners Ltd 1963*
>
> *The facts:* C was an advertising agent acting for a new client, Easipower Ltd. C requested information from Easipower's bank, D, on its financial position. D returned non-committal replies, which expressly disclaimed legal responsibility, and which were held to be a negligent misstatement of Easipower's financial resources.
>
> *Decision:* While D was able to avoid liability by virtue of its disclaimer, the House of Lords went on to consider whether there ever could be a duty of care to avoid causing financial loss by negligent misstatement where there was no contractual or fiduciary relationship. It decided that, had it not been for the disclaimer, D would have been liable for negligence, having breached the duty of care, because a special relationship did exist.

In reaching the decision in *Hedley Byrne*, Lord Morris said the following:

> 'If someone possessed of a special skill undertakes....to apply that skill for the assistance of another person who **relies** on that skill, a duty of care will arise....If, in a sphere in which a person is so placed that others could reasonably rely on his skill....a person takes it on himself to give information or advice to....another person who, as he **knows or should know**, will place reliance on it, then a duty of care will arise.'

As in *Hedley Byrne*, cases involving negligent misstatement are usually concerned with whether or not a duty of care exists (and perhaps also the extent of that duty) rather than questions of breach and causation. The law has come a long way from its post-*Donoghue v Stevenson* stance on financial loss, but it has evolved very much on a case by case basis, in a way that makes it extremely difficult (if not impossible) to extrapolate clearly defined principles that dictate whether or not a duty of care exists in a given situation.

Undoubtedly the concept of a special relationship is still helpful and the considerations outlined in *The Nicholas H* case (see section 2.1) will still be relevant. What is clear is that liability can only arise where the defendant is in the business of giving professional advice and the statement is made within that context. He will not be liable for advice given informally or on a social occasion.

As mentioned above, it is clear from *The Nicholas H* case that, in applying the tests described in that case, the courts will be examining the relationship between the parties in the context of the damage suffered. One consequence of this is that their approach may differ depending on whether, for example, the circumstances involve the preparation of accounts for shareholders or for a potential takeover bidder. The Court of Appeal has recently made it clear that it will be very difficult to prove that a duty of care is owed to sophisticated investors, who are more likely to be considered responsible for their own actions (*Springwell Navigation Corp v J P Morgan Chase Bank 2010*).

Remember that, in addition to establishing that a duty of care exists and has been breached, it will be necessary to show that the loss was caused by that breach. If, in fact, the loss was attributable to another cause or would have been suffered in any event, an action for negligence will not succeed.

> *JEB Fasteners Ltd v Marks, Bloom & Co 1982*
>
> *The facts:* Accountants, in the knowledge that the company was seeking outside finance, prepared accounts negligently showing overvalued stock and inflated profits. The claimant saw the accounts and took over the company.
>
> *Decision:* The claim failed on grounds of causation. It was considered that the claimant should have known from his own enquiries that the figures were inaccurate and that the company was taken over in order to secure the directors' expertise and not purely on the basis of the accounts.

The following cases are described in order to give you a feel for the types of situation that can arise and the courts' approach to determining whether the professionals owe a duty of care in tort. An understanding of the legal considerations is more important than a recall of the facts of any given case.

3.1 No special relationship

It is likely that unless the defendant makes the negligent misstatement in the knowledge or reasonable expectation that an identified bidder would rely on it, then no duty of care is owed to anyone other than the body of shareholders as a whole. This was the position in the following leading case:

> *Caparo Industries plc v Dickman and Others 1990*
>
> *The facts:* Caparo, a shareholder in Fidelity plc, bought more shares and later made a takeover bid, after seeing accounts prepared by the defendants that showed a profit of £1.3m. Caparo claimed against the auditors for the fact that the accounts should have shown a loss of £400,000, arguing that the auditors owed a duty of care to investors and potential investors in respect of the audit. They should have been aware, Caparo argued, that a press release stating that profits would fall significantly had made Fidelity vulnerable to a takeover bid and that bidders might well rely upon the accounts.
>
> *Decision:* The auditor's duty was owed to the body of shareholders as a whole and did not extend to potential investors nor to existing shareholders increasing their stakes.

The House of Lords said that the reason for annual accounts was to enable the shareholders to exercise their rights in respect of the management of the company and not to give advice on the merits of further investment in the company. It would be wrong to impose a duty of care on the auditors because a recipient of the accounts used them for a purpose for which they were not intended, without the auditors' prior knowledge. The House also ruled that, since there was no duty owed to an individual shareholder, there could be none owed to a potential takeover bidder who was not known to the auditors. A company's vulnerability to a takeover could hardly create sufficient proximity between the auditors and any bidder.

Following *Caparo*, therefore, where an individual relies on annual audited accounts to invest in or lend to or bid for a company, unknown to the professional who prepared them, there is no cause of action because no duty of care exists.

Preparing a statement for **general circulation**, which could foreseeably be relied upon by persons unknown to the professional for a variety of different purposes, was not sufficient to give rise to a duty of care. On the other hand, preparing information in the knowledge that a **particular person** was contemplating a transaction and would rely on the information in deciding whether or not to proceed with the transaction would mean that a duty of care was owed.

This approach is also illustrated by *James MacNaughton Papers Group Ltd v Hicks Anderson & Co* 1991, where an accountant prepared draft accounts for a company chairman but the claimant also inspected the accounts and then took over the company. It was held that since the accounts were in draft only and drawn up specifically for the chairman, the accountant only owed a duty of care to the chairman and not to a potential takeover bidder.

3.2 Special relationship

Where financial statements are prepared for the purpose of contesting a proposed takeover bid, the directors and financial advisers will owe a duty of care in respect of them to a known takeover bidder. These were the facts in *Morgan Crucible v Hill Samuel Bank Ltd 1991*.

The claimant's original argument, that it was reasonable that a bidder might rely on them was amended (following the decision in *Caparo*) and instead the claim succeeded because:

- The bidder had been identified to the defendant
- It was intended that the bidder should rely on the accounts, and
- Express representations had in fact been made to the bidder by the defendant.

Likewise, in *Galoo Ltd v Bright Grahame Murray 1995*, the Court of Appeal reiterated that an auditor owes a duty of care to a takeover bidder when he has been expressly informed that the bidder will rely on the accounts for the purpose of determining the value of his bid and the bidder does so rely on them. On the facts of that case, it was considered that the accounts had been prepared not just for audit purposes, but also for the purpose of fixing the takeover price.

The need for a cautious approach (and possibly to issue disclaimers) when giving financial advice in such situations is well illustrated by the following case:

> *ADT Ltd v BDO Binder Hamlyn* 1996
>
> *The facts:* Binder Hamlyn signed off the audit of BSG as showing a true and fair view of the company's position. ADT was thinking of buying BSG and, as a potential buyer, sought Binder Hamlyn's confirmation of the audited results. At a meeting between the Binder Hamlyn audit partner and a director of ADT, the audit partner specifically confirmed that he 'stood by' his firm's audit. ADT proceeded to purchase BSG for £105m. It was subsequently alleged that BSG's true value was only £40m. ADT therefore sued Binder Hamlyn for the difference, £65m plus interest.
>
> *Decision:* Binder Hamlyn assumed a responsibility for the statement that the audited accounts showed a true and fair view of BSG which ADT relied on to its detriment. Since the underlying audit work had been carried out negligently, Binder Hamlyn was held liable for £65m.

The court concerned itself particularly with the **purpose of the statement made at the meeting** and attached great importance to the fact that Binder Hamlyn **assumed responsibility** as a result of the partner's comments.

3.3 Non-takeover situations

The following two cases provide further examples of where a duty of care was said to exist, based on the knowledge of the accountants in preparing a client's accounts:

Law Society v KPMG 2000

The facts: KPMG were retained by a firm of solicitors to prepare annual reports required by the Law Society. The Law Society found that the solicitors had been defrauding clients and amounts had to be made good from a compensation fund of which the Law Society was a trustee. The Law Society sued KPMG for negligence.

Decision: KPMG owed a duty of care to the Law Society and was liable in negligence. It was just and equitable to make KPMG liable since it was entirely foreseeable that an adverse accountant's report could result in intervention by the Law Society for the protection of the public.

Andrew v Kounnis Freeman 1999

The facts: The defendant, Kounnis, prepared the accounts of a travel company which collapsed.

Decision: The accountant had assumed a duty of care to the CAA and was liable in negligence. A reasonable accountant should have known that the CAA would assume the audited accounts had been prepared with due skill and care and would rely on them in deciding whether to renew the company's licence.

In both cases it may be said that it was reasonably foreseeable that the claimant (who could be identified and was not one of a large class of recipients) would rely on the accounts.

3.4 Summary

As the Court of Appeal made clear in the *James MacNaughton* case, there is no single overriding principle that can be applied to the complexities of every case. Rather, as you will have seen from the cases mentioned in this chapter, there are a number of factors which the court will take into account and some will assume a greater significance than others.

The factors with the greatest significance are:

- The **purpose** for which the statement is **made** and **communicated**
- The **relationship** between the professional, the recipient and any relevant third party
- The state of **knowledge** of the professional
- Whether the professional could be said to have **assumed responsibility** to the claimant
- The size of any **class** to which the recipient belonged
- Whether the **third party** was identified and known to the professional
- The extent of **reliance** by the claimant and whether that was foreseeable
- Whether it is **fair and equitable** (and not an offence to public policy) to impose a duty of care

It is worth noting that the increasing litigation against professionals, particularly during the takeover boom period of the late 1980s, led accountants to find ways to limit their potential liability. KPMG, for example, incorporated its audit practice in 1995. Several large audit firms, for example Ernst & Young LLP, have incorporated as Limited Liability Partnerships (which are discussed in Chapter 9).

Any exclusion clause which attempts to exclude liability for negligent misstatement may be subject to the reasonableness test in UCTA (see Chapter 2).

 Interactive question 2: Negligent misstatement   [Difficulty level: Easy]

In order to show that there exists a duty of care not to cause financial loss by negligent misstatement, the claimant must show that

1 The person making the statement did so in a professional capacity
2 The claimant was the only person likely to rely on the statement
3 The claimant was introduced to the person making the statement
4 The claimant actually relied on the statement and suffered loss as a result

A   1 and 4 only
B   1, 2 and 4 only
C   1, 3 and 4 only
D   1, 2, 3 and 4

See **Answer** at the end of this chapter.

3.5 Companies Act liability for auditor's report and audited accounts

In addition to any liability in tort, an auditor also commits an offence under the Companies Act 2006 if he recklessly causes an auditor's report to contain any matter that is misleading or false to a material extent (s 507). Such an offence is punishable by fine.

Also relevant to this question of professional liability are the following provisions of that Act:

* Any provision which exempts an auditor of a company (to any extent) from, or indemnifies him against, liability for negligence (among other things) in relation to providing audited accounts is **void** (save for an indemnity for costs against successfully defending proceedings or where a liability limitation agreement applies), s 532.

* A company may enter into a liability limitation agreement with an auditor, limiting his liability for negligence (among other things) in the course of auditing accounts to a fair and reasonable amount, s 534.

Interactive question 3: Professional advice   [Difficulty level: Exam standard]

Claudia is a trainee accountant employed in an accountancy firm. She meets Daniel at a party and they date for three months. During that time, Daniel asks for some tax advice. Claudia looks up some information at work and then goes home and gives him advice, based on the information she has obtained from the office. She has misinterpreted the tax law and gives incorrect advice to Daniel. A reasonably competent accountant would not have given the same advice to Daniel.

If Daniel decides to sue Claudia, indicate whether or not she could rely on any of the following factors as a complete or partial defence.

		Yes	No
A	She was merely a trainee and therefore the objective standard of care required is lower.	☐	☐
B	She was in a relationship with Daniel, therefore there is a rebuttable presumption that she is not intending him to use her advice professionally.	☐	☐
C	Daniel had intended to do as she advised anyway, so was not affected by her advice.	☐	☐

Daniel might succeed in a claim for negligence against:

		Yes	No
D	Claudia	☐	☐
E	Claudia's firm	☐	☐
F	Claudia's firm and Claudia	☐	☐

See **Answer** at the end of this chapter.

4 Defences and damages

Section overview

- There are **three** defences of particular relevance to the tort of negligence.
- The principal remedy in any case involving negligence will be an award of damages.

4.1 Defences

The three defences particularly relevant to a case involving negligence are:

Defence	Application
Contributory negligence	Where the defendant can show that the damage or loss suffered was partly due to the claimant's fault, the claimant's damages will be reduced by the court in proportion to his degree of fault. For example, if a claimant would have received £100,000 but is found to be 40% contributorily negligent, the damages awarded will be £60,000. (Where there is concurrent liability in tort and contract, this defence will also apply to reduce contractual liability.) The defence is governed by the Law Reform (Contributory Negligence) Act 1945.
Volenti non fit injuria (literally 'to a willing person no injury is done')	This applies where the claimant voluntarily (ie exercising free choice) agrees to undertake the legal risk of loss or damage at his own expense. Effectively it amounts to an agreement by the claimant to exempt the defendant from a duty of care which otherwise would be owed. The fact that a person knows that there is a risk, or even consents to run that risk, does not mean *volenti* necessarily applies. The question is whether the claimant consented to run the risk of having no legal redress. Where UCTA applies, *volenti* cannot be raised to provide a greater exclusion of liability than the Act would allow (for example, to relieve liability for death or personal injury).
Exclusion clauses	Where there is an agreement between the parties that contains a provision seeking to exclude or limit liability for negligence, it may be subject to UCTA. In so far as it relates to business liability for death or personal injury caused by negligence, it will be void. Provisions limiting liability for other types of damage caused by negligence will be subject to the reasonable test. UCTA specifically provides that a person's agreement to, or awareness of, the clause does not necessarily amount to voluntary acceptance of any risk.

4.2 Damages

Damages for negligence are compensatory and are intended to put the claimant in the same position he would have been in had he not suffered any loss. They are normally awarded in a single lump sum. As in contractual claims, damages will not be recovered to the extent that they are considered to be too **remote**. When a person commits a tort with the **intention of causing loss** or harm which in fact results from the wrongful act, that loss can never be too remote.

The loss is too remote unless it can be said that the type of damage that actually did occur was reasonably foreseeable. Provided the kind of damage suffered was reasonably foreseeable, it does not matter that it came about in an unforeseeable way, nor that it was more extensive than could have been foreseen.

> *The Wagon Mound* 1961
>
> *The facts:* A ship was taking on oil in Sydney harbour. Due to negligence, oil was spilled onto the water and it drifted to a wharf 200 yards away where welding equipment was in use. The owner of the wharf carried on working because he was advised that the sparks were unlikely to set fire to furnace oil. Safety precautions were taken. A spark fell onto a piece of cotton waste floating in the oil, thereby starting a fire which damaged the wharf. The owners of the wharf sued the charterers of the ship.
>
> *Decision:* The claim must fail. Pollution was the foreseeable risk, fire was not.

5 Vicarious liability

Section overview

- An employer may be liable for the tortious acts of his 'employee' provided there is a close connection between the relevant act and the employee's employment.

- A principal may be liable for the tortious acts of his agent where they are committed in furtherance of an agency relationship.

- Partners in an ordinary partnership may be vicariously liable for the tortious acts of their fellow partners where they are committed in furtherance of the partnership business.

Vicarious liability is a legal doctrine under which one person can be held legally responsible and liable for the tortious acts of another person. Thus a person may be liable in tort in two ways:

- **Primarily**, if he commits a tort
- **Vicariously**, if his employee or agent commits a tort

Vicarious liability is a legal liability which may be imposed on a person even though he is himself free from blame and **in addition to** the personal liability of the other person who committed the tort.

The doctrine has the advantage of providing an innocent tort victim with recourse against a financially responsible defendant, but at the same time it does impose an additional burden on the business or person held vicariously liable. In the context of employment, for example, this imposition of liability in the absence of fault is a pragmatic recognition of the fact that the employer is likely to have a greater ability to pay damages than the employee, is the best insurer against liability and is able to pass the costs of such liability, or potential liability, to his customers. It has far less to do with any argument that the employer should accept losses alongside the benefits of the employee's work or that he was careless in selecting the employee.

5.1 Vicarious liability and employment

There are two requirements to establish vicarious liability:

- Generally speaking, the wrongdoer (tortfeasor) must be an employee and not an independent contractor.
- The employee must have been acting in the course of his employment.

Employee...

Various tests have been used to distinguish between an *employee* and an *independent contractor*. We will look at them when we look at employment law in Chapter 11, but bear in mind the test may be slightly different when determining whether the person is an employee for the purposes of a tort. The key issues are whether the 'employer' has control over what that person does and how they do it and whether the employee is integral to the business.

However, the courts have shown a willingness to extend vicarious liability to cases where the wrongdoer is not, strictly speaking, an 'employee'.

Likewise, an 'employer' may be found vicariously liable for the acts of an 'agency worker' where the employer temporarily hires the worker from an agency company to act, in effect, as his employee. In such cases, either the 'employer' or the 'agency company' or both can be found vicariously liable, depending on the facts of the case.

...Acting in the course of employment

An employer will only be liable for torts committed by an employee **in the course of his employment**. Otherwise you could have the silly situation of an employer being liable for an employee's motorcycle accident whilst driving a private bike on holiday.

C H A P T E R
4

The law relating to whether an employee was acting in the course of his employment has recently been revised considerably by the following House of Lords case:

Lister and ors v Hesley Hall Ltd 2001

The facts: The warden of a boarding school was found guilty of sexually abusing children resident there.

Decision: The school was vicariously liable. The nature of the warden's work created a sufficient connection between the acts of abuse which he had committed and the work which he was employed to do.

Obviously, in this case, the school did not employ the warden for the purposes of abusing the children. In that sense, he was not acting in the course of his employment when he carried out the abuse. However, the House of Lords concluded that the acts that he carried out were so closely connected with the nature of his work, that it was fair and just to hold the employer liable. In other words, he was employed to look after the children, and the torts committed were in his work time, in the place where he was employed and while he was carrying out his employed duty to care for the children.

Whether this 'close connection' between the employee's tort and his employment exists must be decided by the court on the facts of each case. Two further cases in which the test has been applied since the Lister case are:

Dubai Aluminium Co Ltd v Salaam and ors 2002

The facts: A, a solicitor, drafted bogus agreements.

Decision: The drafting of agreements of this nature (but for a proper purpose) would be within the ordinary course of business for a solicitor. Therefore the dishonest acts were sufficiently closely connected to the course of his business for his employers to be vicariously liable for those acts.

Attorney General v Hartwell 2004

The facts: A police constable in the British Virgin Islands was on duty when he went to a restaurant where his partner worked as a waitress. He fired several shots at his partner and her male companion. One shot hit a British tourist, who sustained serious injuries.

Decision: The Privy Council found that the Attorney General (as the representative of the Government of the British Virgin Isles) was not vicariously liable for the personal injury sustained by the British tourist. The acts of the policeman were not closely connected to his employment, and in fact had nothing to do with his police duties. He was pursuing a personal vendetta.

5.2 Vicarious liability and agency

A principal is vicariously liable for a tort committed by an agent acting within the limits of his authority and carrying out the acts for which he was appointed as agent.

Ormrod v Crossville Motor Services 1953

The facts: A car owner asked a friend to drive his car to Monte Carlo where the owner was going to take part in a rally and then they were going to holiday together after the rally. The friend's negligent driving caused damage to the claimant's bus.

Decision: The owner was vicariously liable for his friend's negligence. It was irrelevant that the friend was driving to Monte Carlo partly for his own purposes.

5.3 Vicarious liability and partnership

A partnership is liable for any wrongful act or omission of any partner acting in the ordinary course of the business of the firm or with the authority of his co-partners which causes loss or injury to another person (s.10 Partnership Act 1890). The question of partners' authority and liability is described in Chapter 9.

Summary

The law gives various rights to persons. When such a right is infringed the wrongdoer is liable in tort

Employers may be held liable for the tortious acts of employees

Principals may be held liable for the tortious acts of their agents

Parners may be held liable for the tortious acts of thier fellow partners

Tortfeasor must be an employee not an independent contractor

Tortious act must be within the course of employment or agency or partnership business

Negligence is the most important modern tort

The law on **negligent professional advice** is currently influenced strongly by the Caparo case, where it was held that the auditors of a public limited company did not owe a duty of care to the public at large who relied upon the audit report in making an investment decision. Note especially how it is different where the professional knows of an identified bidder who has access to the accounts

Remember the criteria applied:
- Purpose made and communicated
- Relationship between parties
- Knowledge of professional
- Reliance
- Size of recipient class

To succeed in an action for negligence and claim damages the claimant must prove that:
- The defendant has a duty of care to avoid causing injury, damage or loss
- There was a **breach of that duty** by the defendant
- In consequence the claimant suffered **injury, damages or loss**

The defendant might be able to rely on volenti or exclusion clause or contributory negligence

In the landmark case of Donoghue v Stevenson 1932 the House of Lords ruled that a person might **owe a duty of care to another with whom he had no contractual relationship** at all. The doctrine has been refined in subsequent rulings, but the principle is unchanged

Whether there is a breach of the duty of care is a question of fact. The standard applied is generally the reasonable man:
- With D's skill
- Ignoring D's disabilities
- Without the benefit of hindsight
- Taking into account any emergency
- Taking account of victim's vulnerability

Finally the claimant must demonstrate that he suffered injury or loss as a result of the breach

The loss must be of a kind that was reasonable forseeable in order not to be too remote

C H A P T E R

4

Self-test

Answer the following questions.

1   In tort no previous transaction or contractual relationship need exist.

    True ☐   False ☐

2   The 'neighbour' principle was established by the landmark case

    A   *Caparo v Dickman 1990*
    B   *Hedley Byrne v Heller 1963*
    C   *Donoghue v Stevenson 1932*
    D   *The Wagon Mound 1961*

3   There are two/three/six essential elements for a negligence claim to be successful. They are

    ....

    ....

4   When the court applies the maxim *res ipsa loquitur*, it is held that the facts speak for themselves and the defendant does not have to prove anything, since the burden of proof is on the claimant.

    True ☐   False ☐

5   What was the leading case on negligent misstatement that allowed recovery of non-physical damage?

6   Which of the following would prevent a claim for negligence from being successful?

    (a)   The claimant followed a course of action regardless of the acts of the defendant.
    (b)   The defendant caused the harm to the claimant.
    (c)   The defendant was not yet fully qualified.
    (d)   The parties were proximate and the harm suffered was reasonably foreseeable.
    (e)   An intervening act broke the 'chain of causation'.
    (f)   The duty of care was restricted by public policy.

7   'A public company's auditors owe no duty of care to the public at large who rely on the audit report in deciding to invest.'

    This is the decision from *Caparo*.

    True ☐   False ☐

8   Name four of the matters to be taken into account by the Court in considering cases of professional negligence.

    •   ....

    •   ....

    •   ....

    •   ....

9   In order for the employer to be vicariously liable the tort must have been committed:

    (1)   ....

    (2)   ....

10 If an agent is liable in tort, the claimant may enforce the vicarious liability of the principal only where he is unable to recover sufficient damages from the agent.

    True ☐   False ☐

Now, go back to the Learning Objectives in the Introduction. If you are satisfied you have achieved these objectives, please tick them off.

Answer to Interactive question 1

D   Any carelessness on the claimant's part may amount to contributory negligence but will not affect the question of whether or not a duty of care exists.

Answer to Interactive question 2

A   2 and 3 are factors that would be taken into account and would be likely to lead to a successful claim, but they are not essential.

Answer to Interactive question 3

A   No – the objective standard of care is the same for a trainee as a qualified accountant.

B   No – there is no such rebuttable presumption (such as there is in contract law). However, the position would be different had Claudia given the advice at the party over a drink or two.

C   Yes – if Daniel's acts and therefore loss were unconnected with her advice then Claudia will not be liable. Daniel will have to prove that the reverse was true.

D   Yes – if he can prove that the loss was due to her advice (ie the defence in (C) is removed).

E   No – Claudia's firm will not be vicariously liable, as although she researched the matter at work, she gave the advice in her own time and away from work premises and therefore not in the course of her employment.

F   No – because of the answer to (E).

CHAPTER

4

1   True

2   C

3   Three: Duty of care
                 Breach of that duty
                 Consequential damage, injury or loss

4   False. *Res ipsa loquitur* means 'the facts speak for themselves' and will lead to an inference that the defendant was in breach of the duty of care.

5   *Hedley Byrne v Heller 1963*

6   (a), (e), (f)

7   True

8
- The purpose for which the statement was made and communicated
- The relationship between the parties
- The size of any class to which the recipient belonged
- The state of knowledge of the maker
- The reliance by the recipient
- Whether the professional assumed responsibility

9   (1)   By an employee

       (2)   The employee must have been acting in the course of his employment (in a way that had a close connection with the scope of his employment).

10   False. The principal's liability is in addition to the agent's liability and exists regardless of the agent's ability to satisfy the claimant.

CHAPTER 5

Companies: the consequences of incorporation

Introduction

Examination context

Topic List

Summary and Self-test

Answers to Interactive questions

Answers to Self-test

Introduction

Learning objectives

Tick off

- To be aware of the different types of company (including off-the-shelf companies) and to understand their characteristics and the concept of corporate personality ☐

- To recognise the circumstances in which the veil of incorporation can be lifted ☐

- To know the procedure for forming a company, what constitutes a company's constitution and how it can be altered ☐

- To be aware of the law relating to promoters and pre-incorporation contracts ☐

- To be familiar with the various administrative requirements which apply as a result of incorporation ☐

Specific syllabus references for this chapter are: 2a, b, c.

Syllabus links

As companies are fundamental in the business world, this chapter is relevant to most papers in your syllabus. Elsewhere, you will study the audit of companies, corporation tax, financial companies, managing companies and preparing company accounts, for example.

Examination context

A large proportion of your exam will relate to company law, as set out in this chapter and Chapters 6, 7 and 8. You might expect around 12 questions to address the areas covered by this chapter.

In the assessment, candidates may be required to:

- Identify the procedure required to form a registered company and identify the advantages and disadvantages of off-the-shelf companies

- Demonstrate an understanding of corporate personality and recognise the circumstances when the veil of incorporation can be lifted

- Identify the administrative consequences of incorporation including requirements regarding statutory books, accounts, meetings and the role of a company secretary

1 Characteristics of a company

Section overview

- A company has a separate legal identity from its members and is, in law, a person in its own right. This is one of the fundamental cornerstones of company law.

- The liability of the members of a company for the debts of the company may be limited. The liability of the company itself is always unlimited.

- The 'veil of incorporation' said to be drawn between the company and its members may be lifted in certain circumstances.

For the purposes of this study manual, a **company** is an entity registered under the Companies Act 2006 ('CA'06') or any earlier Companies Act.

The single largest piece of legislation ever made, the CA'06 is intended to be a comprehensive code of company law, restating and replacing most of the relevant companies legislation that went before it (principally the Companies Acts 1985 and 1989) and also introducing new law. Many of the changes in law were designed to lighten the regulatory and bureaucratic burden on companies (simplifying decision-making processes and capital maintenance provisions, for example), although it remains to be seen whether the burden may actually be increased in some areas, such as communication with nominated holders and the new duty on directors to promote the success of the company (which could lead to differences in the way they conduct their business).

Subject to some very minor restrictions, the Act is now in force. References to 'the Act' are to this statute and section numbers are given for ease of reference only (the exam will not require you to know section numbers).

1.1 Legal personality

A person possesses legal rights and is subject to legal obligations. In law, the term 'person' is used to denote either a **natural person** (ie an individual human being) or an **artificial person** (including companies).

It is a fundamental legal principle that a company is a **legal entity**, separate and distinct from its members. One of the consequences of applying this principle is that the liability of the company's members (not the company itself) for the debts and other liabilities of the company can be limited. It also follows that the property of a company belongs to that company, debts of the company must be satisfied from the assets of that company and the company continues in existence (despite any change in its membership) until such time as it is wound up or otherwise removed from the register.

The first case that clearly demonstrated the separate legal personality of companies is of great significance to any study of company law and is therefore set out in some detail below.

Salomon v Salomon & Co Ltd 1897

The facts: The claimant, Salomon, had carried on business as a leather merchant and boot manufacturer for 30 years. He decided to form a limited company to purchase the business with, he and six members of his family each subscribing for one share. The company then purchased the business from Salomon for £38,782, the purchase price being by way of the issue of 20,000 £1 shares, the issue of debentures for £10,000 (effectively making Salomon a secured creditor) and the balance in cash. The company did not prosper and was wound up a year later, at which point its liabilities exceeded its assets. The liquidator, representing unsecured trade creditors of the company, claimed that the company's business was in effect still the claimant's (since he owned all but six of the issued shares), that he should bear liability for its debts and that payment of the debenture debt to him should be postponed until the company's trade creditors had been paid.

C H A P T E R

5

Decision: The Court of Appeal held that since the other shareholders were 'mere puppets' and that the company had been irregularly incorporated, Salomon should indemnify the company against its liabilities. The House of Lords however held that the business was owned by, and its debts were liabilities of, the company. The claimant was under no liability to the company or its creditors, his debentures were validly issued and the security created by them over the company's assets was effective. This was because once the company had been found to have been formed in compliance with the formal procedures set out in the Companies Act, the company was regarded as a legal entity in its own right, notwithstanding the dominant position of Salomon within the company.

1.2 Liability

As mentioned above, one of the key consequences of the fact that the company is distinct from its members is that its members may enjoy **limited liability**. This means that, in the event of business failure, the members will only be asked to contribute identifiable amounts to the assets of the business, even though they are, essentially, the ones who **own** the business. Not surprisingly, most companies are registered with limited liability.

It is important that you understand that the company itself, on the other hand, is **liable without limit for its own debts**. In an **unlimited company**, there is no limit on the company's **or** the members' liability. Thus, the question of limited liability is important when a **limited** company is unable to satisfy all its debts.

The amounts that members may be required to pay, in the event of a winding up, depend upon the type of limited company, as follows:

Type of company	Amount owed by member at winding up
Company limited by shares	Any outstanding amount of the nominal value of any share which has not been paid either by the original or a subsequent holder of the shares. If the member's shares are fully paid, there is no further liability to contribute. Any premium (over the nominal value) that was agreed to be paid for the share will also be owed to the extent that it has not been paid, unless the shareholder at the time is not the original shareholder (since the amount of premium is a debt that does not pass with the shares).
Company limited by guarantee	The amount they guaranteed to pay in the event of a winding up.

A company, as a separate legal entity, may also have liabilities in tort and crime. However, it is currently extremely difficult to prosecute a company successfully for a criminal offence.

1.3 Veil of incorporation

As a result of the law stated in Salomon's case, a '**veil of incorporation**' is said to be drawn between the members and the company, separating them for the purposes of liability and identification. This often results in protecting the members from the consequences of the company's actions, as you will see below. Occasionally the separate legal personality symbolised by the veil can be problematic as where, for example, an individual incorporated his business but insured the company's property in his own name rather than that of the company. When the property was destroyed by fire, it was held that he had no insurable interest (either as creditor or member) and that the company, as a separate legal entity, should have insured its own assets (*Macaura v Northern Assurance Co Ltd 1925*).

A rigid application of the principle of separate legal personality can sometimes produce harsh or inequitable results and so the law sometimes 'lifts the veil' in order to expose the commercial reality of the situation.

Generally speaking, this may be done by the courts in order to defeat fraud, sharp practices or illegality, although it is difficult to define a set of consistent principles underlying the cases. Examples of where the veil has been lifted by the courts are given below in order to give you a general understanding of the courts' approach. You will not be examined on your recollection of each case.

Groups of companies – where the subsidiary can be regarded as the agent of the holding company	
• To produce tax liability	*Firestone Tyre & Rubber Co Ltd v Lewellin 1957*: English subsidiary (S) deemed to be agent of American holding company (H) (thus rendering H liable to UK tax) where H entered into agreement with distributors under which the distributors should place orders with H, to be carried out by S. In fact, S received orders direct, handled business completely (free from control of H) and forwarded money (less a percentage) to it.
• To give entitlement to compensation	*Smith, Stone & Knight Ltd v Birmingham Corporation 1939*: Compensation for compulsorily-acquired premises was payable to an owner-occupier (H in this case) but not a tenant-occupier(S). Held that S occupied the premises as an agent of H since it was wholly-owned and the directors of H and S were the same.
• To prevent evasion of excise duty	*Re H and others 1996*: Where evasions were alleged to have been committed by H, the court also allowed restraint of S's assets, refusing to recognise the companies as separate.

It is important to note, however, that cases such as these do not mean that groups of companies will generally be regarded as a single entity. There are numerous examples of where the courts have refused to lift the veil between companies within a group, including cases where creditors of an insolvent subsidiary are not paid in full even though the holding company remains solvent or where a claimant proceeds against a subsidiary company that is not as asset-rich as its holding company.

To reveal true national identity and expose illegality	*Daimler Co Ltd v Continental Tyre & Rubber Co (GB) Ltd 1916*: A company was registered and had its registered office in England. However, since all of its members with control of the company (except one) were German, the veil could be lifted to expose the company as an enemy alien. Therefore trading with this company was against the law (in wartime). (See too *Re F G Films* below.)
Quasi-partnership	*Ebrahimi v Westbourne Galleries 1972*: In this case, the courts lifted the veil to reveal a company so completely in the nature of a partnership, that a winding-up of the company could be ordered on the grounds of it being just and equitable, because one of the directors being excluded from the management of the company represented a complete breakdown in the management of the company just, as it would be unlawful in a partnership.
Where a company is a sham	
• To prevent an evasion of obligations	*Gilford Motor Co Ltd v Horne 1933*: An employee was contractually bound not to solicit customers from his ex-employer after leaving its service. In order to get round this, he formed a company and carried on his work, soliciting his ex-employer's customers in the process. The veil was lifted to reveal his company as a 'mere cloak or sham' and an injunction was granted against it and the employee.
• To reveal national identity	*Re F G Films Ltd 1953*: An English company was formed to make an English film. In fact the staff and finance were American, the film was produced in India and there were neither premises nor employees in England. The veil was lifted to expose a 'sham' company with the result that the marketing and other advantages available to British films were not available in this case.

In addition to the courts sometimes exercising their discretion to lift the veil, **legislation** can also provide for the veil to be lifted, usually in order to confer a personal liability on those who run a company for breach of obligations imposed on the company. You should note that the following examples are only legitimate illustrations of the veil being lifted if the directors or others (upon whom liability is imposed) are also members of the company:

STATUTE	
Situation where veil might be lifted	Explanation
Where director is disqualified	Directors who participate in the management of a company in contravention of an order under the Company Directors Disqualification Act 1986 will be **jointly** or **severally liable** along with the company for the company's debts.
Fraudulent and wrongful trading (ss 213, 214 Insolvency Act 1986)	Where a company is being wound up • All persons who are knowingly parties to carrying on business with the intent of defrauding creditors or for some other fraudulent purpose (fraudulent trading) and • Directors who carry on business when they knew or should have known that the company would not avoid insolvent liquidation (wrongful trading) can be held **personally liable** to make such contribution to the company's assets as the court thinks fit.
Trading without a trading certificate (s 767)	A public company must obtain a certificate from the Registrar before it commences to trade. Failure to do so leads to **personal liability** for the directors for any loss or damage suffered by a third party to a transaction entered into by the company in contravention of this section.

Interactive question 1: Lifting the corporate veil [Difficulty level: Easy]

Following the collapse of Forest Ferns Ltd, Sandy is disqualified from being a director for five years. However, after three years, he sets up a company, Beach Holidays Ltd, of which he is a director and 95% shareholder. As a result of a terrorist attack on a passenger jet from Heathrow, the overseas holiday market collapses and Beach Holidays Ltd goes into insolvent liquidation. Which of the following best describes the legal position?

A   Beach Holidays Ltd is a separate legal personality and is therefore solely responsible for its debts.

B   Sandy is liable for Beach Holidays Ltd's debts as a 95% shareholder and the veil will be lifted to reveal the company as a sham, designed to conceal a sole proprietor's business.

C   The veil will be lifted on a statutory basis because Sandy is disqualified and he will be solely liable for the debts of Beach Holidays Ltd.

D   The veil will be lifted because Sandy was acting whilst disqualified and both he and Beach Holidays Ltd will be liable for the debts on a joint and several basis.

See **Answer** at the end of this chapter.

2 Types of company

Section overview

- Public companies are companies limited by shares and registered as public companies.

- Private companies may be unlimited, or limited by shares or guarantee.

- Public companies may re-register as private and *vice versa*.

- Limited companies may re-register as unlimited and *vice versa*.

2.1 Limited and unlimited companies

The liability of the members of a company may be limited or unlimited (s 3) as follows:

Liability	Description
Limited by shares (public or private)	Liability is limited to the amount of the nominal value, if any, unpaid on members' shares held by them (including any premium payable by the current owner in respect of them).
Limited by guarantee (private only)	Liability is limited to such amount as the members undertake to contribute to the company's assets in the event of it being wound up.
	A company limited by guarantee cannot be registered with a share capital. A company limited by guarantee is often a charity or trade association, ie a non-commercial organisation that aims to keep income and expenditure in balance but has the members' guarantee as a form of reserve capital in case of insolvency.
Unlimited (private only)	There is no limit on the members' liability. They can be compelled to contribute as much as may be necessary to pay the company's debts in full.
	An unlimited company does not need to file annual accounts, subject to certain conditions (for example, that it is not a subsidiary or a parent of a limited company (s 448)).

A company may alter its status **once**, as follows (ss 102-111).

- **Limited to unlimited**: with the consent of **all members** of the company.

- **Unlimited to limited**: by passing a **special resolution** to that effect and specifying whether the company is to be limited by shares or guarantee.

In each case, the company must make any necessary changes to its name and articles and apply, with appropriate documentation, to the Registrar of Companies.

A company limited by shares may not re-register as a company limited by guarantee, and *vice versa*.

2.2 Public and private companies

A **public company** is a limited company expressly registered as a public company under the Act. Only a small proportion of companies are public companies.

A **private company** is any registered company (limited or unlimited) that is not stated to be a public limited company. Most private companies are small to medium enterprises in which some, if not all, shareholders are the directors.

The principal differences are that a public company is subject to more stringent rules and regulation than private companies and that only a public company can offer its securities to the public. The principal features of public and private companies can be summarised as follows (at the same time illustrating the differences between them):

Feature	Public	Private
Liability	Must be limited.	May be limited or unlimited.
Share capital	Subject to authorised minimum (currently £50,000).	No minimum.
Ability to commence trading	Must have trading certificate before it can commence trading (s 761).	May commence trading once incorporated.
Public offers	Can offer its securities to the public (and may obtain a listing from the Stock Exchange or other investment exchange).	Prohibited from offering its securities to the public (s 755).
Name	Must end with 'public limited company' or 'plc' (or Welsh equivalent) (s 58).	Must end with 'limited' or 'ltd' (or Welsh equivalent) although certain companies (including charities) may be exempt from this requirement (ss 59–62).
Loans etc	Loans to persons connected with directors and quasi-loans and credit transactions to directors or connected persons need members' approval (ss 198-202).	These rules do not apply (unless the company is associated with a public company).
Directors	Must have at least two directors (s 154).	Must have at least one.
Company Secretary	Must have one (s 271).	Need not have one (s 270).
Written resolutions	Not applicable.	May pass written resolutions instead of calling meetings (s 288).
AGMs	Must hold AGM (s 336).	Need not hold AGM.
Accounts and reports	Must lay these before general meeting.	Need not do so.
	Must file within 6 months (s 442).	Must file within 9 months (s 442).
Small and medium sized companies	Not applicable.	May qualify as small or medium-sized, and take advantage of audit exemptions (small companies) and less stringent regime for filing.
Appointment of auditors	Must appoint auditors each year if necessary (s 489).	Existing auditors may be deemed to be re-appointed, subject to conditions (s 487).
Pre-emption rights	May not be excluded.	May be excluded.
Payment for shares	Additional rules apply to public companies, including that shares must be at least ¼ paid up (s 586) and concerning valuations for non-cash consideration (s 593).	Not applicable.
Reduction of capital	Needs special resolution confirmed by the court (s 641).	Needs only special resolution and directors' solvency statement (s 642).
Power to redeem or purchase shares out of capital	Not applicable.	May do so, subject to conditions (s 709).

In addition, special rules apply to **quoted companies** with regard to publication of details on the company website and directors' remuneration reports.

A private company may apply to the Registrar of Companies to be re-registered as a public company (or a public company as a private company) provided certain conditions and procedures are satisfied (ss 90–101).

Interactive question 2: Types of company [Difficulty level: Exam standard]

Alex, Barry and Carol have operated as a partnership for five years trading in domestic carpets. The business has been successful and they are now considering expanding the business operations by opening three new shops and an additional wholesale unit. The partners are aware that the expansion will require new business capital. They are considering the formation of a company rather than continuing as a partnership.

What types of company may be formed under the Companies Act 2006? Which type of company is suitable for this business?

See **Answer** at the end of this chapter.

3 Formation of a company

Section overview

- There are a variety of documents required to form a company.

- Companies can be bought 'off the shelf'.

- Promoters make business preparations for a new company.

A company may not be formed for an unlawful purpose.

3.1 Registration documents

In order to form a company, the following documents must be sent to the Registrar of Companies:

Document	Description
Memorandum of association	A memorandum in the prescribed form stating that the subscribers (a) wish to form a company and (b) agree to become members of the company and, in the case of a company with a share capital, agree to take at least one share each. It must be authenticated by each subscriber.
Application	This must state • The company's proposed name (which is subject to certain rules designed to prevent the company misleading the public regarding its identity and/or activities) • Whether the liability of the members is to be limited and, if so, whether by shares or guarantee • Whether the company is to be private or public • Whether the registered office is to be in England and Wales or Wales or Scotland or Northern Ireland • The intended address of the registered office (the registered office is the address for delivery of legal documents which may need to be served on a company and also where company registers must or may be kept (see section 6)).

Document	Description
Statement of capital and initial shareholdings (applicable to a company with a share capital)	It must state • The total number of shares • Their aggregate nominal value • Details of individual classes of shares • The amount to be paid and unpaid on each share This is essentially a snapshot of the company's share capital at the time of registration.
Statement of guarantee (applicable to a company limited by guarantee)	It must state the maximum amount which each member undertakes to contribute to the net assets of the company if the company is wound up while he is a member or within one year thereafter.
Statement of proposed officers	This must give particulars of and the consent of • The first director(s) of the company • The first company secretary (optional in the case of a private company).
Statement of compliance	This is a statement that the requirements of the Act have been complied with.

Articles of association may also be submitted, but if none is supplied, the default articles will apply (see section 5 below).

If the Registrar is satisfied that the registration requirements of the Act have been complied with, he will register the documents and issue a **certificate of incorporation**, naming and describing the company and giving its date of incorporation and registered number.

This certificate is conclusive evidence that the company is registered in accordance with the Act and is a body corporate. If irregularities in formation procedure or an error on the certificate are later discovered, it is nonetheless valid and conclusive (*Jubilee Cotton Mills Ltd v Lewis 1924*).

Note that a **public company** also needs to obtain a **trading certificate** before it can commence trading. It must submit:

- An application stating (amongst other things) that the nominal value of the company's allotted share capital is not less than the 'authorised minimum' and

- A statement of compliance (s 762).

Any transaction in **contravention** of this provision will render any company officer in default liable to a fine but the transaction will remain valid. Failure to obtain a trading certificate within a year of incorporation may result in a compulsory winding up (s 122 Insolvency Act 1986).

3.2 Companies 'off-the-shelf'

It is possible to buy a company that has already been incorporated. There are two principal advantages to such 'off-the-shelf' companies:

- It is obviously a quicker way of achieving the result of having a company 'ready to go'.

- It avoids any potential liability arising from pre-incorporation contracts (see section 3.3 below) as the company already exists.

There are disadvantages, however, since the following changes may need to be made:

- Change of name
- Transfer of subscribers' shares
- Change of directors and possibly company secretary
- Alteration of articles

3.3 Promoters and pre-incorporation contracts

In addition to the person who takes the procedural steps to get a company incorporated, the term 'promoter' includes anyone who makes **business preparations** for the company. However a person who acts merely in a professional capacity in company formation, such as a solicitor or an accountant, is not on that account a promoter.

A **promoter owes certain duties to** the company:

- A general duty to exercise **reasonable care and skill**

- A **fiduciary duty** to disclose any personal interest in a transaction and, sometimes, to account for monies received. Generally speaking, any profits which he makes from promoting the company and fails to disclose must be surrendered to the company. However, if he discloses them and the company gives consent, he may retain any legitimate profits.

  In the case of a public company, disclosure is made through the listing particulars or prospectus. Disclosure in a private company should be to existing and prospective members or to the board of directors, provided it is independent of him.

Since a company has no capacity to enter into contracts prior to its coming into existence, if a promoter makes a contact on the company's behalf prior to incorporating (a '**pre-incorporation contract**'), the following will apply:

- The **company cannot ratify** the contract since it did not exist when the contract was made *(Kelner v Baxter 1866)*

- The **company is not bound by it** even after incorporation and even if it has derived some benefit from it *(Re National Motor Mail Coach Ltd, Clinton's Claim 1908)*

- The **company cannot enforce the contract** against the third party unless the promoter and third party have given rights of action to the company under the Contracts (Rights of Third Parties) Act 1999

- The contract takes effect (subject to any agreement to the contrary) in the same way as one made with the **promoter** and he is **personally liable** on it (s 51).

A promoter can **avoid potential liability**, most usually by

- Not making contracts until the company has been incorporated, or

- Using an off-the-shelf company, or

- Agreeing a draft only with the third party on the basis that the company, once formed, will enter into the agreed form with the third party.

Where a promoter is already liable on a pre-incorporation contract, he may be able to arrange for the company to **novate** the contract (ie enter into a new contract on identical terms), in which case he should also secure the third party's consent to the promoter thereupon being released from personal liability.

Note that giving rights to the company under the Contracts (Rights of Third Parties) Act 1999 does not also remove a promoter's liability since the Act provides that the original parties remain liable on the contract.

A promoter usually incurs **expenses** in preparations, such as drafting legal documents, made before the company is formed. He cannot legally claim any remuneration or indemnity for his services or expenses but, in practice, will generally arrange that the first directors, of whom he may be one, agree that the company shall make such payment to him.

Interactive question 3: Pre-incorporation contracts   [Difficulty level: Exam standard]

Imran is in the process of setting up a new company, Silver Stumps Ltd. Before submitting the application for registration, he enters into a contract on behalf of the company with Greenfields plc for the purchase of a cricket ground on the banks of the River Avon. Shortly after the company is registered and a certificate of incorporation issued, Silver Stumps Ltd finds that it is unable to raise sufficient funds and so fails to complete on the purchase on the due date.

Which of the following best describes the legal position?

A   Greenfields plc may enforce the contact against Silver Stumps Ltd because Silver Stumps Ltd automatically assumes responsibility for contracts entered into on its behalf upon incorporation.

B   Provided Silver Stumps Ltd ratifies the contract with Greenfields plc, Greenfields plc may enforce the contract against Silver Stumps Ltd.

C   Greenfields plc may enforce the contract against Imran personally because Silver Stumps Ltd cannot ratify the contract.

D   Imran's liability on the contract ceased because he has transferred all rights to Silver Stumps Ltd in accordance with the Contracts (Rights of Third Parties) Act 1999.

See **Answer** at the end of this chapter.

4   A company's name

Section overview

- There are rules which restrict a company's freedom to choose any name.

- A company's name may be changed either through the company's choice or as directed by the Registrar.

- A company's name must be disclosed in accordance with the Act.

The Act sets out rules which provide for certain company names to be prohibited, for a name to be changed and requiring disclosure of a company's name and business name (exceptions are set out in ss 60-62).

4.1   Prohibited names

You have already learned that the name of a public company should end with 'public limited company' (or 'plc') and that a private limited company should end with 'limited' or 'ltd'.

In addition, the name of a company should be chosen with care, having regard to the following rules (contained in Part 5 of the Act):

- The company will not be registered if the Registrar considers the name to be **offensive**, or if its use could constitute a **criminal offence**.

- The approval of the Secretary of State is required if the name is **sensitive** in some way or likely to suggest some **connection** with central or local government, or any public authority. Words such as 'British' or 'International', for example, are only likely to be sanctioned if the size of the company matches its pretensions.

- Words which indicate that the company is of another **type or legal form** are not permitted.

- A company cannot be registered if its name is the **same as** or virtually the same as the name of an existing company.

4.2   Change of company name

A company may **choose** to alter its name at any time by passing a special resolution to that effect or otherwise as provided for in its articles (s 77). The company must notify the Registrar accordingly and obtain a new certificate of incorporation. The change does not affect any rights, obligations or proceedings of the company.

The Secretary of State may order a company to change its name for a number of reasons, including where it is considered to be the **same as** or virtually the same as an existing company name or that it might otherwise **mislead** the public.

Interactive question 4: Formation of company　　　　[Difficulty level: Exam standard]

What are the documents that must be delivered to the Registrar on formation of a private company limited by shares?

See **Answer** at the end of this chapter.

4.3 Disclosure of company name

The name of the company must be displayed in certain locations and on certain documents in accordance with regulations made by the Secretary of State (s 82). The name must also be engraved legibly on the company seal (s 45). Breach of either provision may result in a fine.

4.4 Business names

Most companies carry on business under their registered names. However, a company, just like an individual or partnership, may adopt a 'business name'.

Business names are subject to similar rules as to words or names that are misleading or otherwise prohibited or that require the approval of the Secretary of State in the case of company names.

5 Articles of association

Section overview

- Every company is required to have articles of association ('articles') and model articles apply where a company does not register its own.

- Articles prescribe regulations governing the management of the company's affairs, the rights of the shareholders and the powers and duties of the directors.

- Articles form part of the constitution of a company and bind the company and its members.

- Articles may be altered by the company in general meeting.

A company's articles form part of its constitution, along with all special resolutions and other relevant resolutions and agreements (s 17). Sometimes a power conferred on a company by the Act is expressed to be subject to any restriction or prohibition contained in the company's articles (for example, the power of a private limited company to reduce its capital). Where the Act prohibits something permitted by the articles, the Act will prevail.

5.1 Model articles

'Model articles' prescribed by the Secretary of State in respect of different types of companies, will apply wherever a company is formed without registering articles or insofar as it registers articles that do not exclude or modify the model articles. The prescribed articles thus operate as **default** articles. 'Table A articles', for example, are commonly adopted by companies limited by shares, either in their entirety or with small amendments. Listed companies must have their own full-length articles containing a number of special provisions as required by Stock Exchange rules.

5.2 The contractual effect of a company's constitution

Under s 33 CA06, the provisions of a company's constitution (ie articles and relevant resolutions and agreement) bind the company and its members as if each had covenanted to the other to observe those provisions. They do not bind the company to third parties.

This principle applies only to rights and obligations which affect members **in their capacity as members**. Thus it applies to defeat an action when an outsider, who is also a member, seeks to rely on the articles in support of a claim made **as an outsider**.

This point can be illustrated by the following case:

Eley v Positive Government Security Life Assurance Co 1876

The facts: Eley, a solicitor, drafted the original articles and included a provision that the company must always employ him as its solicitor. Eley became a member of the company some months after its incorporation. He later sued the company for breach of contract in not employing him as a solicitor.

Decision: Eley could not rely on the article since it was a contract between the company and its members and he was not asserting any claim **as a member**.

S 33 gives to the constitution the effect of a contract made between (a) the company and (b) its members individually. It also acts as a contract on the members **in their dealings with each other**.

In certain cases, if a contract contains no specific term on a particular point but the articles do, then the **contract may be deemed to incorporate the articles** to that extent. In one case, for example, a director's contract with the company was silent as to remuneration but the articles provided that directors would be paid £1,000 per annum. The court held that although the articles did not constitute a contract between the company and the director (in his capacity as director) they could be used to imply the term as to remuneration into his contract *(Re New British Iron Co, ex parte Beckwith 1898)*.

Generally speaking, if a contract incorporates terms of the articles, it is subject to the company's **right** to **alter** its articles. However, where rights have already accrued under a contract, say for services rendered **prior** to the alteration, those rights will be unaffected by any alteration of the articles.

5.3 Alteration of articles

A company may normally alter its articles by passing a special resolution to that effect (s 21). However, where the articles contain '**provision for entrenchment**' such provisions can only be altered with the agreement of all company members or by court order (s 22). Such a provision for entrenchment might, for example, require that certain articles can only be changed if particular conditions are met or procedures followed that are more restrictive than the usual requirement for a special resolution. A company cannot provide that a provision for entrenchment can never be replaced or amended and must give notice to the Registrar whenever one is included or removed.

A copy of any amended article must be sent to the Registrar within 15 days.

A member will not be bound by any alteration made after he became a member insofar as the alteration requires him to take more shares or increases his liability in any way to pay money to or contribute to the company (s 25).

6 Administrative consequences of incorporation

Section overview

Incorporation necessitates compliance in a number of areas including the ownership, management and financing of companies dealt with in subsequent chapters. There are also administrative consequences, including:

- The need to maintain registers and records
- The need to submit certain documents to the Registrar of Companies
- The need to produce audited accounts and reports.

6.1 Company records

The term '**company records**' refers to any register, agreement, minutes, accounting records or other documents required to be kept by the Act. They may be kept in hard copy or electronic form. In each case, the company record is to be kept at the company's registered office or at any other place specified in regulations made by the Secretary of State. The Act sets out rules relating to rights of inspection (and sometimes rights to receive copies) for members and others. Generally speaking, any contravention of any of these provisions renders the company and every company officer in default guilty of an offence and liable to a fine.

In particular, a company is required to keep the following company records:

- A register of members

- A register of directors and (if applicable) company secretaries

- A register of directors' residential addresses (this information is 'protected information' and must not be made available for public inspection.)

- Copies of directors' service contracts and indemnity provisions restricting directors' liabilities

- Records of resolutions and minutes (for a period of ten years)

- Directors' statement and auditor's report

- A register of charges and copies of charges

In addition, a company is required to give copies of the company's articles, and certain other documents of constitutional importance, free of charge upon request (s 32). A company is not required to keep a register of debenture holders but, if it does, it must comply with the provisions concerned with its availability for inspection (s 743).

6.2 The register

The Registrar of Companies maintains a '**register**' in respect of each company at Companies House. This register contains:

- The certificate of incorporation

- The trading certificate (if it is a public company)

- Certificates of registration of charges

- The information contained in documents delivered to the Registrar in accordance with any statutory provision, including annual accounts and return, special and some ordinary resolutions and changes of directors.

The Registrar is required to keep certain information in electronic form (including the articles, annual accounts and reports, annual return, statements of capital and statement of directors), but otherwise may keep the register in such form as he thinks fit.

Subject to exceptions listed in the Act (s 1087), any person has the right to inspect the register and, with payment of a fee, to require a copy of any material on the register. The exceptions to this right to inspect include the following:

- Protected information on directors' residential addresses
- The contents of any charges

Any person also has the right to a copy of any certificate of incorporation and the right to inspect the Registrar's index of company names.

6.3 Accounts and reports

Generally speaking, every company must keep accounting records and must produce annual accounts which normally require to be audited (see 6.4 below). In addition, the directors are responsible for producing a report. These accounts and reports need then to be circulated to members and filed at the registry. You should be familiar with the following framework, although be aware that there are many exceptions and points of detail which may be relevant in practice.

Document	Notes
Accounting records (s 386)	'Adequate accounting records' that are sufficient to show the company's financial position at any time with reasonable accuracy, including: • Daily entries of income and expenditure • Record of assets and liabilities • (If applicable) statements of stock and stocktakings
Annual accounts (s 393)	ie a balance sheet and profit and loss account. Consolidated group accounts are normally required where the company is a parent company. The accounts must give a 'true and fair view' of the company's financial position in respect of its financial year. Notes to the accounts must deal with employee numbers and costs and directors' benefits. The accounts must be approved by and signed on behalf of the board of directors.
Directors' Report (s 415)	In respect of the financial year, the • Names of directors • Principal activities of the company • Statement that the auditor is not unaware of any relevant audit information A recommended dividend and business review, (including principal risks and uncertainties facing the company) are usually included although not always (for example small companies). (A consolidated report should be produced where group accounts are prepared). The directors' report must be approved by and signed on behalf of the board of directors.
Directors' Remuneration Report (s 420)	This applies to **quoted companies only** and is subject to the members' approval.
Auditor's Report (s 495)	Where accounts are audited (see section 6.4 below) the report must • Identify the accounts audited and the financial reporting framework applied in their preparation • Describe the scope of the audit • State that, in the auditor's opinion, the accounts give a true and fair view of the company's financial affairs • State that the directors' report is consistent with the accounts
Annual return (s 855)	The return must state the date to which it is made up and contain information including • The address of the company's registered office • Prescribed particulars of the directors and any company secretary • The type of company and its principal business activities • The address(es) of where the register of members and any register of debenture holders may be inspected (if not kept at the registered office) • A statement of capital and prescribed particulars concerning the members and the shares in the company The return must be signed by a director or secretary and delivered to the Registrar within 28 days of the return date (usually the anniversary of the date of incorporation).

Non-compliance with these provisions may render the company and any relevant officer liable to a fine and, in some cases, imprisonment.

A company's accounts and reports must be publicised in compliance with the Act, including filing them at the Registry within **9 months** (**private** company) or **6 months** (**public** company) after the end of the relevant accounting reference period.

You should be aware that a less stringent regime applies to **small and medium-sized companies** (for example, they may file 'abbreviated accounts'). Broadly, these are private companies which comply with two or more of the following requirements (s 382):

	Small	Medium
Turnover	≤ £6.5m	≤ £25.9m
Balance sheet	≤ £3.26m	≤ £12.9m
Employees	≤ 50	≤ 250

6.4 Audit requirements

Generally speaking, a company is required to appoint auditors to carry out an audit of its annual accounts. Some companies are exempt, namely:

- Small companies (that satisfy the small company criteria in 6.3 above)
- Dormant companies

  } but not certain companies, including insurance or banking companies

- Non-profit-making companies subject to public sector audit

- Subsidiary companies whose parent company guarantees their liabilities outstanding at the balance sheet date

Even where an exemption applies, an audit can be required by 10% or more of the members or by members representing at least 10% of the nominal value of the company's issued share capital.

An auditor or auditors must be **appointed** for each financial year and can be appointed by the directors or by the members passing an ordinary resolution or, in the event of default, by the Secretary of State. The auditor's remuneration should be fixed by those appointing him. An auditor of a private company is deemed to be re-appointed unless the company decides otherwise (s 487).

The auditor has a **right of access** at all times to the company's books and accounts. He has a **duty** to carry out a proper investigation in preparing his report. He may be **removed** by ordinary resolution, subject to **special notice** being given and the auditor having the right to make representations.

Any person who knowingly or recklessly causes an auditor's report to include any matter that is misleading, false or deceptive commits an **offence** punishable by a fine. (See also Chapter 4 regarding auditors' liability for negligent misstatement.)

6.5 Company secretary

Every **public company** must appoint a company secretary who satisfies the qualification requirements contained in the Act (s 273). Private companies may choose to have a company secretary but are not obliged to do so. The company secretary is usually appointed by the directors.

A company secretary is an employee of the company. He is also an 'officer' of the company and therefore faces potential civil and criminal liability where the Act so provides in the event of contravention by the company of legislative requirements.

The Act does not define the role of the company secretary and it will vary according to the size and nature of each company. However, typically, a company secretary will convene the meetings of the board of directors, issue the agenda and draft the minutes. He will also be responsible for the various statutory registers and for filing documents with the Registrar. In a smaller company, he is also likely to act as general administrator and compliance manager and might even be responsible for the accounts and taxation aspects of the company's business.

The company secretary is recognised as having the power to contract on behalf of the company in respect of its administrative operations, including the employment of office staff and management of the office generally. Thus he may bind the company by his actions on the basis of implied actual authority as well as any express or ostensible authority. However, a company secretary's implied authority is limited and does not extend to buying land, for example, nor to borrowing money, nor to doing other acts usually undertaken by the directors.

Summary

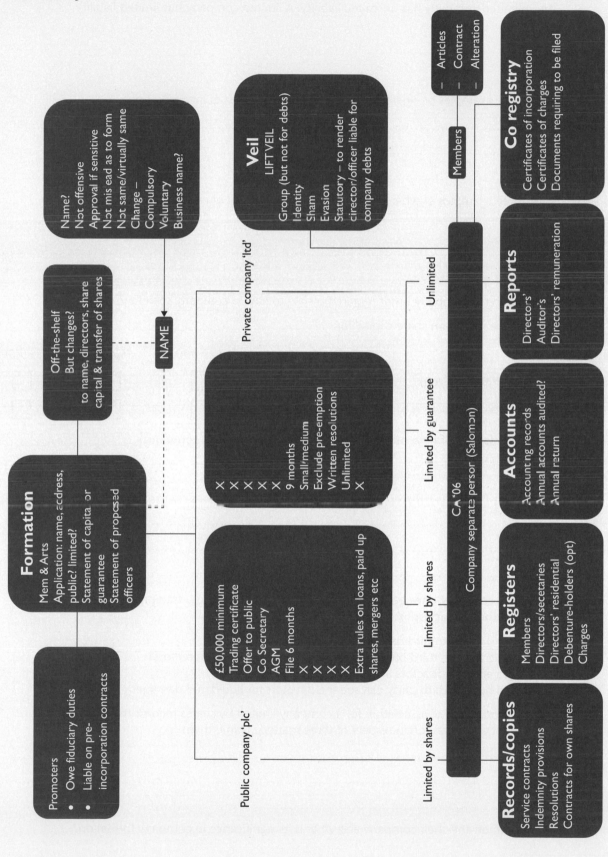

Formation
Mem & Arts
Application: name, address,
public? limited?
Statement of capital or
guarantee
Statement of proposed
officers

Off-the-shelf
But changes?
to name, directors, share
capital & transfer of shares

NAME

Name?
Not offensive
Approval if sensitive
Not mislead as to form
Not same/virtually same
Change –
Compulsory
Voluntary
Business name?

Promoters
• Owe fiduciary duties
• Liable on pre-
incorporation contracts

Veil
LIFT VEIL
Group (but not for debts)
Identity
Sham
Evasion
Statutory – to render
director/officer liable for
company debts

Private company 'ltd'
× × × × ×
9 months
Small/medium
Exclude pre-emption
Written resolutions
Unlimited
×

Public company 'plc'
£50,000 minimum
Trading certificate
Offer to public
Co Secretary
AGM
File 6 months
×
×
×
×
Extra rules on loans, paid up
shares, mergers etc

CA '06
Company separate person (Salomon)

Unlimited

Limited by guarantee

Limited by shares

Limited by shares

– Articles
– Contract
– Alteration

Members

Co registry
Certificates of incorporation
Certificates of charges
Documents requiring to be filed

Reports
Directors'
Auditor's
Directors' remuneration

Accounts
Accounting records
Annual accounts audited?
Annual return

Registers
Members
Directors/secretaries
Directors' residential
Debenture-holders (opt)
Charges

Records/copies
Service contracts
Indemnity provisions
Resolutions
Contracts for own shares

CHAPTER

5

ICAEW

Self-test

Answer the following questions.

1 Define a company.

2 What was the name of the case that is generally cited as establishing the principle of corporate personality?

3 An unlimited company has unlimited liability. A limited company has limited liability.

☐ True

☐ False

4 Give three examples of where the courts might lift the veil of incorporation.

- ....
- ....
- ....

5 Give three examples of where statute provides for the veil of incorporation to be lifted.

- ....
- ....
- ....

6 Is it true that a company is not required by law to have a company secretary?

7 What is the minimum share capital for:

	No minimum	£20,000	£50,000	£100,000
(1) A private company?	☐	☐	☐	☐
(2) A public company?	☐	☐	☐	☐

8 List ten examples of how public companies differ from private companies.

- .... · ....
- .... · ....
- .... · ....
- .... · ....
- .... · ....

9 If a public company does business or borrows before obtaining a trading certificate from the Registrar, the transaction is

A Invalid and the third party cannot recover any loss
B Invalid but the third party can recover any loss from the directors
C Valid and the directors are punishable by a fine
D Valid but the third party can sue the directors for liquidated damages

10 The memorandum of association for a company limited by shares records the subscribers' agreement and intention in respect of three matters. Name them.

- ....
- ....
- ....

11 What is an off-the-shelf company and what is its significance in company formation?

12 (1) A company can ratify a pre-incorporation contract thus releasing the promoter from any personal liability.

☐ True

☐ False

(2) A promoter should avoid personal liability by utilising the Contracts (Rights of Third Parties) Act 1999 and giving rights of enforcement to the company as third party.

☐ True

☐ False

13 A company cannot be registered unless it submits a copy of its articles of association when applying for registration

☐ True

☐ False

14 How can a company change its articles of association?

15 In the event of conflict which prevails: the articles or the Act?

16 Which one of the following is not compulsory?

- Register of members
- Register of directors
- Register of secretaries
- Register of debenture-holders
- Register of charges

17 What are the 'accounting records' that a company is required to maintain?

18 Small companies and dormant companies are not required to have their accounts audited.

☐ True

☐ False

Now, go back to the Learning Objectives in the Introduction. If you are satisfied you have achieved these objectives, please tick them off.

ICAEW

Answers to Interactive questions

Answer to Interactive question 1

D   Directors who participate in the management of a company whilst disqualified will be liable for the company's debts on a joint and several basis. Where the director is also a member, as here, this is an example of the corporate veil being lifted.

Answer to Interactive question 2

The main categories of companies which may be formed under the CA'06 are a public company limited by shares, and a private company, which may be limited by shares or by guarantee or be an unlimited company.

A private company limited by shares is the most suitable type for a small business venture of this kind. It offers the advantages of being a corporate entity separate from its members, giving them the protection of limited liability. This means that on a winding-up of the company, each shareholder would only have to contribute any amount that was not already paid up on their shares.

The main restriction on a private company is that it may not offer its shares or debentures to the public. However, it is subject to fewer restrictions than a public company including not needing a company secretary or an AGM. It may use capital to finance the purchase of its own shares and it may give financial assistance for the purchase of its shares. If the company ranks as a small or a medium-sized company for the purposes of its annual accounts, the accounts delivered to the registrar need not contain all the material required in the accounts of a public company and need not be audited.

Answer to Interactive question 3

C   There is no automatic assumption of responsibility for promoters' contracts on incorporation. A company cannot ratify a contract entered into by a promoter before the company is formed because a principal must have been in existence at the time the contract was made in order to be capable of ratifying it. The reference to Imran's rights being transferred by the Act in D is inappropriate.

Answer to Interactive question 4

- Memorandum of association

- Application stating name, domicile and intended address of registered office, and a statement describing the liability of the members as limited by shares and whether the company is to be public or private

- Copy articles of association (although if none is submitted, prescribed default articles will apply)

- Statement of capital and initial shareholdings

- Statement of proposed directors (and company secretary if applicable)

- Statement of compliance

Answers to Self-test

1   A company is an entity registered under the Companies Act 2006 or any earlier Act.

2   *Salomon v Salomon & Co Ltd 1897*.

3   False. Any company has unlimited liability for its debts. In a limited company, the liability of the members (not the company) is limited to the amount outstanding on their shares or the amount of any guarantee.

4
- Where a subsidiary company can be regarded as an agent of the holding company.
- To reveal the true national identity of a company.
- Where the company is a quasi-partnership.
- Where a company is a sham.

5
- Where a public company trades without a trading certificate.
- In cases of fraudulent or wrongful trading.
- Where a director carries on business when he is disqualified.
- Where directors form a new company with a name identical or similar to that of an insolvent company.

6   This is true in the case of private companies but a public company must have a company secretary.

7   (1) £0
        (2) £50,000

8   See table in section 2.2 of this chapter.

9   C

10
- Their wish to form a company
- Their agreement to becoming members of the company
- Their agreement to subscribe for at least one share each

11   It is a dormant company available for purchase by those wishing to set up a company. It avoids the usual formation formalities and the problems associated with pre-incorporation contracts do not arise.

12   (1) False, since the company was not in existence at the time of the contract.
        (2) False. The Act provides that the original parties remain liable on the contract.

13   False. Where articles are not registered, model ('default') articles prescribed by the Secretary of State will apply.

14   By special resolution, unless there is provision for entrenchment, in which case unanimous consent or a court order is required.

15   The Act

16   Register of debenture-holders.

17   Adequate accounting records, that are sufficient to show the company's financial position at any time with reasonable accuracy, including daily entries of income and expenditure, a record of assets and liabilities and (if applicable) statements of stock and stocktakings.

18   True (although not if the company is an investment or banking company).

CHAPTER

5

CHAPTER 6

Companies: ownership and management

Introduction

Examination context

Topic List

    1   Directors

    2   Members

    3   Majority rule and minority protection

    4   Meetings and resolutions

Summary and Self-test

Answers to Interactive questions

Answers to Self-test

Introduction

Learning objectives

- To know how directors are appointed and removed and to understand their role in the management of the company ☐

- To be familiar with the powers and duties of directors ☐

- To recognise the consequences of directors being in breach of their duties ☐

- To appreciate the role of the members of a company and in particular to understand in what circumstances they can exercise control over the directors ☐

- To understand the principle of majority rule and when minority shareholders can take action ☐

- To know the various rules concerning company meetings and resolutions ☐

Specific syllabus references for this chapter are: 2c, g, h, j, k, l.

Syllabus links

The issue of a director's authority to bind the company relates to agency, which you studied in Chapter 3.

You will come across references to the members of a company passing resolutions in many areas of company law, including insolvency and in relation to share capital. This chapter explains how such resolutions come to be passed, whether in general meeting or otherwise.

Examination context

You should expect exam questions on each of the learning objectives stated.

In the assessment, candidates may be required to

- Identify the various statutory rights of shareholders to challenge the management of the company

- Identify the ways in which a director may be appointed and removed

- Identify directors' duties and explain the consequences of any major breach

- Identify the powers of directors and in what circumstances they will bind the company in a contract with third parties

- Recognise how members can influence the management of a company through meetings and resolutions, including the members' right to requisition a meeting

1 Directors

Section overview

- The directors of a company manage the company's business.

- The Companies Act 2006 and a company's articles of association together dictate who can and cannot be a director and how directors are appointed and removed.

- The Act and company articles also determine the extent of a director's powers and his authority to bind the company.

- Directors owe a number of duties to the company and face potential civil and criminal liability in the event of breach.

References to 'the Act' and section numbers refer to the Companies Act 2006 ('CA'06') unless otherwise stated. Section numbers are given for reference only.

1.1 Directors and their appointment

The term 'director' refers to every person who occupies the position or fulfils the role of director (ie to conduct the company's affairs), whatever he is called (s 250).

Every company is required to have at least one director who is a natural person and a public company must have at least two directors (s 154). Generally speaking, a director should be aged sixteen or more (although there are exceptions) and he does not need to hold any particular qualifications. However, certain persons may be **disqualified** from acting, either by the Company Directors Disqualification Act 1986 or by the articles of association. A sole director cannot also hold the position of auditor of the company. You should be familiar with the following types of director:

Director	How such a director comes to be in office
Director (on incorporation or subsequently)	As provided by the articles, usually appointed • By existing directors or • By ordinary resolution (directors of public companies should be voted on individually (s 160))
De facto director (literally 'director in fact')	ie anyone who acts as a director, although not validly appointed as one. He becomes a director (and subject to all provisions concerning directors) by virtue of his conduct, rather than by formal appointment. He has the same powers as a properly appointed director.
Shadow director	ie someone 'in accordance with whose directions or instructions the directors are accustomed to act' save where that person is merely giving advice in a professional capacity, for example lawyers and accountants. Whether someone is a shadow director is a question of fact.
Alternate director	The articles usually provide that a director may appoint an alternate director to attend and vote at board meetings which he himself is unable to attend. The alternate director may be another director or an outsider. Some articles provide for such an appointment to be subject to the approval of the board.
Executive director	ie a director who is also charged with performing a specific role, eg a finance director, usually as an employee of the company. The articles usually provide for the directors to appoint one or more of their number to any executive function and on such terms as to remuneration and powers as they see fit. If an executive director ceases to be a director, his office will also terminate, but without prejudice to any claim he may have for breach of any service contract.

Director	How such a director comes to be in office
Non-executive director	ie a director (appointed or otherwise as above) who does not have a particular function but generally just attends board meetings. Directors' duties apply to non-executive directors in the same way as to executive directors.
	Many directors of public companies are non-executive and it is generally regarded as a great strength for a company to have a board consisting of both executive and non-executive directors. They are seen as helpful in contributing an independent view to the board's deliberations and ensuring the continuing effectiveness of the executive directors and their management of the company's affairs.
	A company normally appoints a **chairman** of the board of directors who also acts as chairman at general meetings. He is usually regarded as a non-executive director.
Managing director (MD)	The articles usually provide for the directors to appoint one or more of their number to be managing director(s), charged with carrying out day-to-day management functions.

A director's actions are valid even if his appointment is subsequently found to have been defective or void (s 161).

Any **change in the directors** of a company should be recorded in the company's register of directors and notified to the registrar within 14 days.

1.2 Directors' vacation of office

A director might leave office in any one of the following ways:

- Death of the director or winding up of the company

- Removal (see below)

- Disqualification (see 1.8 below)

- Resignation

- Not offering himself for re-election, where the articles provide for retirement and re-election of directors. (In the case of public companies, for example, Table A provides that one third of all non-executive directors (those who have been in office the longest) shall retire each year and be eligible for re-election.)

In addition to any provision in the articles for removal, a company may **remove a director** from office by passing an **ordinary resolution** to that effect (s 168). **Special notice** (of 28 days) must be given of the intended resolution and the director then has the right to address the meeting and to request that any written representations that he makes be circulated to members or read out at the meeting.

Note that **removal** of a director may entitle the director to sue for **breach of contract** if he also has a contract of service with the company. Note too that this power of removal may be limited in the following ways

- A director who is also a member may have weighted voting rights given to him under the constitution for such an eventuality, so that he can automatically defeat any motion to remove him as a director *(Bushell v Faith 1970)*.

- It is possible to draft a shareholders' agreement stating that a member holding each class of share must be present at a general meeting to constitute a quorum. If so, a member holding shares of a certain class could prevent a director from being removed by not attending the meeting.

Interactive question 1: Directors [Difficulty level: Easy]

(1) Which of the following terms describes a person in accordance with whose directions or instructions the directors are accustomed to act'?

    A   Alternate director
    B   Shadow director
    C   De facto director
    D   Non-executive director

(2) Which of the following accurately states the requirements for the removal of a director?

    A   Special resolution with ordinary notice
    B   Ordinary resolution with special notice
    C   Ordinary resolution with ordinary notice
    D   Special resolution with special notice

See **Answer** at the end of this chapter.

Section 1 of the Company Directors Disqualification Act 1986 provides that a court may formally **disqualify** any person from being (without leave of the court) a director (including a shadow director), liquidator, administrator, receiver or manager of a company's property or in any way directly or indirectly being concerned or taking part in the promotion, formation or management of a company. Disqualification is considered at section 1.8 below.

In addition, the **articles** may provide that a director must vacate office if he becomes bankrupt or of unsound mind, or if he is absent from board meetings for, say, 6 consecutive months and the directors resolve that he should vacate office on that account.

Interactive question 2: Resolution for removal of director [Difficulty level: Exam standard]

A company has three members who are also directors. Each holds 100 shares. Normally the shares carry one vote each, but the articles state that on a resolution for a director's removal, the director to be removed should have 3 votes per share. On a resolution for the removal of Jeremy, a director, Jeremy casts 300 votes against the resolution and the other members cast 200 votes for the resolution. Has Jeremy validly defeated the resolution?

A   No, the articles are invalid insofar as they purport to confer extra votes.

B   Yes, the proceedings and articles are valid.

C   Yes. Whilst the articles are invalid and the voting is therefore 200 to 100 in favour, a special resolution is required and the necessary 75% majority has not been obtained.

D   No. A director is not entitled to vote on a resolution for his own removal.

See **Answer** at the end of this chapter.

1.3 Directors' powers

The powers of the directors are defined by the company's articles. Normally directors are authorised, in general terms, to manage the business of the company and to exercise all the powers of the company. The old requirement for companies to specify their objects (as charitable companies are required to do under charities legislation and community interest companies might choose to do) was removed by the Act and companies now have **unrestricted objects** (and, therefore, more extensive powers) unless the articles specifically restrict them (s 31). The directors' powers are to be exercised properly and within the company's' constitution, but the directors are not agents of the members and subject to their instruction as to how to act. There are, however, a number of restrictions on these powers, some of which result in powers being placed in the hands of the members rather than the directors.

Restriction	Explanation
Statutory (general)	The directors are statutorily bound to exercise powers only 'for the purpose for which they are conferred' (see section 1.5 below).
Statutory (specific)	For example alteration of the articles and reduction of capital need a special resolution, which the directors must secure from the shareholders in general meeting before they can act. Directors' actions which expressly require members' approval are detailed in section 2.3 below.
Articles	For example the articles may set a maximum amount that the directors are entitled to borrow, any greater amount needing approval of the company in general meeting. (As to whether such a restriction will be effective against a third party, see section 1.4 below.)
Members	The members can exercise control over the directors' powers • By passing a special resolution to alter the articles, thereby re-allocating the powers between the board and the general meeting • Ultimately by removing directors from office

The directors' powers are vested in them as a **collective body** and are exercised by the directors in board meetings. Generally speaking, it is considered sufficient if the directors are in communication with each other, usually by telephone, rather than necessarily being in one place at the same time and articles may make such provision. Equally, even if the directors are assembled together, there can be no board meeting if any of the directors object to a meeting being held in those circumstances.

1.4 Directors' authority and managing directors

If the board acting collectively or one director acting on his own has **authority** to enter into a contract on behalf of the company, then the contract will be binding on the company. You will recall from Chapter 3 that a director's authority may be express or implied (actual authority) or it may be ostensible or apparent authority. The position is as follows:

Authority	Explanation
Express	Binding
Implied	Binding. **Managing directors**, and to some extent other executive directors (such as sales directors or finance directors), are much more likely to bind the company by their actions, since greater powers are usually delegated to them. Thus a managing director has implied usual authority to make general business contracts on behalf of the company (in addition to any actual authority given to him by the board). There is little guidance from statute or case law, on the other hand, on what authority might be deemed to attach to non-executive directors or directors in lower or middle management, but it will not be as wide ranging as that attaching to a managing director. (Indeed such case law as there is suggests that it is very limited indeed.)
Ostensible	Binding. If the board permits a director to behave as if he were a managing director or give the impression that he is one, that director will have the **apparent or ostensible** authority to enter into all commercial contracts relating to the business as a managing director would have and to bind the company in respect of them.

It might be helpful to revise the principles of agency outlined in Chapter 3 and in particular the case of *Freeman & Lockyer v Buckhurst Park Properties (Mangal) Ltd 1964* in respect of managing directors. Where a director would have authority but for a restriction placed on it, the position is governed by s 40. This provides that 'in favour of a person dealing with a company in good faith, the power of the directors to bind the company or authorise others to do so, is deemed to be free of any limitation under the company's constitution (s 40).

Note in particular:

- The section relates to **any transaction or dealing** between the company and a third party (ie not just to contracts)

- The other party is **deemed to be acting in good faith** unless the contrary is proved (and will not be deemed to be acting in bad faith just because he knows of the limitation)

- The **limitations to be disregarded** include any imposed on the directors by resolution or agreement of the members.

Section 41 provides that s 40 will not apply where the person dealing with the company is a director or person connected with a director. In such cases, the transaction becomes voidable at the instance of the company and that party is liable to account for any gain and to indemnify the party against any loss.

Interactive question 3: Directors' authority   **[Difficulty level: Easy]**

Under the articles of association of Farming Ltd the directors of the company need the consent of the general meeting by ordinary resolution to borrow sums of money in excess of £50,000.

Mary has been appointed managing director of the company and she holds 1% of the issued shares of the company. Mary has recently entered into two transactions for the benefit of Farming Ltd. First, she arranged to borrow £100,000 from Conifer Bank Ltd, secured by a floating charge on the company's assets. However she failed to seek the approval of the members as required by the articles. Second, she placed a contract worth £10,000 with Saw Ltd to buy some agricultural machinery.

Advise the directors of Farming Ltd whether they are bound by the agreements with Conifer Bank Ltd and Saw Ltd.

A   The company is not bound by either contract
B   The company is bound by both contracts
C   The company is only bound by the contract with Conifer Bank Ltd
D   The company is only bound by the contract with Saw Ltd

See **Answer** at the end of this chapter.

1.5   Directors' duties

For the first time, the Act provides a **statutory code** of most **directors' duties** which take effect 'in place of' the common law rules and equitable principles which used to make up the law on directors' duties, but which will depend on those rules and principles for their interpretation and application (s 170).

There are, of course, **specific statutory duties** owed by directors, such as the obligation to prepare the directors' report, and other common law duties may remain that have not been codified, such as a duty to consider creditors' interests when insolvency is inevitable. Of course directors of listed companies are required to comply, or to explain any non-compliance, with the UK Corporate Governance Code and directors of unlisted companies are also advised to have regard to various corporate governance guidelines and objectives. However, the duties listed below are of more general application (indeed the Act refers to them as '**general duties**') and they are expressly stated to apply to shadow directors also.

Duty	Explanation
To act within powers (s 171)	A director must • Act in accordance with the company's **constitution** • Exercise powers only for the **purpose for which they were conferred** If the directors infringe this rule by exercising their powers for a collateral purpose, the transaction will be invalid **unless** it is approved or ratified by the **company** in **general meeting**. If the irregular use of directors' powers is the allotment of shares, the votes attached to the new shares may not be used in reaching a decision in general meeting to sanction it.

Howard Smith Ltd v Ampol Petroleum Ltd 1974

The facts: Shareholders who held 55% of the issued shares intended to reject a take-over bid for the company. The directors honestly believed that the bid's success was in the company's interest and so allotted new shares to the prospective bidder so that the shareholders opposed to the bid would then have less than 50% of the enlarged capital and the bid would succeed.

Decision: The allotment was invalid. 'It must be unconstitutional for directors to use their fiduciary powers over the shares in the company purely for the purpose of destroying an existing majority or creating a new majority which did not previously exist'.

If the majority approve what has been done (or have authorised it in advance) however, that decision is treated as a proper case of majority control to which the minority must normally submit (see section 3 below).

Bamford v Bamford 1969

The facts: The directors of Bamford Ltd allotted 500,000 unissued shares to a third party to thwart a take-over bid. A month after the allotment, an ordinary resolution was passed ratifying the allotment, the holders of the newly-issued shares not voting. The claimants (minority shareholders) alleged that the allotment was not made for a proper purpose.

Decision: The ratification was valid and the allotment was good. There had been a breach of fiduciary duty but the act had been validated by an ordinary resolution passed in general meeting.

Duty	Explanation
To promote the success of the company (s 172)	A director must act in the way he considers, in **good faith**, would be most likely to **promote the success** of the company **for the benefit of its members** as a whole. He should have regard to • The likely **long term consequences** of any decision • The interests of the company's **employees** • The need to foster the company's **businesses relationships** with suppliers, customers and others • The impact of the company's operations on the community and the **environment** • The desirability of the company maintaining a **reputation** for high standards of business conduct • The need to act **fairly** as **between members** of the company The duty is expressed to be subject to any legal rule or provision which requires directors, in certain circumstances, to have regard to the interests of creditors. What will promote the success of the company is a matter for the directors' good faith judgement.
To exercise independent judgment (s 173)	It does not mean that he is **not** exercising independent judgment where he acts in accordance with • An agreement duly entered into by the company that restricts the future exercise of discretion by its directors, or • The company's constitution

ICAEW

Duty	Explanation
To exercise reasonable care, skill and diligence (s 174)	ie the care, skill and diligence that would be exercised by a **reasonably diligent person** with

• The general knowledge, skill and experience that may **reasonably be expected** of a person performing **his functions** as director

• His **actual** general knowledge, skill and experience

Thus it is no excuse for a director to say that he lacked expertise if a reasonable director in his position would have that expertise. Further more, his **actual** expertise may result in a **higher** standard than that of the reasonable director. The courts have held, for example, that a director who signs an insurance proposal without reading it may be liable in negligence.

An executive director with expertise in a particular area, or even a non-executive director who is qualified or experienced in a relevant discipline, will be expected to show a higher standard of care than simply attending board meetings. Even someone with no commercial or business experience or qualification is required (by the Act) to demonstrate the care that may be expected of a person fulfilling his director's role. Simply attending board meetings and not attending to the company's interests in between meetings is unlikely to be sufficient (unless it can be shown that a director's failure to prevent a fellow director's wrongdoing did not cause or contribute to the loss suffered).

Lexi Holdings plc (in administration) v Luqman 2009

The facts: Two sisters and their brother were directors of a company. The brother had convictions for offences of dishonesty in the past. The sisters knew this but played no part in the company, demanded no explanations from their brother of his business dealings and did not advise the other directors, auditors and the bank of his convictions. The brother took nearly £60m in fictitious loans, false facility letters and by misappropriation of company funds.

Decision: The Court of Appeal held that the sisters were, or ought to have been, aware of various matters in relation to the fraud perpetrated on the company by their brother. As a result, they were liable as they were in breach of their fiduciary and common law duties of care owed to the company.

Duty	Explanation
To avoid conflict of interest (s 175)	A director must avoid a situation in which he **has or can have** a **direct or indirect interest** that **conflicts or possibly may conflict** with the **interests of the company** or **another duty**. This duty is particularly applicable to the exploitation of any property, information or opportunity, (regardless of whether the company could actually take advantage of it) but is expressly stated not to apply to any conflict arising in relation to a transaction or arrangement with the company (where ss 177 and 182 apply, see below).

Towers v Premier Waste Management Ltd 2012

The facts: A company director accepted a personal loan of equipment from a customer without charge and without disclosing the transaction or seeking approval of it. The customer then invoiced the company, which sued the director for breach of duty.

Decision: The Court of Appeal held that the director had gained an advantage from a potential conflict and had disloyally deprived the company of the opportunity to object to an opportunity being diverted from the company to the director personally. It was irrelevant that the company had suffered no loss or that the director had no corrupt motive.

The **duty is not infringed** if the matter has been **authorised by the directors**. This may happen

- In a **private** company, provided the company's constitution does not invalidate such authorisation

- In a **public** company, provided the company's constitution expressly allows such authorisation

In each case, the relevant director cannot be counted towards a quorum and his votes will not be included in determining whether the authorisation is given.

If such authorisation is given there is no need for further approval by the members unless the company's constitution so provides.

If the case falls within the statutory provisions for matters requiring members' approval (and these provisions are satisfied), then the director does not also need to comply with this duty.

Duty	Explanation
Not to accept benefits from third parties (s 176)	A director must not accept a benefit from a third party by reason of his - Being a director or - Doing (or not doing) anything as director Unless the acceptance of the benefit cannot reasonably be regarded as likely to give rise to a conflict of interest. If the case falls within the statutory provisions for matters requiring members' approval (and these provisions are satisfied), then the director does not also need to comply with this duty.

Duty	Explanation
To declare interest in proposed transaction or arrangement (s 177)	Provided the director is, or ought reasonably to be, aware of the situation, he must **declare the nature and extent of any such interest** (direct or indirect) **to the other directors**, unless it cannot reasonably be regarded as likely to give rise to a conflict of interest. The notice may be made • At a board meeting • By notice in writing or • By a general notice, ie that he has an interest in the third party and is therefore to be regarded as interested in any transaction or arrangement with that third party (in which case he should take reasonable steps to ensure that such general notice is brought up at the next board meeting). Provided such declaration is made, there is no need for approval by the members or the board, unless the company's constitution so provides or unless it is an arrangement between a director and the company for the transfer of a 'substantial non-cash asset' (see section 2.3 below). (Note that a specific duty exists likewise in relation to **existing** transactions or arrangements as soon as is reasonably practicable (s 182). This duty applies also to shadow directors (s 187). Breach of this specific duty is punishable by fine.)

A person may continue to be subject to the duties in ss 175 and 176 even after he ceases to be a director, in certain circumstances (s 170 (2)).

One or more of the general duties may overlap, in which case each will apply. For example, taking a bribe from a third party would contravene the duty not to accept benefits from third parties (s 176). It might also amount to a failure to promote the success of the company for the benefit of its members (s 172) and/or a failure to exercise independent judgment (s 173).

Worked example: Directors' duties

Xray Ltd intends to enter into a contract for the supply of medical supplies from a firm in which Xavier, a director of Xray Ltd, is a partner. The terms of the contract are no less onerous than those of contracts between the company and other suppliers, but nonetheless Xavier is concerned that he may commit an offence if the contract goes ahead due to his interest in the firm. Advise Xavier.

Solution

Xavier is under a duty to avoid any situation in which he has an interest that, even potentially, conflicts with the company's interests, even if the company is not actually prejudiced as a result (it may even fair better as a result). However, this duty does not apply to a conflict of interest arising in relation to a transaction with the company, as is the case here. The relevant duty, with which Xavier must comply, is a duty to disclose his interest to the other directors pursuant to s 177. He should make such disclosure at a board meeting or in writing. He could provide a general disclosure of the nature and extent of his interest in the firm, so that he is to be regarded as interested in any transaction with it. Such general notice should be given at a board meeting or brought up at the next meeting following it. If he fails to do so, the contract will be voidable at the instance of the company and he could be liable to indemnify the company against any loss.

1.6 Breach of directors' duties

A director in breach of any of the duties imposed on him may be required to make good any loss suffered by the company, including accounting for any secret profits. Any contract entered into between the company and a director may be rendered voidable by the director's breach of duty. Any property taken by the director from the company can be recovered if it is still in his possession. It may be recoverable from a third party unless that third party required it for value and in good faith.

Where the breach has not yet occurred or is continuing, an injunction might be an appropriate remedy.

If another director, or directors, is or are also in breach then their liability will be joint and several. In the absence of any breach, however, a director will not be jointly liable with another who is in breach.

Legal action in respect of a breach of directors' duties is most likely to be pursued under s 260 (see section 3.3 below).

The articles of a company may impose **more onerous** requirements on its directors. They cannot, however, **dilute** the duties except to the extent that is permitted by certain provisions. For example:

- s 173: that a director will not be in breach of the duty to exercise independent judgement if he has acted in a way authorised by the constitution

- s 175: some conflicts of interest by independent directors may be permitted, subject to the constitution

- s 180 preserves any rule of law that would otherwise be a breach of duty.

Any **ratification** of conduct amounting to negligence or other breach of duty by a director (or former director or shadow director) must be made by an ordinary resolution of the members, disregarding the votes of that director and any member connected with him (s 239).

Note that any provision to exempt a director from or indemnify him against liability for breach of duty or negligence (or default or breach of trust) is **void** (s 232), save that a company may provide insurance and qualifying indemnity in respect of third parties.

In any proceeding for negligence, default, breach of duty or breach of trust against an officer of the company (or auditors), the court may relieve him of any liability if it considers that he acted **honestly and reasonably** and that, having regard to all the circumstances of the case, he **ought fairly to be excused** (s 1157).

> *Re D'Jan of London Ltd 1993*
>
> *The facts:* D, a director of the company, signed an insurance proposal form without reading it. The form was filled in by D's broker. An answer given to one of the questions on the form was incorrect and the insurance company rightly repudiated liability for a fire at the company's premises in which stock worth some £174,000 was lost. The company became insolvent and the liquidator brought this action under s 212 of the Insolvency Act 1986 alleging D was negligent.
>
> *Decision:* In failing to read the form D was negligent. However, he had acted honestly and ought therefore to be partly relieved from liability. The fact that D owned a 99% shareholding was relevant, as the risk he took might have been seen as more unreasonable if he had owned a lower stake in the company. (This case was brought on a provision from CA 1985 in line with s 1157 CA 06.)

1.7 Wrongful and fraudulent trading

In addition, a director faces personal civil and criminal liability and possible disqualification (see 1.8 below) where he engages in wrongful or fraudulent trading.

Wrongful trading applies only where a company goes into insolvent liquidation and the liquidator can show that, at some time before the commencement of the winding up, the director(s) knew or should have known that there was no reasonable prospect that the company could have avoided going into insolvent liquidation. However, no declaration of wrongful trading will be made where the court is satisfied that the director(s) took every step that he or they ought to have taken in order to minimise the potential loss to creditors (s 214 Insolvency Act 1986).

The standard applied is that of a **reasonably diligent person** with the general knowledge, skill and experience that might reasonably be expected of a person carrying out that particular director's duties (ie a reasonable occupant of a similar post). Where a director has greater skill and experience than a 'normal' director, he is also judged by reference to his own capacity. Thus the standard expected of a listed company director would be higher than for the director of a small owner-managed private company.

Where a director is liable under s 214 the court can order him to 'make such contribution to the assets of the company as the court thinks proper'. The fact that wrongful trading is not based on fraud is not a reason for giving a nominal or low figure of contribution, although the figure should be assessed in the light of all the circumstances of the case.

Fraudulent trading occurs where any business of a company is carried on with intent to defraud creditors of the company (or of another person) or for any fraudulent purpose. The offence is committed by any person who is knowingly a party to the business being carried in that manner. Note that only persons who **take the decision** to carry on the company's business in this way or play some active part are liable. **'Carrying on business'** can include a single transaction and also the mere payment of debts as distinct from making trading contracts. The criminal offence (s 993 CA 06) may be committed whether or not the company has been or is in the course of being wound up and is punishable by a fine and/or imprisonment for up to 10 years. It also gives rise to a civil liability for the company's debts on a winding up (s 213 Insolvency Act 1986). Thus, as in the case of wrongful trading, a director may be ordered to make such contribution to the assets of the company as the court thinks fit.

The assets available for distribution in a winding-up will (potentially) be much increased by a large directors' contribution. It serves as a warning to directors to take professional advice sooner rather than later, as the prospect of making a personal contribution may prove much more expensive than winding-up at the appropriate stage.

1.8 Disqualification of directors

The Company Directors Disqualification Act 1986 (CDDA) was introduced in response to public disquiet with directors of failed companies being able to walk away from the wreckage of a company with no personal liability, regardless of the reasons for which the company failed. In many cases they would then go on to start new, very similar companies (so-called 'phoenix' companies) which had no liability to the previous creditors, who usually ended up with nothing.

The CDDA provides that a court may disqualify a person from being a director or insolvency practitioner or receiver or manager of a company and from being concerned in the promotion, formation or management of any company except with leave of the court. In some circumstances an order is in the courts' discretion; in others, it is mandatory:

Grounds	
A disqualification order for up to **15 years may** be made:	Where a person is **convicted** of a **serious offence** (usually in connection with the promotion, formation, management or liquidation of a company).
	Where it appears in the course of the **winding up** of a company that a person has been guilty of **fraudulent trading** (though not necessarily convicted of the offence).
	Where the **Secretary of State** considers it to be **in the public interest**.
	Where a director is guilty of certain **breaches of competition law**.
	Where a director has participated in **wrongful trading**.
A disqualification order for up to **5 years may** be made:	Where a person has been **persistently in default** in relation to provisions of **company legislation** (and three convictions for default in five years are conclusive evidence of persistent default).

A disqualification order **must** be made, for a minimum of 2 years and a maximum of 15 years:	Where a person has been a director of a company which has at any time become insolvent (whether while he was a director or subsequently) and his conduct as a director of that company makes him **unfit to be concerned in the management of a company**. (The courts may also take into account his conduct as a director of other companies, whether or not these other companies became insolvent.) Directors can be disqualified under this section even if they take no active part in the running of the business. In uncontested cases, and where it is considered expedient in the public interest, the Secretary of State may accept a disqualification undertaking instead of seeking a disqualification order (ie an undertaking that the director will not act as a director etc or be concerned in the management etc of a company).

Note that a **bankruptcy order** made against a person **automatically disqualifies** him from acting as a director of a company or being concerned in the management or promotion of a company (s 11).

Offences for which directors have been disqualified include the following:

- Insider dealing
- Failure to keep proper accounting records
- Failure to read the company's accounts
- Loans to associated companies on uncommercial terms to the detriment of creditors

The courts' approach has been to view 'ordinary commercial misjudgement' as insufficient to justify disqualification.

Re Uno, Secretary of State for Trade and Industry v Gill 2004

Facts: A group consisting of two furniture companies carried on trading while in serious financial difficulties, while the directors tried to find a way out of the situation. Uno continued to take deposits from customers for furniture to fund its working capital requirements.

Decision: The directors were not disqualified for acting in this way as their behaviour was not dishonest or lacking in commercial probity and did not make them unfit to manage a company. They had been trying to explore realistic opportunities to save the businesses and were not to blame for the eventual collapse of the businesses and the subsequent loss of customers.

A **lack of commercial probity,** or gross negligence or total incompetence, however, might render disqualification appropriate.

Secretary of State for Trade and Industry v Thornbury 2008

Facts: A director failed to carry out any further investigation after receiving verbal assurances from other directors regarding the financial status of the company. The company was in breach of its statutory obligations to pay HMRC.

Decision: Although the director had not been dishonest, it had not been reasonable for him to leave matters in the other directors' hands to such a degree. He was held to be unfit to be concerned in the management of a company and disqualified for two years.

Note that recent guidance from the Office of Fair Trading has signalled a greater willingness to disqualify directors of companies which are in breach of competition law. It seems that a director's active involvement in the breach will no longer be required. Rather, a director may face disqualification if it can be shown that he had reasonable grounds to suspect a breach but failed to take steps to prevent it, or even where he did not know of the breach but should, in all the circumstances (including his own skill and experience) have known of it.

Breach of a disqualification order can result in a fine and/or imprisonment.

The following circumstances may result in the court imposing a lower period of disqualification **in mitigation**:

- Lack of dishonesty
- Loss of director's own money in the company

- Absence of personal gain (such as excessive remuneration)
- Efforts to mitigate the situation
- Low likelihood of re-offending

Administrators, receivers and liquidators all have **a statutory duty to report** to the Department for Business, Innovation and Skills (BIS) on directors of companies in whose affairs they have become involved, where they believe the conditions for a disqualification order have been satisfied. The Secretary of State then decides whether to apply to the court for an order, but if he does decide to apply, he must do so within **two years** of the date on which the company became insolvent.

Interactive question 4: Directors' disqualification　　　　　　　　[Difficulty level: Easy]

Match the correct periods of disqualification with the following scenarios (in two cases the period is the same):

				Years
A	Persistent default in filing annual returns			
B	Fraudulent trading	1	2–15 years
C	Wrongful trading	2	≤ 5 years
D	Where the court considers that his conduct makes him unfit to be considered in the management of a company	3	≤ 15 years

See **Answer** at the end of this chapter.

2 Members

Section overview

- Shareholders, being members of a company with a share capital, effectively own the company.
- The members exercise control over the directors where required by law and the company's articles.

Any subscriber of a company's memorandum and any person entered on the company's register of members is a member of the company. A single member limited company must include a statement on its register that there is only one member. Subject to limited exceptions, a company cannot be a member of its holding company. Where a member owns shares in a company, he is called a 'shareholder'.

2.1 Regulation of the members

The members are regulated internally by the **articles of association**. These may be supplemented by a **shareholders' agreement** which deals with members rights and duties and which often offers more protection to the individual or minority shareholders, for example by requiring unanimous consent to an alteration to the articles, rather than the usual 75% majority. One advantage of a shareholders' agreement is that it is a private document not requiring registration. Thus it might cover the following matters in a wish to keep them off the public record:

- Confidentiality undertakings and non-competition restrictions, the right of certain shareholders to appoint directors and dispute resolution.

- Choice of bankers, cheque signatories and the company's policy on loans and borrowing.

A shareholders' agreement is of course, a binding contract and therefore enforceable in and subject to the courts' jurisdiction. It is particularly common in the case of companies which were formerly, or are in the nature of, a partnership.

2.2 Members' rights and communication

Members have a number of rights including the right

- To be sent a copy of annual accounts and reports
- To require directors to call a general meeting
- To appoint a proxy

A member may be entitled, under the company's articles, to nominate another person to exercise all or any of those rights in place of him.

Subject to any contrary provision in the company's articles, a company may send communications in electronic form, provided the member has agreed (generally or specifically).

A member of a **listed company** who holds shares on behalf of another person may nominate that other person to enjoy **information rights**, ie the right to receive a copy of all communications required to be sent to members, including accounting reports (s 146). Such information can be provided electronically unless a request is made for hard copies.

A member may take action to **enforce personal rights of membership** for example the right to vote (*Pender v Lushington 1877*) or receive a due dividend. Note that this is not a derivative action, on behalf of the company, but a personal action.

2.3 Approval of directors' actions

As mentioned in section 1, the Act provides for certain matters concerning directors (and shadow directors) to require the approval of the members in general meeting in order to be valid. These are:

Matter requiring approval	Notes	Consequences of breach
Service contracts (s 188)	Approval is required if the service contract provides for a director's employment to be a **guaranteed term of two years or more** (ie not terminable by the company in a lesser period or only in specified circumstances). A written memorandum setting out the proposed contract must be provided to the members prior to the resolution being passed.	The provision is void and the contract is thereafter deemed to include a term entitling the company to terminate it at any time on giving reasonable notice.
Substantial property transactions (s 190)	Approval is required for any arrangement where a director is to acquire from the company (or the company from the director) a **substantial non-cash asset**, ie one (or more) whose (aggregate) value • Exceeds 10% of the company's asset value and is more than £5,000 or • Exceeds £100,000 The section does not apply to transactions permitted under a relevant service contract or to payments for loss of office. There are other exceptions applicable to group companies, companies in winding up or administration and to transactions on recognised investment exchanges.	The company faces no liability for failure to obtain approval. The transaction is **voidable** at the instance of the company except in specified circumstances, unless the members give approval within a reasonable period. The director (and possibly others) is liable to account to the company for any gain and to indemnify the company against any loss or damage.
Loans to directors etc (s 197)	Approval is required for **any loan** by a company to a director or for any **guarantee** or **security** by a company in connection with a loan made by another party to a director. A written memorandum setting out the details of the transaction proposed must be given to the members.	The transaction is **voidable** at the instance of the company, except in specified circumstances, unless it is approved by the company within a reasonable period.

Matter requiring approval	Notes	Consequences of breach
There are similar provisions dealing with quasi-loans to directors and loans and quasi-loans to persons connected with directors, credit transactions (public companies only) and transactions related to any of the above	There are exceptions for • Expenditure on company business, defending proceedings or regulatory action or investigation • Minor transactions or ones in the ordinary course of business • Intra-group transaction • Money-lending companies	The director (and possibly others) is liable to account to the company for any gain and to indemnify the company against any loss or damage.
Payments for loss of office (s 217)	Approval is required for **payments or benefits** to be made on **loss of office or retirement**. A written memorandum of the proposed payment (or other benefit) must be sent to all members. There are exceptions for small payments and payments in discharge of legal obligations. ('Small payments' are currently those of £200 or less, although the Secretary of State does have power to increase this figure.)	The payment is held **on trust** for the company. Any director who authorised the payment is liable to indemnify the company for any loss.

Note that the general duties still apply even if one of these provisions applies (s 180) so that, for example, the directors should only approve a loan to a director if they are confident that it will not offend the duty to promote the success of the company. On the other hand, if members' approval is obtained under one of these provisions (or an exception applies so that approval is not needed) then the duties to avoid conflicts of interest and not to accept benefits from third parties (ss 175 and 176) will not apply (s 180), (but the other duties will still apply). For example, if a director fails to obtain authorisation from the directors or members for a loan in respect of legal defence costs, he will not be acting in breach of his duty to avoid conflicts of interest.

3 Majority rule and minority protection

Section overview

• Generally speaking the company is controlled by the will of the majority. If the minority objects to the majority's actions, the basic rule is that it has no recourse because the company is the proper claimant.

• However, the minority is given the right by statute to object in certain circumstances.

• Any member may also bring an action against the directors (on behalf of the company) for breach of duty or negligence against the directors.

• Any member may apply to the court for relief where the affairs of the company have been conducted in an unfairly prejudicial manner.

• Any member may, as a last resort, petition the court to wind up the company on the ground that it is just and equitable to do so.

3.1 The rule in Foss v Harbottle

Although the directors can be said to 'manage' the company, it is the members who ultimately 'control' the company. Usually a 75% majority gives complete control and a majority of over 50% gives considerable influence, including the power to appoint and remove directors.

Furthermore, unlike directors, members may exercise their votes in their own interests and are not required to act for the benefit of the company. Generally speaking, if the minority is unhappy with a decision made by a majority, it has no recourse: the company (being a separate legal person) is the proper claimant with the action vested in it. This is sometimes referred to as 'the rule in Foss v Harbottle'.

> *Foss v Harbottle 1843*
>
> *The facts*: A shareholder (Foss) sued the directors of the company alleging that the directors had defrauded the company by selling land to it at an inflated price. The company was by this time in a state of disorganisation and efforts to call the directors to account at a general meeting had failed.
>
> *Decision*: The action must be dismissed.

- The **company** as a person separate from its members is the **only proper claimant** in an action to protect its rights or property.

- The **company** in **general meeting** must decide whether to bring such legal proceedings.

A minority can, however, take action in certain cases, in particular:

- Where statute specifically provides for a minority to have a particular power or to apply to the court for example. The permitted minority is normally measured by being a minimum number of members or by members holding a specified percentage of the company's share capital or voting rights (see 3.2 below).

- A derivative action for negligence, **breach of duty**, default or breach of trust by the directors under s 260 (see section 3.3 below).

- A derivative action in respect of **unfairly prejudicial conduct** by the majority under s 994 (see 3.4 below).

- To petition the court for the company to be **wound** up on the grounds that it is **just and equitable** to do to so (see 3.5 below).

Note too that a minority member may also pursue a personal action to enforce his rights of membership.

3.2 Statutory rights of minorities

A minority of members is given a number of **specific** statutory rights, including the following:

Subject	Required
Variation of class rights	Holders of ≥15% of class of shares (or ≥15% of members where no share capital) can apply to court for cancellation (s 633)
Company meeting	Can be requisitioned by holders of (usually) ≥5% of company's paid up capital with voting rights (or ≥5% of voting rights where no share capital) (s 303)
Notice of members' resolutions	Must be given by company on requisition of members holding ≥5% of voting rights (s 292)
Payment out of capital by private company for the redemption or purchase of its shares	Any member (or creditor) can apply to court to prohibit the transaction (s 721)
Registration of limited company as unlimited	Can be prevented by individual members

3.3 Derivative action on behalf of the company

A **director's duties** are **owed to the company** which means that the **company is the proper claimant** in any proceedings for relief and a member cannot sue a director for breach of duty. However, under s 260, a member may bring a **derivative claim** on behalf of the company in respect of an actual or proposed act or omission by a director (or former director or shadow director) which involves negligence or breach of duty (or default or breach of trust).

It is not necessary to show that the wrongdoing directors control the majority of the company's shares. The member must first make out a *prima facie* case to the court and obtain permission to continue the claim (or to take over a claim begun by the company or another member).

The member will be refused permission where the court is satisfied that:

- The relevant act or omission has been **authorised by the company** beforehand or ratified by the company subsequently, (remembering that any decision to ratify must be made not counting the votes of the director concerned or any connected person, s 239)

- A person acting in accordance with the duty to promote the success of the company would not seek to continue the claim.

In deciding whether to grant or refuse permission, the court will have regard to the following:

- Whether the member is acting in **good faith**

- The importance that a person **promoting the success of the company** would attach to it

- Whether **authorisation** or ratification by the company by the company is **likely**

- Whether the **company** has decided not to pursue the claim

- Whether its member could pursue the claim in **his own right** rather than on behalf of the company

- The views of members with **no personal interest** in the matter

Kiani v Cooper 2010

The facts: K, a shareholder and director in Company X, sought permission to continue a derivative action against C, the other shareholder and director, on behalf of Company X, in respect of certain actions taken by C.

Decision: C had failed to produce any evidence in corroboration of his defence against K's allegations and permission was granted to pursue a derivative claim. The court took account of the fact that K had acted in good faith throughout and considered that a hypothetical director would wish to continue the claim against C. Although the court considered that K could have petitioned for unfair prejudice (see below), the possibility of an alternative action was only one factor and did not deny K the right to pursue a derivative claim under s.260.

Interactive question 5: Derivative action [Difficulty level: Easy]

In a derivative claim against the directors of a company under s 260 CA'06, the court will consider many factors. What are the THREE factors that will lead to a claim being unsuccessful in any event?

A   That the act was ratified by the company

B   That the claimant was not acting in good faith

C   That the company authorises the act beforehand

D   That a person acting in accordance with the duty to promote the success of the company would not pursue the claim

See **Answer** at the end of this chapter.

3.4   Application for relief on the grounds of unfairly prejudicial conduct

Any member (including someone to whom shares have been transferred by operation of law, for example on death) or the **Secretary of State** may apply to the court for relief under s 994 on the grounds that the company's affairs are being or have been conducted in a manner which is **unfairly prejudicial** to the interests of the members **generally or of some part** of the members' interests. Application may also be made in respect of an actual or proposed act or omission that would be similarly prejudicial.

There is **no** statutory definition of what constitutes unfairly prejudicial conduct, although it is specifically provided that the removal of a company's auditor from office on improper grounds (including a divergence of opinion on accounting treatments or audit procedures) shall be treated as unfairly prejudicial. It does not need to be illegal, nor even intentional or discriminatory; it is the **effect** of the conduct that is considered.

The following are examples of conduct that has been held to be unfairly prejudicial in contravention of the identical provision in earlier legislation (s 459 CA 1985):

- **Exclusion** and **removal** from the **board** where the company was one in which the director had a legitimate expectation of being involved in management, ie a quasi-partnership company.

  Re Bird Precision Bellows Ltd 1986

  The facts: A minority with 26% of the shares suspected the MD of this 'quasi-partnership' company of concealing bribes paid to secure contracts. When the DTI refused to investigate the minority was removed from the board. They claimed that this unfairly amounted to prejudicial conduct.

  Decision: The claim was allowed as it was a 'quasi-partnership'.

- **Improper allotment** of shares, for example, an allotment by a majority shareholder simply to increase his holding

- Making an **inaccurate statement** to shareholders, for example misleading them by recommending acceptance of a bid by another company which the directors owned

- **Diversion of a company's business** to a director-controlled company

Actions brought claiming that the following matters constituted unfairly prejudicial conduct **failed**:

- **Failure** by a parent company **to pay** the **debts** of a **subsidiary**

- **Non-compliance** with the **Stock Exchange rules**, the City Code and the Cadbury Code.

- **Failure** by a fellow director and majority shareholder **to increase the petitioner's shareholding** (see *O'Neill v Philips 1999* below). However, where the excluding party has made a **reasonable offer to buy out the shares of the excluded shareholder**, the exclusion is unlikely to be regarded as unfairly prejudicial (provided the shares are properly valued and without applying a discount to reflect the fact that it is a minority shareholding).

Whatever the reason for the application, the complaint must be based on prejudice to the member **as a member** and not as an employee, nor as an unpaid creditor.

O'Neill v Phillips 1999

The facts: P owned a 75% shareholding, although O managed the company (following P's decision to take a less active role in the affairs of the company) and, at P's suggestion, took 50% of the profits. The possibility of increasing O's shareholding to 50% was discussed but never acted upon. When business declined, P resumed control. He demoted O to the position of branch manager and withdrew his profit share. However, O remained a director. O claimed unfair prejudice for the withdrawal of his profit share and the alleged repudiation of an agreement to increase his shareholding.

Decision: The House of Lords held that there was no firm agreement to increase O's shareholding and so he had no legitimate expectation of such action that the law would enforce. It was considered quite fair that P should retain a majority shareholding and exercise control in the way he did. Lord Hoffman did say (obiter) that if there had been an actual agreement in O's favour, his capacity as member (and not just as employee) might have founded a claim since he had invested time and money in the company.

The courts will not generally intervene in cases of dispute about **management** (even bad management) save possibly where it results in serious financial damage to the company and the minority's interests. A breach of company law will not necessarily mean that there is unfairly prejudicial conduct. However, where company law has been fully complied with, it may be said that relief under s 994 is unlikely to be given unless there are equitable considerations that make it fair in all the circumstances. The provision cannot simply be invoked by shareholders when they do not like the way a company is run.

Re A Company 1983

The facts: The petitioners' grievance was the directors' refusal to put forward a scheme of reconstruction or a proposal to purchase their shares (by the company). The directors were preoccupied with plans for diversification of the business.

Decision: The directors' duty was to manage the company to its advantage as they saw it. It was not a case of 'unfair prejudice'.

The courts may also take **the petitioner's conduct** into account when deciding whether certain actions are unfairly prejudicial.

Re R A Noble & Sons (Clothing) Ltd 1983

The facts: C had provided the capital but left the management in the hands of the other director on the understanding that he would be consulted on major company matters, but he was not consulted. He confined himself to enquiries of the other director on social occasions and accepted his vague assurances that all was well. The petition followed from a breakdown of the relationship.

Decision: C's exclusion from discussion of company management questions was largely the result of his own lack of interest. His petition was dismissed.

When a petition is successful, the court may make such order it thinks fit for giving relief in respect of the matters complained of, including:

- Regulating the **future conduct** of the company's affairs (for example that a controlling shareholder shall conform to the decisions taken at board meetings)

- Authorising any person to bring **legal proceedings** on behalf of the company

- Requiring the company to do an act that it has omitted to do or to **refrain from doing** an act complained of

- Providing for the **purchase of shares** of the **minority** by other members or by the company itself

- Requiring the company to make any (specified) alterations to its articles, or not to make such alterations without leave of the court.

Perhaps the most common type of relief is an order that either the controlling shareholder or the company shall purchase the petitioner's shares at a fair price. This ends a relationship which has probably broken down beyond repair. The **court** may determine what is **fair** and need not make any allowance for the fact that the shares to be bought are only a minority holding and do not give control. The shares should be valued on the basis of their **worth before** it was diminished by the controlling shareholders' conduct. Where the articles provide a method for valuing shares, it should be used unless it would be unfair to the petitioner.

Interactive question 6: Unfairly prejudicial conduct   [Difficulty level: Exam standard]

Are the following likely to amount to unfairly prejudicial conduct under s 994 CA'06?

		Yes	No
A	Failure of a parent company to pay the debts of its subsidiary	☐	☐
B	Diversion of the company's business to a director-controlled company	☐	☐
C	Failure to call a general meeting	☐	☐
D	Late presentation of the company's accounts	☐	☐

See **Answer** at the end of this chapter.

3.5 Just and equitable winding up

A member who is dissatisfied with the directors or controlling shareholders over the management of the company may petition the court for a winding up on the grounds that it is **just and equitable** to do so. The member must show that **no** other remedy is available, since winding up what may be an otherwise healthy company is a drastic step. It is very much a remedy of last resort.

Re A Company 1983

The facts: The parties' working relationship had completely broken down and they agreed that they would settle the dispute by a sale of the minority's shares to the majority. This settlement broke down however, because they could not agree on the price and the minority then petitioned on the just and equitable ground.

Decision: An order for liquidation on this ground may only be made 'in the absence of any other remedy'. As the parties had agreed in principle that there was an alternative to liquidation the petition must be dismissed.

Orders have been made for winding up in the following situations:

- Where the company was formed for an **illegal or fraudulent purpose**.

- Where there is a **complete deadlock** in the management of its affairs.

Re Yenidje Tobacco Co Ltd 1916

The facts: Two sole traders merged their businesses in a company of which they were the only directors and shareholders. They quarrelled bitterly, refused to speak to each other and conducted board meetings by passing notes through the hands of the secretary. One sued the other for fraud and he petitioned for compulsory winding up.

Decision: 'In substance these two people are really partners' and by analogy with the law of partnership (which permits dissolution if the partners are really unable to work together) it was just and equitable to order liquidation.

- Where the directors deliberately **withheld information** so that the shareholders had no **confidence** in the company's management.

Interactive question 7: Minority action [Difficulty level: Exam standard]

Austen Ltd has three directors. Darcy, Bingley and Bennett. Together they own 85% of the shares in the company. They agree to sell a plot of land to Wickham for £50,000 which is what they honestly believe it to be worth. They do not, however, have the land professionally valued until later when it is shown to be worth nearer £100,000. Elizabeth and Jane are two minority shareholders who are considering bringing an action against the directors and the company.

In what type of action are Elizabeth and Jane most likely to be successful?

A   An action for relief on the grounds that the company's affairs have been conducted in a manner which is unfairly prejudicial to the members (s 994)

B   An action claiming breach of duty and negligence (s 260)

C   A petition for winding up the company on the just and equitable ground (s 122 IA 1986)

D   A personal action to enforce their rights as members

See **Answer** at the end of this chapter.

4 Meetings and resolutions

Section overview

- Decisions affecting the existence, structure, and constitution of a company are reserved to the company in general meeting, rather than the directors.

- Certain matters to be carried out by the directors also require a decision in general meeting.

- A decision of a company in general meeting is only valid and binding if the meeting is properly convened by notice and if the business of the meeting is fairly and properly conducted. Therefore the statutory rules on notice, quorum, proxies and voting need to be followed.

- The decision may need to be passed by an ordinary or a special resolution (depending on the subject matter).

- Private companies are permitted to pass written resolutions, which means that they do not need to hold general meetings except in very limited circumstances.

- There are also rules governing class meetings and single member companies.

Note that there are special rules in relation to 'traded companies', ie companies with shares which carry voting rights and are admitted to trading on a regulated market in an EEA State by or with the consent of the company . (These rules are found in The Companies (Shareholders' Rights) Regulations 2009.)

4.1 General meetings

A general meeting of the company **may** be called by

- The directors

- 5% of the members

- The court (of its own motion or on the application of a director or member)

- An auditor who gives notice of his resignation accompanied by a statement of the circumstances connected with his resignation and requesting a meeting (s 518).

A general meeting of a **public** company **must** be called where the net assets fall to half or less of its called up share capital.

A meeting may be required and may specify any proposed resolution by members representing at least 5% of the paid up capital of the company that carries voting rights or (where there is no share capital) at least 5% of the voting rights (s 303).

Within 21 days of any such requirement, the directors must call a meeting to take place within a 28-day notice period. If they fail to do so, the members who requested the meeting (or any of them representing over 50% of the total voting rights) may call a meeting to take place within 3 months of the initial request to the directors. A lesser number may require the company to circulate a statement of up to 1,000 words in respect of any resolution or other business to be dealt with at the meeting (s 314).

Notice of at least 14 days (or longer if required by the articles) must be given unless **shorter notice** is agreed to by at least 90% (or up to 95% if so required by the articles) of the nominal value of the shares with voting rights or (where there is no share capital) at least 90% of the voting rights (95% in the case of public companies).

Notice must be given to **every member** and **every director** (s 310). The notice must state the **time, date and place** of the meeting and the **general nature of the business** to be dealt with. Note that in particular cases, special notice may be required (see 4.4 below).

Interactive question 8: General meetings   [Difficulty level: Easy]

Bonanza Ltd is a company limited by shares which last held a general meeting 6 months ago. Which of the following cannot now call a further general meeting?

A   The directors
B   Members representing at least 5% of the paid up capital with voting rights
C   An auditor
D   A company secretary

See **Answer** at the end of this chapter.

4.2   Annual general meetings

Every **public company** must hold an annual general meeting ('AGM') once a year, during the 6 months following its accounting reference date (s 336). Failure to do so renders every officer of the company who is in default liable to a fine.

Notice of at least 21 days must be given unless **all the members** entitled to attend and vote agree to **shorter notice**. The notice must state that the meeting is an AGM.

The members of a public company may require the company to give notice of a resolution to be moved at the meeting, provided they represent at least 5% of the total voting rights or number at least 100 with shares on which there is paid up an average of £100 or more per member (s 338).

The directors of a public company must lay its annual accounts and reports before the company in general meeting (s 437). This is normally done at the AGM. Typically other business will include the declaration of a dividend and the appointment of directors and auditors.

A private company is not required to hold an AGM.

Interactive question 9: Notice periods   [Difficulty level: Easy]

In a public company, what percentage of the voting rights or nominal value of shares with voting rights must consent to a notice period of less than 14 days?

	A For a general meeting	B For an AGM
51%	☐	☐
75%	☐	☐
90%	☐	☐
95%	☐	☐
100%	☐	☐

See **Answer** at the end of this chapter.

4.3   Resolutions at general meeting

Section 281 provides that resolutions can only be passed in accordance with the Act, namely:

*   **Private** companies: as a written resolution or at a general meeting

*   **Public** companies: at a general meeting

*   Where a resolution is required but not specified, an **ordinary resolution** will be required (unless a higher majority is required by the articles).

These are two types of resolution which might be passed by the company in general meeting:

Type of resolution	Required majority of the votes cast	Business	Rules
Ordinary	>50%	Any business for which a special resolution is not specifically required by enactment or the articles	
Special	≥75%	Where special resolution is specifically required by enactment or the articles, for example: • Change of name • Alteration of the articles • Reduction of share capital • Winding up the company	The notice of the meeting must include the text of the resolution and specify that it is to be moved as a special resolution. All special resolutions must be filed with the Registrar within 15 days.

4.4 Written resolutions

The members or directors of a private company (but **not** a public company) may propose a **written resolution** without the need to hold a meeting in respect of any matter **except**

• Removal of a director
• Removal of an auditor
} before the expiration of his period of office

The same majority of votes is required for any written resolution as would be required if the resolution were passed in general meeting. The expression 'written resolution' does not mean that there is a requirement for writing in the sense of hard copy. The members or directors (as the case may be) must comply with the procedural steps for resolutions laid down by the Act, but the Act specifically acknowledges that meetings may be held without persons being physically together in the same place (s.360A).

A written resolution must be passed within **28 days** from its circulation (or any other period specified in the articles). Once signified, a member's agreement to a written resolution cannot be revoked. A written resolution is passed once the necessary majority has signified agreement to it. Articles cannot override a private company's power to pass written resolutions (s 300).

4.5 Notice and special notice

As has been mentioned, 14 days' notice is required for general meetings except

• For AGMs of a public company, which require 21 days
• Where special notice (of 28 days) is required to be given

The number of days always refers to **clear days**, that is excluding the day of the meeting and the day on which notice is given or a request is received. Thus, for an AGM of a public company on Thursday 25th, notice must be given on Wednesday 3rd.

Special notice of at least **28 days** needs to be given where a resolution is proposed

• To remove an auditor (s 510) or
• To remove a director or to appoint a substitute upon his removal (s 168)

The relevant director or auditor may submit written representations and require that they be circulated to members with notice of the meeting or read out at the meeting. They are also entitled to be heard at the meeting at which the resolution is proposed and/or the ensuing vacancy is filled.

4.6 Proceedings at meetings

Quorum

A quorum is the minimum number of persons required to be present at a general meeting. Generally speaking (and subject to the company's articles), a company must have a quorum of two members or proxies or corporate representatives, save that a single member company may have a quorum of one.

If the required number is not present, the meeting is said to be **inquorate**. Normally the articles provide for an automatic and compulsory adjournment in such cases.

Voting

The rights of members to vote and the number of votes to which they are entitled in respect of their shares are fixed by the articles. One vote per share is normal but some shares, for instance preference shares, may carry no voting rights in normal circumstances. Voting may be either:

- By a **show of hands**, ie where each member (or his proxy) has one vote irrespective of the number of shares held and exercises that vote by raising hands, or

- (More commonly) **by poll**, ie where each member and **proxies** representing absent members, may use as many votes as his shareholding grants him. If a poll is taken, the result of the previous show of hands is disregarded. (The Act provides that a poll may be demanded by a certain contingent of members (s 321).)

In voting, either by show of hands or on a poll, the number of votes cast determines the result. Votes which are not cast, whether the member who does not use them is present or absent, are simply disregarded. Hence the majority vote may be much less than half (or three quarters) of the total votes which could be cast.

Proxies

Every member of a company has a statutory right (s 324) to appoint one or more persons as his 'proxy', to exercise all or any of his rights to attend, speak and vote at a meeting of the company and any more extensive rights conferred by the articles.

Records

As noted earlier, every company must keep the following records for ten years (s 355) and available for inspection by members.

- Copies of all resolutions passed otherwise than at general meeting
- Minutes of all general meetings
- Details of decisions by sole member companies

Quoted companies must also publish on a website the results of polls at general meetings (s 341).

4.7 Class meetings

Class meetings may be held in respect of individual classes of shareholders or debenture holders and the rules for these are usually found in the articles or the debenture trust deed respectively.

Generally speaking, most statutory provisions relating to meetings and resolutions also apply to class meetings.

4.8 Single member private companies

Similarly, any enactment or rule of law applicable to companies with two or more members applies equally to sole member companies (with any necessary modifications) (s 38). A single member may conduct business informally without notice or minutes. However, he must still provide a written record of any decision that should have been taken in general meeting (or written resolution) and must comply with filing requirements in the normal way.

Summary and Self-test

Summary

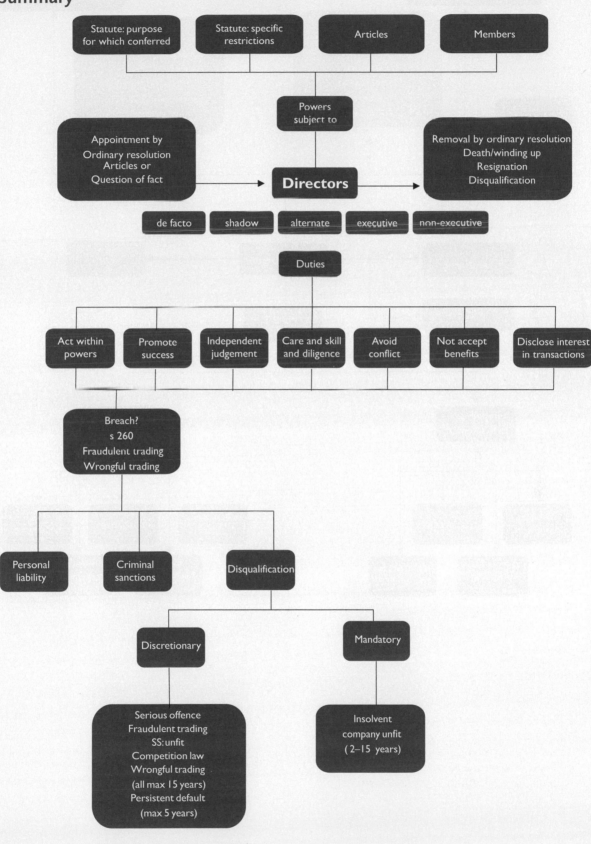

ICAEW

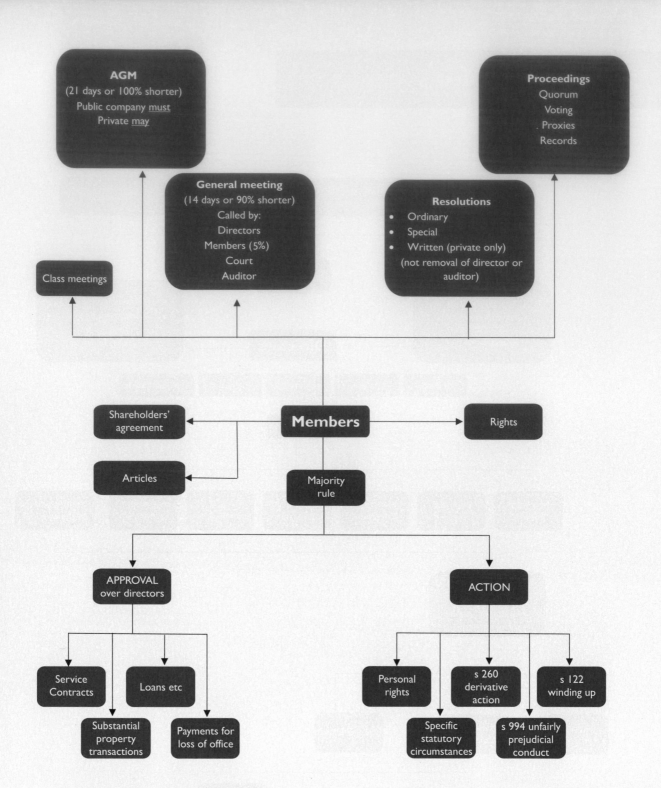

AGM
(21 days or 100% shorter)
Public company <u>must</u>
Private <u>may</u>

Proceedings
Quorum
Voting
Proxies
Records

General meeting
(14 days or 90% shorter)
Called by:
Directors
Members (5%)
Court
Auditor

Resolutions
- Ordinary
- Special
- Written (private only)
(not removal of director or
auditor)

Class meetings

Shareholders'
agreement

Members

Rights

Articles

Majority
rule

APPROVAL
over directors

ACTION

Service
Contracts

Loans etc

Personal
rights

s 260
derivative
action

s 122
winding up

Substantial
property
transactions

Payments for
loss of office

Specific
statutory
circumstances

s 994 unfairly
prejudicial
conduct

Self-test

Answer the following questions.

1   How many directors must a company have?

☐ Public company

☐ Private company

2   What is a shadow director?

3   A company may remove a director by special resolution provided it gives special notice.

☐ True

☐ False

4   Name TWO ways which indicate that the power of the directors is subject to the will of the members in general meeting.

•   ....

•   ....

5   List SIX of the general duties imposed on directors by CA'06.

•   ....

•   ....

•   ....

•   ....

•   ....

•   ....

6   The test of whether a director exercised reasonable care, skill and diligence is partly objective, ie the standard reasonably to be expected of someone performing his role as director, but also partly subjective if having regard to his actual general knowledge, skill and experience would require a higher standard.

☐ True

☐ False

7   The offences of wrongful trading and fraudulent trading only apply when a company goes into insolvent liquidation and may give rise to a personal liability on the part of a director.

☐ True

☐ False

8   In what circumstances might the Secretary of State accept a disqualification undertaking instead of seeking a disqualification order?

☐   Where the director has participated in wrongful trading

☐   Where the director is considered unfit to be concerned in the management of a company

☐   Where the director has been in persistent default of company law filing requirements

9   What is the principal advantage of a shareholders' agreement?

10 Name THREE matters which concern directors but require approval of the members in general meeting and state briefly the consequences of breach.

Matter	Consequence of breach

11 State the rule in Foss v Harbottle.

12 What are the THREE possible actions available to a minority who is unhappy with the action of the majority?

   • ....

   • ....

   • ....

13 Under what TWO circumstances is a public company required to call a general meeting?

   • ....

   • ....

14 Name THREE instances when a written resolution cannot be used.

   • ....

   • ....

   • ....

15 Where special notice is required, how many days' notice must be given?

   ☐ 7 days

   ☐ 14 days

   ☐ 21 days

   ☐ 28 days

16 If the voting on a show of hands results in 58% in favour of a resolution and voting on a poll results in 61% in favour, which result counts?

Now, go back to the Learning Objectives in the Introduction. If you are satisfied you have achieved these objectives, please tick them off.

ICAEW

Answer to Interactive question 1

(1) B   Shadow director

(2) B   Ordinary resolution with special notice

Answer to Interactive question 2

B   This was confirmed in *Bushell v Faith 1970.* A is therefore wrong. C is wrong in stating the articles are invalid *and* that a special resolution is needed; an ordinary resolution will suffice to remove a director. A director can vote on his removal if he is a member; therefore D is incorrect.

Answer to Interactive question 3

B   The company is bound by both agreements (assuming there is no lack of good faith on the bank's part). The transaction is beyond the authority of the managing director, Mary, in that she failed to obtain an ordinary resolution of the company as required by its articles of association. However s 40 provides that, in favour of a person dealing in good faith with a company, the power of the board of directors to bind the company or (importantly in this case) to authorise others to do so, shall be deemed to be free of any limitation under the company's constitution. Therefore the restriction placed on her actual authority (by the article requiring an ordinary resolution) shall be deemed not to exist in favour of the third party, Conifer Bank Ltd.

Farming Ltd will also be bound by the contract with Saw Ltd, as this was within her implied usual authority as managing director.

Answer to Interactive question 4

A   2   Persistent default in filing annual returns ≤ 5 years

B   3   Fraudulent trading ≤ 15 years

C   3   Wrongful trading ≤ 15 years

D   1   Where the court considers that his conduct makes him unfit to be
          considered in the management of a company, 2–15 years

Answer to Interactive question 5

A, C and D. If any of these matters are present, the claim will be unsuccessful. Whether or not the claimant is acting in good faith (B) is one of the matters taken into consideration by the court, but is not conclusive in the same way.

Answer to Interactive question 6

A   No

B   Yes

C   Yes

D   No

Answer to Interactive question 7

B   Elizabeth and Jane could consider a derivative action, under s 260 CA'06. Under the common law, prior to the Act, they would be unlikely to succeed. The facts of this case resemble those of *Pavlides v Jensen 1956* where it was held that mere negligence did not justify a minority action to protect the company's rights since, in the absence of fraud, the sale could legitimately be approved by a majority of the shareholders. However, the new statutory provision covers negligence by the directors and so a remedy may be given. It remains to be seen how the courts will interpret and apply s 260.

Answer to Interactive question 8

D   The company secretary has no power to call a meeting

Answer to Interactive question 9

A   For a general meeting 95%

B   For an AGM 100%

1   A public company must have at least 2 directors. A private company must have at least 1 director.

2   A shadow director is someone in accordance with whose directions or instructions the directors are accustomed to act.

3   False. Special notice is required but only an **ordinary** resolution is needed.

4
- Alteration of the articles requires special resolution
- Reduction of capital requires special resolution
- Borrowing power may need ordinary resolution
- Directors' office is subject to members' power to remove by ordinary resolution

5
- To act within the company constitution and to exercise their powers only for the purposes for which they were conferred
- To promote the success of the company
- To exercise independent judgement
- To exercise reasonable care, skill and diligence
- To avoid conflicts of interest
- Not to accept benefits from third parties
- To declare any interest in a proposed transaction or arrangement

6   True

7   False. Fraudulent trading applies whether or not a company has been or is in the course of being wound up. It is true, however that the commission of both offences can lead to a personal liability to contribute to the company's debts.

8   Where the director is considered unfit to be concerned in the management of a company.

9   It does not need to be registered or open to public inspection.

10

Matter	Consequence of breach
Service contracts	Provision is void and contracts deemed to include provision for termination on reasonable notice
Substantial property transactions	Contract is voidable, director liable to account for any gain and indemnify against any loss
Loans to directors etc	Contract is voidable, director liable to account for any gain and indemnify against any loss
Payments for loss of office	Payment is held on trust for the company, director liable to indemnify for any loss

11   In order to redress a wrong done to a company or its property or to enforce its rights, the proper claimant is the company itself and not a member or members of the company.

12
- Derivative action under s 260 (if majority represented by directors)
- Derivative action under s 994 for unfairly prejudicial conduct
- Petition for the winding up of the company on the just and equitable ground (s 122 IA '86)

13
- An AGM every year
- Wherever its net assets are half or less of its called up share capital

14
- In a public company
- To remove an auditor
- To remove a director

15 28 days

16 The vote on a poll. If a poll is taken, the result of the previous show of hands is disregarded.

CHAPTER 7

Companies: finance

Introduction

Examination context

Topic List

1   Shares

2   Share capital

3   Loan capital and charges

Summary and Self-test

Answers to Interactive questions

Answers to Self-test

Learning objectives

- To understand the key types of shares in a company, including the procedures for the issue, payment and transfer of shares ☐

- To identify different types of share capital and know how share capital can be altered ☐

- To understand the key issues in relation to capital maintenance ☐

- To learn about loan capital and debentures ☐

- To recognise fixed and floating charges and to know the rules relating to their registration and priority ☐

Specific syllabus references for this chapter are: 2d, e, f and m.

Syllabus links

In the previous chapter, you learned about companies limited by shares and this chapter now explores the financing of such companies. You will learn about loans and charges over companies' assets and, in the next chapter, consider further what happens when a company defaults on such arrangements.

Examination context

You can expect around four or five questions on the subject matter of this chapter on your exam paper.

In the assessment, candidates may be required to:

- Identify the procedures for the issue of shares, including issues at a premium and pre-emption rights

- Identify aspects of capital maintenance including reduction of capital, redemption and purchase of a company's own shares, financial assistance for the purchase of a company's own shares and distribution of profit.

- Identify share transfer requirements and disclosure requirements

- Identify the nature of fixed and floating charges and the procedures for registering them

1 Shares

Section overview

- The most common types of share are ordinary shares and preference shares. A company may also issue redeemable shares (which may take the form of ordinary or preference shares).

- Shares which have certain rights not enjoyed by other shares in the company are grouped in a class and are said to have class rights.

- Generally speaking, shares may be allotted provided authority is given in the articles or by ordinary resolution and they must first be offered to existing shareholders in proportion to their existing holdings.

- Shares must be paid for in money or money's worth. They can be issued at a premium but not, as a general rule, at a discount.

- Shares are generally freely transferable and may be transferred in a paper or paperless format.

A **share** is a transferable form of personal property, carrying rights and obligations, by which the interest of a member of a company limited by shares is measured. A member of a company who holds one or more shares is a **shareholder**. References to 'the Act' are to the Companies Act 2006 unless otherwise stated.

1.1 Types of shares

If the constitution of a company states no differences between shares, it is assumed that they are all ordinary shares. However, often a company will choose to confer different rights on different classes of share. You will remember that the statement of capital submitted on formation (or on subsequent actions of the company that have an effect on share capital) includes the prescribed particulars of the rights attached to each type of the company's shares. Details are also likely to be included in the company's articles.

The most common types of share are ordinary shares and preference shares. They (and redeemable shares) are described below:

Share	Feature
Ordinary	Ordinary shareholders have an automatic right to have their capital repaid and to participate in the distribution of profit, when the company is wound up, provided the company has surplus assets once creditors have been satisfied.
	Dividends are payable to ordinary shareholders only according to declarations made by the directors and they are not cumulative (whereas dividends payable on preference shares are normally cumulative).
	It is the ordinary shareholders who are normally offered the benefit of rights issues and bonus issues.
	All ordinary shareholders have statutory pre-emption rights (see section 1.4 below).
Preference	Preference shareholders also have a right to have their capital repaid on a winding up (unless the articles provide otherwise). If there is a surplus after repayment of capital, ordinary and preference shareholders will share equally. Where preference shares are expressed to carry a priority or preferential right to return of capital, the amount paid up on each preference share is to be repaid before anything is repaid to ordinary shareholders. In these circumstances, however, if there is a surplus after repayment of capital, the preference shareholders will have no right to share in that surplus.

Share	Feature

Typically preference shares will carry a prior right to a fixed dividend, in which case

- It is not a right to compel payment of a dividend, simply to receive a dividend at the specified rate before any other dividend is paid or declared.

- The right to receive a preference dividend is deemed to be cumulative unless the contrary is stated.

- On liquidation, the preference shareholders cease to be entitled to any unpaid preference dividends unless

  - A dividend has been declared though not yet paid when liquidation commences and

  - The articles (or other terms of issue) expressly provide that in a liquidation arrears are to be paid in priority to return of capital to members

- Holders of preference shares have **no entitlement** to participate in any **additional dividend** over and above their specified rate unless that is expressly provided.

Preference shares are usually expressed **not to carry a right to vote** (or only in specified circumstances, such as failure to pay the preference dividend, variation of their rights or a resolution to wind up). If there is no express provision, they carry the same voting rights as ordinary shares.

Preference shareholders do not have rights of pre-emption unless they are specifically conferred by the company's articles of association or terms of issue of the shares.

Redeemable	A redeemable share is one which is issued on terms that it can be bought back by the company at the option of the company or the shareholder (see section 2.4 below).

1.2 Class rights

Any share which has different rights from others is grouped with the other shares carrying **identical** rights to form a class. The rights that attach to shares in that class which are different from the rights enjoyed by all shareholders are called 'class rights'.

The rights attached to a class of shares (or members' rights generally in a company without a share capital) can be **varied** only in accordance with the articles or (if they contain no such provision) according to the procedure set out in the Act (s 630), namely

- A special resolution of the relevant class or written consent from at least 75% in nominal value of the issued shares of that class.

- The holders of at least 15% of the issued shares of the class in question (who have not themselves consented to or voted in favour of the variation) may apply to the court, within 21 days of the consent being given by the class, to have the variation cancelled.

  The court can either confirm the variation as made or cancel it as 'unfairly prejudicial'. It cannot, however, modify the terms of the variation. A variation will be 'unfairly prejudicial' where it is shown that the majority who voted in favour was seeking some advantage to themselves as members of a different class instead of considering the interests of the class in which they were then voting (*Re Holders Investment Trust, 1971*). A copy of the court order must be forwarded to the Registrar within 15 days.

- A notice giving particulars of any variation, or creation of a new class, must be delivered to the Registrar within one month of the variation.

Note that the fact that the value of existing rights may be affected will not concern the court if the **rights themselves** are unchanged. A class right is varied only if the right itself is altered. An alteration which affects how the right 'operates', but which leaves the right unchanged is not a variation.

For example, where shares of one class are subdivided with the incidental effect of increasing the voting strength of that class, the class rights of another class are not varied as a result, even though the rights of the non-altered shares are, in practice. less valuable:

Greenhalgh v Arderne Cinemas Ltd 1946

The facts: The company had two classes of ordinary shares, 50p shares and 10p shares. Every share carried one vote. A resolution was passed to subdivide each 50p share into five 10p shares, thus multiplying the votes of that class by five.

Decision: The rights of the original 10p shares had not been varied since they still had one vote per share as before.

Interactive question 1: Types of share   [Difficulty level: Exam standard]

Which type(s) of share

		Ordinary	Preference
A	Carries statutory rights of pre-emption in the absence of any express provision?	☐	☐
B	Carries a right to a dividend at a specified rate which is deemed to be cumulative in the absence of any express or implied provision to the contrary?	☐	☐
C	Carries an automatic right to have capital repaid in the event of the company being wound up?	☐	☐
D	Carries a right to vote in the absence of any express provision?	☐	☐

See **Answer** at the end of this chapter.

1.3   Allotment of shares

Shares are **allotted** when a person acquires the unconditional right to be included in the company's register of members in respect of those shares (s 558). Shares are generally said to be **issued** once the allottee receives a letter of allotment or share certificate as evidence of his title. Once his name is entered on the register of members, he is then a member of the company.

The general rule is that the directors of any company may allot shares on the following basis (s 551)

(1)   There must be authority given either

- By the articles or
- By ordinary resolution

It can be general or specific, conditional or unconditional.

(2)   The authority must

- State the maximum number of shares to be allotted

- State the expiry date for the authority, which must be not more than five years after the authority (ie after the incorporation or resolution)

The authority may be given, varied, renewed or removed by an **ordinary resolution**, even if this constitutes an alteration of the articles (which would normally require a special resolution).

The rule does not apply to the allotment of shares in pursuance of an employees' share scheme.

In addition, the directors of a **private** company **with only one class of shares** may allot shares of that class **unless** (and to the extent that) it is prohibited by the company's articles (s 550).

Any director who knowingly contravenes or allows a contravention commits an offence punishable by a fine.

A **rights issue** is an allotment of additional shares made to existing members, usually *pro rata* to their existing holding in the company's shares. If the members do not wish to subscribe for additional shares under a rights issue they may be able to sell their rights and so obtain the value of the option.

A **bonus issue** is the capitalisation of the reserves of a company by the issue of additional shares to existing shareholders, in proportion to their holdings. Such shares are normally fully paid-up with no cash called for from the shareholders.

1.4 Rights of pre-emption

Whenever a company proposes to allot 'equity securities' (usually ordinary shares for cash), it is required to offer those shares first to holders of similar shares **in proportion to their holdings** (s 561) and on the same or more favourable terms. These rights of existing company shareholders to be offered new equity shares issued by the company *pro rata* to their existing holding of that class of shares are called **pre-emption rights**.

The offer must be made in writing or in electronic form and must specify a period of not less than **21 days** during which the offer may be accepted. Equity securities which have been offered to members in this way but are not accepted may then be allotted on the same (or less favourable) terms to non-members.

If equity securities are allotted in breach of these rules the members to whom the offer should have been made may, within two years from delivery of the return of allotment, recover compensation for their loss, if any, from those in default (s 563). The allotment will generally be valid.

These pre-emption provisions **do not apply** in the following cases:

Reason	Explanation
Exceptions	The Act provided that the provisions do not apply to allotments of • Bonus shares • Securities to be wholly or partly paid up otherwise than in cash • Securities relating to an employees' share scheme
Exclusions	A private company may exclude all or any of the provisions in its **articles**, either generally or in relation to allotments of a particular description
Disapplication	Directors of a private company **with only one class of shares** may be authorised to allot equity securities as if s 561 did not apply by either • The articles or • Special resolution Where directors are given **authority** by the company to allot shares, they may also be given the **power** to allot equity securities as if s 561 did not apply by either • The articles (where a general authority is given) or • Special resolution

1.5 Shares at a discount

As a general rule, shares cannot be allotted at a discount to (or for a price which is less than) the nominal value (s.580). If shares are allotted at a discount, the allottee is liable to pay the company an amount equal to the amount of the discount, together with interest.

The no-discount rule only requires that, in allotting its shares, a company shall not fix a **price** which is less than the nominal value of the shares. It may leave part of that price to be paid at some later time. Thus £1 shares may be issued at a price of £1 but only partly paid – 75p on allotment and 25p when called for or by instalment. The unpaid capital passes with the shares, if they are transferred, as a debt payable by the holder at the time when payment is demanded.

More specifically (s 552), a company is prohibited from applying any of its shares or capital money in paying any commission, discount or allowance to any person in consideration of his subscribing for shares (or procuring subscriptions or agreeing to subscribe or procure subscriptions). This prohibition applies regardless of how the shares or money are to be applied, whether in addition to the purchase price of property acquired by the company or the contract price of work to be carried out for the company or in being paid out of the nominal purchase money or contract price or otherwise.

There is one exception, however, which entitles a company to pay a commission to someone who agrees to subscribe or to procure subscriptions for shares, provided the company's articles contain the relevant authority and provided the commission paid does not exceed 10% of the issue price of the shares or the amount authorised by the articles, whichever is less.

1.6 Shares at a premium

Shares may be issued at a premium, for cash or otherwise. In such cases, a sum equal to the premium on each share must be transferred to a **share premium account**. If a company allots 100 of its £1 (nominal) shares for £1.50 in cash, £1 per share is credited to the share capital account, and 50p to the share premium account. The allotment would be shown in the balance sheet as follows:

	Before share issue £	After share issue £
Cash	100	250
Share capital	100	200
Share premium	–	50
	100	250

That amount so transferred may be used to **write off the expenses** of the issue of those shares and any commission lawfully paid on the issue. The account may also be used to pay up new shares to be allotted to members as **fully paid bonus shares**. There are also special rules for group reconstruction relief and merger relief, which relieve companies from the requirement to transfer any premium to a share premium account. Thus if an acquiring company secures at least 90 per cent of the equity capital of another company as consideration for an allotment of its shares, any premium obtained from the excess of the other company's assets over the nominal value of its shares need not be transferred to the share premium account.

Otherwise, the share premium account is treated as part of the company's paid up share capital and is subject to rules on the reduction of capital set out in the Act. For example, a company cannot distribute part of its share premium account

- As a dividend
- To write off expenses incurred in connection with the formation of the company, nor
- To write off expenses incurred in connection with an issue of debentures

1.7 Payment for shares

Shares must be paid up in **money or money's worth** (including goodwill and know how). Thus payment may be cash or a **'non-cash' consideration** of sufficient value. For instance, a company may issue shares in payment of the price agreed in the purchase of a property. Whilst a blatant and unjustified overvaluation will be declared invalid, the courts generally will not wish to intervene in a directors' valuation of an asset acquired for shares if it appears reasonable and honest. To issue shares **'at par'** is to obtain consideration equal to the nominal value. The prohibition on offering of shares at a discount on *nominal* value does not prevent a company from issuing shares at a price which is below *market* value.

Shares are deemed to be allotted or paid up in **cash** where the company receives

- Cash
- An undertaking to pay cash to the company (but not to another person) at a later date
- A cheque
- A release of its liability for a liquidated sum

There are additional rules which apply to **public companies**, as follows:

Rule	Explanation
Subscribers (s 584)	Shares taken by subscribers must be paid up in cash.
Services (s 585)	Shares cannot be paid for by an undertaking by someone to do work or perform services for the company or any other person.
1/4 paid up (s 586)	Shares must be paid up at least as to one-quarter of the nominal value plus the whole of any premium payable (except for shares allotted in pursuance of an employees' share scheme).
Long-term undertaking (s 587)	Shares cannot be allotted as fully or partly paid up otherwise than in cash if the payment is or includes an undertaking which may be performed more than five years after the allotment.
Valuation of non-cash consideration (s 593)	Any payment otherwise than in cash must be independently valued (subject to certain exceptions concerning mergers or an arrangement with another company).

Generally speaking, where an allotment is made in contravention of these provisions, the allottee is liable to pay an amount equal to the nominal value of the allotted shares together with interest. He may apply to the court for relief from such liability and the court may grant relief where it considers it just and equitable to do so.

Interactive question 2: Issue of shares   [Difficulty level: Exam standard]

The directors of Starwake plc propose to allot 1,000 shares with a nominal value of £5 each for cash.

	Yes	No
A Can the company amend its articles of association to incorporate a provision excluding the statutory rights of pre-emption?	☐	☐
B Is an authority to allot shares given by ordinary resolution sufficient?	☐	☐
C Can any of the shares be sold for £4.50 each on a fully paid-up basis?	☐	☐
D Can any of the shares be sold for £5.50 each?	☐	☐

See **Answer** at the end of this chapter.

1.8   Transfer of shares

Shares are generally freely transferable in accordance with and subject to any restrictions contained in the company's articles (s 544).

Unlisted shares

Once the member-transferor and the transferee have reached agreement, the transferor holds the shares as trustee for the transferee until registration but remains a member of the company with the right to vote as he chooses. Once the transferee pays for the shares, the transferor must vote as directed by the transferee. Once the transferee's name is entered on the register of members, the transferor ceases to be a member and the transferee acquires all the member's rights.

The transferor executes a stock transfer form in favour of the transferee and gives it to him with the share certificate. Both are sent to the company for registration. Once the company receives a proper instrument of transfer, it must either register the transfer and prepare a share certificate or give notice of refusal to the proposed transferee, with reasons for the refusal, **within two months**. Where notice of refusal is given, the transferee's beneficial interest is not affected (that is, he is still entitled to any dividend or return of capital on winding up), but he cannot exercise all members' rights, including

ICAEW

voting rights, until the transfer is registered and his name is entered on the register of members. He is also entitled to such information as he may reasonably require as to the reasons for the refusal (but he is not entitled to minutes of directors' meetings). Where the company fails to comply with these provisions, it and its officers are guilty of an offence punishable by a fine.

There is no requirement for certification where shares are transmitted by operation of law, for example where a bankrupt member's trustee in bankruptcy or a deceased member's personal representative becomes entitled to the member's shares.

Listed shares

Securities may be transferred without a written instrument.

CREST Co Ltd is a private company owned by a number of firms connected with all sections of the equities market. The company is currently the approved operator of an electronic system which enables shareholders to hold and transfer their securities without the need for written instruments of transfer. Under the CREST system, a member appoints a custodian broker to hold his shares under a customer agreement, which provides for the broker to deal with the shares only in accordance with the shareholder's directions. Any transfer of shares is normally completed in three days.

Regulations under the Act (made by either the Treasury or the Secretary of State) may provide that companies may be **required** (rather than just permitted) to adopt such a paperless holding and transfer of shares (s 785). Such regulations might impose such a requirement in relation to particular types of company or security or provide for the company to pass an ordinary resolution to that effect.

You should be aware that there are very detailed rules for the disclosure of substantial interests in the relevant share capital (essentially voting shares) of public companies. For example, in the case of companies listed on the Official List or AIM, issuers are obliged to publish their total share capital and voting rights at the end of each calendar month in which a change has occurred. A shareholder must notify the issuer (by completing a notification form) where his percentage of voting rights reaches 3% of the total voting rights of the company, and each 1% thereafter. It follows that this threshold may be reached even where a shareholder does not actually deal in the shares. He is therefore obliged to make the notification within two trading days of when he became or should have become aware of the notifiable change. These provisions are set out in the Disclosure and Transparency Rules (published by the Financial Services Authority).

2 Share capital

Section overview

- The capital which is invested in a company limited by shares by shareholders is called its share capital.

- A company's share capital can be increased and altered in a number of ways, but there are strict controls on any reduction of capital.

- In certain circumstances a company may acquire its own shares, by redemption or purchase, and private companies may be permitted to fund such an acquisition out of capital.

- Private companies may give financial assistance for the acquisition of their shares but public companies are prohibited from doing so, save in certain circumstances.

- Dividends represent a return on capital invested and, generally speaking, must be paid out of distributable profits only.

It is a fundamental principle of company law that limited companies should utilise their share capital only for the purposes of the business and should not be allowed to diminish or return any part of that capital to the detriment of company creditors or minority shareholders. This **maintenance of capital** principle is upheld by various provisions in the Act which limit capital reduction schemes, restrict the freedom of a company to purchase its own shares and give financial assistance to aid share purchases, strictly control the circumstances in which capital may be used for the redemption and purchase of shares, as well as restricting the scope for making dividend payments and utilising payments of share premiums.

Remember too that a **public company** must satisfy the authorised minimum share capital requirement (currently £50,000).

2.1 Types of capital

The word capital is used in different ways in relation to companies. You should be familiar with the following terms:

Term	Meaning
A company having a share capital	A company that has power under its constitution to issue shares (s 545)
Issued or allotted share capital	Shares that have been issued or allotted as the case may be (s 546) (including shares taken by the subscribers on the formation of the company). A company need not issue all its share capital. Any part of it not issued is called **unissued share capital**.
Called-up share capital	So much of the share capital as equals the aggregate amount of the calls made on its shares plus share capital that is paid up without being called and share capital to be paid at a specified future date under the articles or terms of allotment of the relevant shares (s 547).
Equity share capital	The issued share capital excluding any part of it that, neither as respects dividends nor as respects capital, carries any right to participate beyond a specified amount in a distribution (ie usually a company's ordinary share capital, since preference shares usually carry a right to a fixed return).
Loan capital	Loan capital describes the company's borrowed money.

Worked example: Types of capital

Portions Ltd has 100 £1 (nominal shares) of which it has issued 80. It has received 25p per share on application and has called on the holders for a further 15p per share.

Its share capital is £100. Its issued share capital is £80. Its called-up share capital is £32 and its paid up share capital is £20.

2.2 Reduction of share capital

A company may wish to reduce its share capital where, for example, its capital exceeds the company's needs or where the company's net assets have fallen in value to below the amount of its capital (as recorded in the accounts) and that position is likely to be permanent. A reduction in share capital may be achieved by various means, including reducing the liability on partly paid shares or by reducing the amount of paid up share capital and either returning it to shareholders or applying it to another purpose.

Companies are only permitted to reduce their share capital in accordance with the two methods prescribed by the Act (s.641). These are designed to reassure creditors with regard to capital invested in the company but also to give directors sufficient flexibility in managing the business effectively and to return unused capital in an appropriate manner. Both methods are subject to any restriction or prohibition contained in the company's articles of association:

- **Any limited company** may reduce its capital by special resolution confirmed by the court. In most cases, any such confirmation is subject to creditors' rights to object to the reduction and to the court being satisfied that all creditors so entitled have either consented to the reduction or had their subsisting debts or claims discharged or secured. If a reduction is confirmed for a public company that results in the nominal value of the allotted share capital falling below the authorised minimum, the company must be re-registered as a private company unless the court directs otherwise

ICAEW

- A **private company** may reduce its capital by special resolution supported by a solvency statement given by all of the directors in a prescribed form (within 15 days prior to the resolution being passed) confirming the company's ability to pay its debts over a period of twelve months (s.643). This method is only permissible where there is at least one member remaining who holds a non-redeemable share (so that a private limited company cannot reduce its share capital to nothing without the court's approval)

A copy of the resolution and a statement of capital, together with a copy of the solvency statement or court order must be filed with the Registrar.

If the net assets of a **public company** are (or fall to) half or less of the company's called up share capital, the directors must call a general meeting in order to consider whether any steps need to be taken to deal with the situation.

Members' liability is reduced accordingly following a permitted reduction in capital. Any reserve arising from a reduction of capital may be treated as a realised profit for the purposes of distributions.

2.3 Other alteration of share capital

A company may, however, increase or alter its share capital as follows and in each case must give notice to the Registrar of the alteration, accompanied by a statement of capital, within one month:

Alteration	Rule
Increase (s 617)	By allotting more shares (see 1.3 above).
Subdivision or consolidation (s 618)	A limited company may pass an ordinary resolution to: • Subdivide its shares into shares of a smaller nominal amount than its existing shares or • Consolidate and divide its share capital into shares of a larger nominal amount than its existing shares The proportion between the amount paid and amount unpaid on the original shares must remain the same. For example, if £1 is unpaid on a £10 share that is subsequently subdivided into 10 £1 shares, there will then be 10p unpaid on each of those 10 shares.

(Note that a company's share capital may also be altered as a result of a redenomination from one currency to another (s 622). Such a redenomination may also result in a reduction of capital in order to round up or down nominal values in the new currency. If such a reduction is needed, it must not exceed 10% of the nominal value of the reduced allotted share capital and a special resolution is required.)

2.4 Redemption of shares

A public limited company must contain authority in its articles to issue redeemable shares and a private company may exclude or restrict the issue of redeemable shares in its articles (s 684). The directors' authority to determine the terms, conditions and manner of redemption may also be given by an ordinary resolution (even if it has the effect of amending the company's articles). Redeemable shares can only be issued when there are other shares issued that are not redeemable.

Redeemable shares may not be redeemed unless they are fully paid. Unless the terms of redemption provide otherwise, the shares must be paid for on redemption.

Redeemable shares may only be redeemed out of:

- Distributable profits of the company or
- The proceeds of a fresh issue of shares made for the purposes of the redemption

Save that a **private limited company** may redeem shares **out of capital** subject to certain conditions (which apply also to a purchase of shares described in section 2.5 below).

These provide that the company may make a 'permissible capital payment' in such amount as is required for the redemption or purchase after applying for that purpose

- Any available profits and
- The proceeds of any fresh issue of shares made for the purpose of the redemption or purchase

For these purposes, 'available profits' has the same meaning as in the case of distributions but whether the company has profits so available is determined in accordance with different provisions (s.711).

A payment out of capital can only be made where the directors' statement and auditor's report support the payment and it is approved by a special resolution (disregarding the voting rights of shares to which the resolution relates). Any proposed payment out of capital must be publicised appropriately and creditors must be given an opportunity to apply to court for the cancellation of the resolution. The payment must be made within five and seven weeks after the resolution is passed.

When shares in a limited company are redeemed, the shares are treated as cancelled and the amount of the company's issued share capital is diminished by the nominal value of the shares redeemed. Notice of redemption, together with a statement of capital, must be given to the Registrar within one month.

2.5 Purchase of own shares

Generally speaking a company is prohibited from acquiring its own shares save in limited circumstances (s 658), namely the:

- Redemption or purchase of shares in accordance with the Act

- Acquisition of shares in a permitted reduction of capital

- Purchase of shares in complying with a court order (eg buying out an unfairly prejudiced minority)

- Forfeiture or surrender of shares in accordance with a company's articles where there is failure to pay for them

A company's ability to purchase its own shares may be attractive to individual investors who might otherwise be concerned that shareholders might not have sufficient resources to buy them out. It also enables the resolution of disputes and difficulties where one member wishes to retire or resign and the remaining shareholders do not wish to (or cannot) purchase his shares and do not want an outsider brought in.

A limited company may purchase its own shares in accordance with the provisions of the Act, subject to any restriction or prohibition contained in its articles and subject to there being issued shares of the company other than redeemable shares or treasury shares. It can only purchase its own shares where the shares are fully paid and the shares must be paid for on purchase.

A limited company may only purchase its own shares out of

- Distributable profits of the company or
- The proceeds of a fresh issue of shares made for the purpose of financing the purchase

Save that a **private company** may use capital to purchase its own shares provided certain conditions are met. (These are the same as the requirements described in 2.4 above with regard to redemption of shares out of capital.)

A market purchase, ie one made on a recognised investment exchange, must be authorised by a resolution of the company which specifies the maximum number of shares that can be acquired and states a maximum and minimum price that can be paid for them.

An off-market purchase, ie one that is not conducted through a recognised investment exchange, must be authorised by a contract approved by (or conditional upon approval by) a special resolution (disregarding the voting rights of the shares to which the resolution relates).

A return giving details of the purchase must be sent to the Registrar of Companies within 28 days. Purchased shares are usually cancelled, although in some cases (generally speaking where the shares are listed or traded on the AIM or regulated market) the company may elect to hold them 'in treasury'. Treasury shares may be sold at a later date without obtaining prior authority from the company's members for the sale.

Where shares are redeemed or purchased out of a company's profits, the amount by which the company's issued share capital is diminished when shares are cancelled must be transferred to the capital redemption reserve. That reserve is treated as part of the company's paid up share capital, except that it may be used to pay up new shares to be allotted to members as fully paid bonus shares.

2.6 Financial assistance for the purchase of shares

Under the Act, private companies are no longer prohibited from giving financial assistance for the acquisition of their shares. However, public companies remain subject to restrictions.

Financial assistance may be given in various ways, including by way of gift or a gift of money to buy them or by guaranteeing or providing security for a loan given by a third party for the purposes of purchasing shares. (Lawful dividends and distributions on liquidation, permitted reductions of capital or redemption of shares, allotments of bonus shares and anything done in pursuance of a court order or arrangement with creditors are not prohibited by the rules on financial assistance (s 681).)

A **public company** (or its subsidiary) is prohibited from giving financial assistance at or before the time of an acquisition of shares in the public company, unless the principal purpose of the assistance is something other than the proposed acquisition (s.678) or the giving of assistance is only an incidental part of some larger purpose and (in either case) it is given in good faith in the interests of the company. The same prohibition applies to any financial assistance to be given by a public company for the acquisition of shares in its private holding company.

However, financial assistance *may* be given for the purpose of certain transactions (outlined below) by

- Private companies

- Public companies where the assistance does not reduce the company's net assets or, to the extent that they are reduced, the assistance is given out of distributable profits

The permitted transactions include:

- Where the lending of money is in the company's ordinary course of business

- Where the financial assistance is given in good faith in the interests of the company for the purposes of an employees' share scheme

- The making of loans to employees (not directors) in good faith to enable them to acquire fully paid shares in the company

Breach of the financial assistance rules is a criminal offence (s 680), punishable by fine and/or imprisonment, and is also likely to affect the contracts concerned and result in civil liability for breach of directors' duties.

Interactive question 3: Maintenance of capital   [Difficulty level: Exam standard]

Might the following transactions by a retail limited company be permitted under the Companies Act 2006?

	Public company	Private company
A The buy-back of redeemable shares out of capital	☐	☐
B The purchase of a company's own shares out of capital	☐	☐
C The provision of a loan to a director for the purpose of acquiring shares in the company	☐	☐
D A reduction of capital authorised by the court	☐	☐

See **Answer** at the end of this chapter.

2.7 Dividends

A dividend is one type of distribution of a company's assets to members of the company. The general rule is that any distribution can only be made **out of profits** that are available for the purpose and not out of capital.

Profits available for distribution are accumulated realised profits (which have not been distributed or capitalised) less accumulated realised losses (which have not been previously written off in a reduction or reorganisation of capital).

A dividend is a debt only when it is declared and due for payment. A shareholder (ordinary or preference) is not entitled to a dividend unless it is declared in accordance with the procedure prescribed by the articles and the declared date for payment has arrived. The directors may decide to withhold profits and cannot be compelled to recommend a dividend.

A **public company** may only make a distribution if its **net assets are**, at the time, not less than the aggregate of its called-up share capital and undistributable reserves. The dividend which it may pay is limited to such amount as will leave its net assets at not less than that aggregate amount (s 831).

Undistributable reserves are defined as

- Share premium account

- Capital redemption reserve

- Any surplus of accumulated unrealised profits over accumulated unrealised losses (known as a revaluation reserve)

- Any reserve which the company is prohibited from distributing by statute or by its articles.

If a distribution is made in contravention of the Act and the receiving member knows or has reasonable grounds for believing that the distribution is made unlawfully, that member will be liable to repay it (or a sum equal to its value where the distribution is made otherwise than in cash) (s 847). The directors may also be liable to repay the amount of the dividend as a result of the breach of directors' duties which will have occurred.

In *Bairstow v Queens Moat Houses plc 2000,* nearly £27 million of dividend was authorised by directors when there were insufficient distributable profits. The directors were held to be in breach of their fiduciary duties and liable to repay the amount of the dividends to the company. Members with actual or constructive knowledge of the unlawful payments were also liable to repay the dividends received.

3 Loan capital and charges

Section overview

- A company may choose to raise loan capital rather than share capital. A debenture is the document that records the terms of any loan.

- A company may enter into a fixed or floating charge by way of providing security for its borrowing.

- The lender or debentureholder is then a secured creditor and will rank in priority to unsecured creditors in any liquidation of the company.

- Charges need to be registered.

3.1 Debentures and rights of debentureholders

A **debenture** is the written acknowledgement of a debt by a company, which normally contains provisions as to repayment of capital and interest. A debenture may be secured on some or all of the assets of the company by the creation of a **charge** over the company's assets. However a document relating to an unsecured loan is also a debenture in company law. A debenture is usually a formal legal document.

Like shareholders, debentureholders own transferable company securities which are usually long-term investments in the company and the procedure for issue and transfer of shares and debentures is very similar.

There are however important differences:

Factor	Shareholder	Debenture holder
Role	Is a member or owner of the company	Is a creditor of the company
Voting rights	May vote at general meetings	May not vote
Cost of investment	Shares may not be issued at a discount	Debentures may be offered at a discount
Return	Dividends are only paid out of distributable profits and when directors declare them	Interest must be paid when it is due
Redemption	Statutory restrictions on redeeming shares	No restriction on redeeming debentures
Liquidation	Shareholders are the last people to be paid in a winding up	Debentures must be paid back before shareholders are paid

From the investor's standpoint, debenture stock is often preferable to preference shares since the former offers greater security and yields a fixed income.

From the company's standpoint, raising capital by borrowing has obvious advantages but it has to bear in mind also the disadvantages of the rate of interest payable and, in particular, the liability imposed by any charge which is created in order to secure the loan.

A **charge** is an encumbrance upon real or personal property granting the holder certain rights over that property, usually as security for a debt owed to the charge holder. The most common form of charge is by way of legal mortgage, used to secure the indebtedness of borrowers in house purchase transactions. In the case of companies, charges over assets are most frequently granted to persons who provide loan capital to the business. A charge **secured** over a company's assets gives to the creditor (called the 'chargee') a prior claim over unsecured creditors (and may give him priority over other secured creditors) to payment of his debt out of those assets. Charges are of two kinds, fixed and floating.

3.2 Fixed charges

A **fixed charge** is a form of protection given to secured creditors relating to specific assets of a company. It attaches to the relevant asset as soon as the charge is created. By its nature a fixed charge is best suited to fixed assets which the company is likely to retain for a long period.

A company is not permitted to deal with, or dispose of, assets that are subject to a fixed charge without the consent of the chargeholder. If the company does dispose of the asset it will either repay the secured debt out of the proceeds of sale so that the charge is discharged at the time of sale, or transfer the asset to the purchaser still subject to the charge.

The charge grants the holder the right of enforcement against the identified asset in the event of default in repayment so that the creditor may realise the asset to meet the debt owed. Fixed charges rank first in order of priority in liquidation.

When he comes to enforce the charge, the chargee may find that the value of the asset does not fully discharge the debt. In a liquidation, the unpaid balance then falls to be an unsecured debt.

Note that if a fixed charge is created to secure a debt within six months before a company becomes insolvent, then it **may** be invalid as a preference (see Chapter 8).

3.3 Floating charges

Unlike a fixed charge, a floating charge permits a company to deal with the charged assets without the permission of the chargeholder until such time as the charge crystallises (thereby becoming a fixed charge). The nature of a floating charge can be described as

- A charge on a class of assets of a company, present and future

- Which class is, in the ordinary course of the company's business, changing from time to time and

- Until the holders enforce the charge, the company may carry on business and deal with the assets charged.

A floating charge is often created by express words but no special form of words is essential. If a company gives to a chargee rights over its assets while retaining freedom to deal with them in the ordinary course of business, that will be a charge which 'floats'. The particular assets subject to a floating charge cannot be identified until the charge attaches by **crystallisation**, at which point the floating charge is converted into a fixed charge on the company's assets. A floating charge is not restricted however to current assets such as book debts or stock in trade. A floating charge over 'the undertaking and assets' of a company (the most common type) applies to future as well as to current assets. For this reason it is not possible to identify the assets to which a floating charge relates (until crystallisation).

Events causing crystallisation are as follows.

- The **liquidation** of the company

- **Cessation** of the company's **business** (which may occur on the crystallisation of another floating charge)

- **Active intervention** by the chargee, generally by way of appointing a receiver

- Any **event specified** in the charge, such as non-payment of interest on the due date or notice given by the chargee that the charge is converted into a fixed charge (on whatever assets of the relevant class are owned by the company at the time of the giving of notice)

A charge may provide for automatic crystallisation when a **specified event** – such as a breach of some term by the company – occurs, whether or not the chargee learns of the event and whether or not the chargee wants to enforce the charge as a result of the event. If the relevant clause specifies that, on the event happening, the floating charge is converted to a fixed one, then it is likely to be valid. However, if the clause provides only that a company is to cease to deal with charged assets on the occurrence of a particular event, it may not be valid.

3.4 Identification of charges as fixed or floating

It is not always immediately apparent whether a charge is fixed or floating and whatever **label** is given to it by the parties is **not conclusive**. Chargees often do not wish to identify a charge as being floating when it was created since this means that, if a receiver is appointed, preferential creditors must first be paid out of the charged assets (s 40 IA 1986).

The general rule is that a charge over assets will not be registered as fixed if it envisages that the company will still be able to deal with the charged assets without reference to the chargee.

Charges expressed to be fixed but which cover present and future book debts are particularly problematic. In the relatively recent landmark case of *National Westminster Bank plc v Spectrum Plus Limited 2005*, the House of Lords made it clear that, although a fixed charge over book debts is conceptually possible, if the chargor retains the right to deal with the book debts in the ordinary course of business in any way (including being able to withdraw amounts from a designated account into which collected book debts have had to be paid), then the charge (whatever it is called) will be a floating charge. In order to be a fixed charge, it is likely that the chargor must be prevented from dealing with the book debts altogether, perhaps by assigning them to the chargee or having to pay collected debts into a 'blocked account' with the chargee (essentially requiring the chargee's consent to any withdrawals).

Additionally a floating charge, if created within **twelve months** before liquidation, may become **void** automatically on liquidation (s 245 IA 1986).

3.5 Comparison of fixed and floating charges

A fixed charge is normally the more satisfactory form of security since it confers immediate rights over identified assets. However, a floating charge has some advantage in being applicable to current assets which may be easier to realise than fixed assets subject to a fixed charge. If for example a company becomes insolvent, it may be easier to sell its stock than its empty factory.

The principal **disadvantages** of floating charges are as follows.

- The holder of a floating charge cannot be certain until the charge crystallises (often through the company failing) which assets will form his security.

- Even when a floating charge has crystallised over an identified pool of assets the chargee may find himself **postponed** to the claim of other creditors as follows.

  - A **judgment creditor** or landlord who has seized goods and sold them may retain the proceeds if received before the appointment of the debentureholder's receiver (s 183 IA).

  - **Preferential debts** (for example remuneration and holiday pay owed to employees) may be paid out of assets subject to a floating charge unless there are other uncharged assets available for this purpose (ss 40 and 175 IA).

  - The holder of a **fixed charge** over the same assets will usually have priority over a floating charge on those assets even if that charge was created before the fixed charge (see below).

  - A creditor may have sold goods and delivered them to the company on condition that he is to retain legal ownership until he has been paid (a **Romalpa** clause).

  - The Enterprise Act 2002 also introduced a clause into the Insolvency Act 1986 stating that a **'prescribed part'** of the company's net property will be **available to unsecured creditors**, regardless of any charges over that property. This introduces an element of 'proportionality' for unsecured creditors. The amount of money that is to be so prescribed, or **'ring-fenced'**, is set by the Secretary of State.

- As noted above, **a floating charge** may become invalid automatically if the company creates the charge to secure an existing debt and goes into liquidation within a year thereafter (s 245 IA); the period is only six months with a fixed charge.

Interactive question 4: Charges [Difficulty level: Easy]

1 What is the term used to describe the point at which a floating charge is converted into a fixed charge?

2 What is meant by 'ring-fencing'?

See **Answer** at the end of this chapter.

3.6 Priority of charges

Where different charges over the **same** property are given to different creditors, their priority must be determined. Thus, if charges are created over the same property to secure a debt of £5,000 to X and £7,000 to Y and the property is sold yielding only £10,000 then either X or Y is paid in full and the other receives only the balance remaining out of £10,000 realised from the security (unless they rank equally).

Leaving aside the question of registration (discussed below), the main points to remember in connection with the priority of any charges are as follows:

- Legal charges rank according to the order of creation (ie the one created first takes priority).

- Equitable charges also take priority according to the order of creation.

- A legal charge created before an equitable one has priority.

- An equitable charge created before a legal charge will only take priority over the latter if, when the latter was created, the legal chargee had notice of the equitable charge.

A creditor to whom a floating charge is given may seek to protect himself against losing his priority, by including in the terms of his floating charge a prohibition against the company creating a fixed charge over the same property, which would otherwise take priority (sometimes called a 'negative pledge clause'). In the absence of such a clause, however, the fixed charge will rank first since, although created later, it attaches to the property at the time of creation (whereas the floating charge attaches at the time of crystallisation). Once a floating charge has crystallised it becomes a fixed charge and a fixed charge created subsequently ranks after it.

3.7 Registration of charges

A company must keep available for inspection

- A copy of every instrument creating a charge which is required to be registered and

- A register of charges, listing all fixed and floating charges and giving the names of the chargees, the amount of the charge and a short description of the property charged

either at the company's registered office or at another place specified in regulations and notified to the Registrar. They must be available for inspection by any creditor or member free of charge and by any other person on payment of a fee.

When a company creates a charge specified in the Act, it must also deliver prescribed particulars, together with the instrument by which the charge is created or evidenced, to the Registrar (s 860) within 21 days, beginning on the day after the charge is created (s 870). Registration may, alternatively, be effected by a person interested in the charge, rather than the company.

The Registrar enters details of the charge in the register (including its date, the name of the chargee, the amount secured and short particulars of the property charged). He then issues a **certificate of registration** of the charge, which is conclusive evidence that the registration requirements have been satisfied. The company must then endorse a copy of that certificate on any debenture issued by the company thereafter, the payment of which is secured by the registered charge (s 865).

Failure to register is an offence punishable by fine, although the court may extend the period for registration where it is satisfied that the failure (or mistake) was inadvertent or not likely to prejudice the company's creditors or shareholders, or otherwise just and equitable (s 873).

Failure to register will also affect the validity of the charge. Non-compliance with s 860 renders the charge **void** against any

- Liquidator
- Administrator and
- Creditor

of the company. The money secured by the (void) charge is then immediately payable.

3.8 Lender's remedies

An unsecured creditor may sue the company for the debt or apply to the court for the appointment of an administrator or petition for a compulsory winding-up. A secured creditor may, in addition, appoint a receiver in respect of the property charged.

Liquidation, administration and receivership are addressed in Chapter 8.

Summary and Self-test

Summary

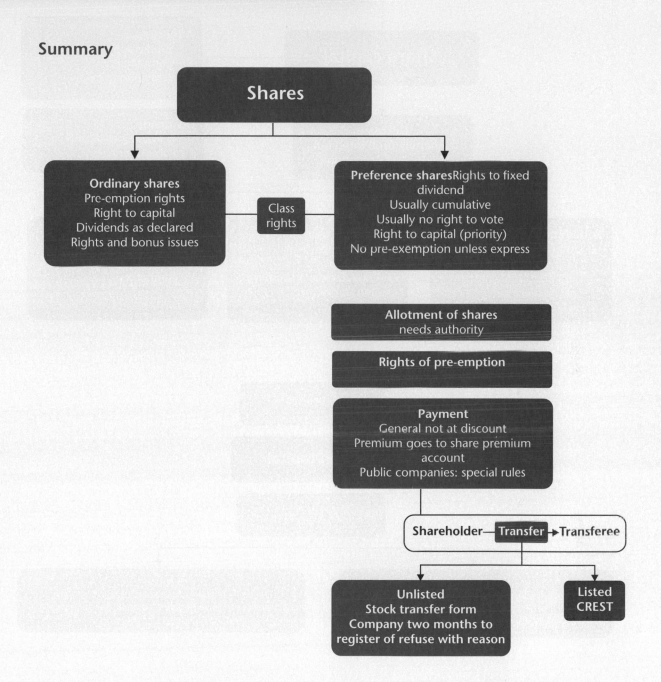

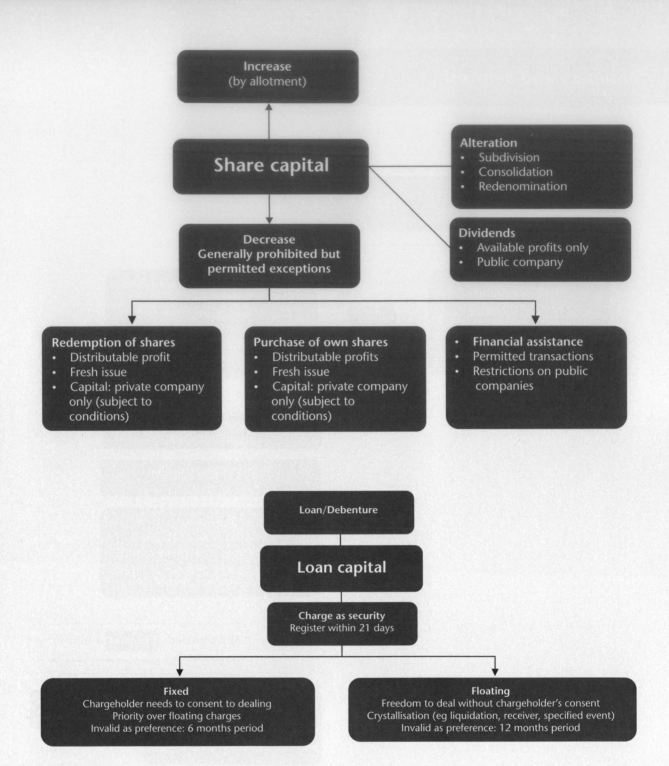

Increase
(by allotment)

Share capital

Alteration
- Subdivision
- Consolidation
- Redenomination

Decrease
Generally prohibited but
permitted exceptions

Dividends
- Available profits only
- Public company

Redemption of shares
- Distributable profit
- Fresh issue
- Capital: private company
  only (subject to
  conditions)

Purchase of own shares
- Distributable profits
- Fresh issue
- Capital: private company
  only (subject to
  conditions)

- **Financial assistance**
- Permitted transactions
- Restrictions on public
  companies

Loan/Debenture

Loan capital

Charge as security
Register within 21 days

Fixed
Chargeholder needs to consent to dealing
Priority over floating charges
Invalid as preference: 6 months period

Floating
Freedom to deal without chargeholder's consent
Crystallisation (eg liquidation, receiver, specified event)
Invalid as preference: 12 months period

ICAEW

Self-test

Answer the following questions.

1   If a company fails to pay preference shareholders their dividend, they can bring a court action to compel the company to pay the dividend.

☐ True   ☐ False

2   Which of the following are rights of preference shareholders (unless excluded by the articles)?

A   The right to receive a dividend is cumulative.

B   If the company goes into liquidation, preference shareholders are entitled to claim all arrears of dividend from the liquidator.

C   As well as rights to their preference dividends, preference shareholders can share equally in dividends payable to ordinary shareholders.

D   Preference shareholders have a priority right over ordinary shares for the return of their capital.

E   Preference shareholders have equal voting rights to ordinary shareholders.

3   What is meant by 'called-up share capital'?

4   What is the majority of the relevant class required to consent to a variation of class rights?

☐ 51%   ☐ 75%

☐ 90%   ☐ 100%

5   What minimum percentage of shareholders in a class may apply to the court for a variation of class rights to be cancelled?

☐ 5%   ☐ 10%

☐ 15%   ☐ 20%

6   Where authority to allot shares is given to directors in the company's articles, what type of resolution is required to vary or renew that authority given that it results in an alteration of the articles?

7   **Fill in the blanks** in the statements below.

A .... issue is an allotment of additional shares to existing members in exchange for consideration payable by the members.

A .... issue is an allotment of additional shares to existing members where the consideration is effectively paid by using the company's reserves.

8   Do rights of pre-emption apply in the following cases?

A A bonus issue	☐ Yes	☐ No
B An allotment of ordinary shares for cash	☐ Yes	☐ No
C An allotment of shares to be partly paid up otherwise than in cash	☐ Yes	☐ No
D An allotment of shares pursuant to an employees' share scheme	☐ Yes	☐ No

9   Can a company issue shares

A At a discount?	☐ Yes	☐ No
B At a premium?	☐ Yes	☐ No
C Otherwise than for cash?	☐ Yes	☐ No

10 A share premium account can be used for bonus issues of shares or discounts on the issue of debentures.

☐ True   ☐ False

11 When a company receives an instrument of transfer, it must register the transfer or give notice of refusal within what time period?

12 Name TWO ways in which a private company may lawfully reduce its share capital.

- ....

- ....

13 Name THREE ways in which a company's share capital can be altered (but not reduced).

- ....

- ....

- ....

14 What type of resolution is required to authorise the redemption of shares?

15 Name three safeguards that are required for a private company to be authorised to redeem or purchase its shares out of capital.

16 What restrictions, if any, apply to a private company providing financial assistance for the purchase of its shares?

17 Can a private company purchase its own shares where they are partly paid up, provided it has sufficient distributable profits?

18 **Fill in the blanks** in the statements below.

A public company cannot make a distribution if it would reduce the company's net assets to below the aggregate of its .... and ....

19 Which of the following are correct statements about the relationship between a company's ordinary shares and its debentures?

A   Debentures do not confer voting rights, whilst ordinary shares do.
B   The company must pay interest on debentures and dividends on ordinary shares.
C   A debentureholder takes priority over a member in liquidation.

20 What are the principal characteristics of a floating charge?

21 Company law requires a company to maintain a register of charges and to make it available for inspection by the public, not just members and creditors.

☐ True   ☐ False

22 In which of the following situations will crystallisation of a floating charge occur?

A   Liquidation of the company
B   Disposal by the company of the charged asset
C   Cessation of the company's business
D   After the giving of notice by the chargee if the contract so provides

23 Within how many days of creation do most charges need to be registered?

☐ 7 days   ☐ 21 days

☐ 14 days   ☐ 28 days

24 What particulars of a charge must the Registrar be sent when the charge is registered?

25 What main remedies are available to a secured debentureholder to enforce his security?

Now go back to the Learning Objectives in the Introduction. If you are satisfied you have achieved these objectives, please tick them off.

Answers to Interactive questions

Answer to Interactive question 1

A   Ordinary shares

B   Preference shares

C   Ordinary and preference shares

D   Ordinary and preference shares

Answer to Interactive question 2

A   No. Only a private company may do so.

B   Yes. Authority may be given either in the articles or by ordinary resolution.

C   No. Shares cannot be allotted at a discount.

D   Yes. Shares may be allotted at a premium.

Answer to Interactive question 3

	Public company	Private company
A	No	Yes
B	No	Yes
C	No	Yes
D	Yes	Yes

Answer to Interactive question 4

1   Crystallisation

2   A certain percentage (prescribed by the Secretary of State) of a company's net property is 'ring-fenced' and made available for unsecured creditors, notwithstanding any charges over that property.

1 False. The company may decide not to pay any dividend, or may be unable to because it does not have any distributable profits. What the preference shareholders have is a right to receive their dividends before other dividends are paid or declared.

2 A and E are implied rights; the others have to be stated explicitly.

3 A company's called-up share capital is so much of the share capital as equals the aggregate amount of the calls made on its shares plus share capital that is paid up without being called and share capital that is to be paid at a specified future date.

4 75%. A special resolution of the relevant class or written consent from at least 75% in nominal value of the issued shares of that class.

5 The holders of at least 15% of the issued shares of the class in question (who have not themselves consented to the variation)

6 An ordinary resolution, even though an alteration in the articles takes place (which would normally require a special resolution). Remember that authority to allot need not be given in the articles, it can be given by ordinary resolution.

7 A **rights** issue is an allotment of additional shares to existing members in exchange for consideration payable by the members.

A **bonus** issue is an allotment of additional shares to existing members where the consideration is effectively paid by using the company's reserves.

8 A No
   B Yes
   C No
   D No

9 A At a discount, no

   B At a premium, yes

   C Otherwise than for cash, yes. However note that the non-cash consideration must be independently valued in the case of a public company

10 True

11 Two months

12 • By a special resolution approved by the court
   • By a special resolution supported by a directors' solvency statement

13 • Allotment of more shares
   • Subdivision
   • Consolidation

14 An ordinary resolution

15 A directors' statement
   An auditors' report
   A special resolution
   Public notice of the proposed payment

16 None

17 No, a company can only purchase its own shares when they are fully paid

18 Called-up share capital and undistributable reserves

19 A and C are correct. Whilst the company has a contractual duty to pay interest on debentures, there is no necessity for it to pay dividends on shares. B is therefore incorrect.

20   A floating charge can be described as:

- A charge on a class of assets, present and future

- Which class is in the ordinary course of the company's business changing from time to time

- Until the holders enforce the charge, the company may carry on business and deal with the assets charged

21   True

22   A, C and D are true. As the charge does not attach to the asset until crystallisation, B is untrue.

23   21 days

24   • A copy of the charge
      • The date that the charge was created
      • The amount of the debt which it secures
      • The property to which the charge applies
      • The person entitled to it

25   • Take possession of the asset subject to the charge and sell it
      • Appoint a receiver of it

CHAPTER 8

Insolvency law: corporate and personal

Introduction

Examination context

Topic List

Summary and Self-test

Answers to Interactive questions

Answers to Self-test

Introduction

Learning objectives

Tick off

- To recognise when administration of a company might be appropriate and how it is achieved ☐

- To know how the winding up of a company is brought about and what happens in a liquidation ☐

- To understand the rationale for and workings of company voluntary arrangements ☐

- To understand issues relating to personal bankruptcy that can have implications for sole traders, partners and directors ☐

- To understand the rationale for and workings of individual voluntary arrangements ☐

Specific syllabus references for this chapter are: 2n and o.

Syllabus links

Chapter 5 addressed how a company is formed. This chapter looks at the termination of a company by winding-up and dissolution (but also compulsory voluntary arrangements and administration, which are both designed to avoid termination). In discussing the rights of secured and unsecured creditors, it also follows Chapter 7 where you studied debentures and company charges.

Examination context

The legal issues discussed in this chapter could be examined in conjunction with other areas of company law, for example the incorporation of a company, fraudulent and wrongful trading and financing by loan capital. You might be asked to advise on appropriate courses of action available to members or creditors in a scenario involving a company in financial difficulties. An awareness of personal bankruptcy and individual voluntary arrangements may be needed in the context of discussing partners' liabilities.

In the assessment, candidates may be required to:

- Identify the nature and function of administration, receivership and company voluntary arrangements

- Identify the principal means of termination of companies, including voluntary and compulsory winding-up

- Describe the priorities on a liquidation of a distribution of assets, including the rights of creditors and employees

- Identify the main implications of bankruptcy and individual voluntary arrangements

When a company is in financial difficulties, there are several courses of action open to its members and creditors. Some are aimed at rescuing the company as a going concern, others are aimed at bringing the life of the company to an end, whether insolvent or not. Thus administration is designed to rescue the company as a going concern or, at least, to secure a better result for the company's creditors as a whole than would be likely on a winding-up. A secured creditor may appoint a receiver to realise the charged assets and satisfy the debt secured. Company voluntary arrangements are also designed to rescue the company and prevent it from being wound up. Liquidation, on the other hand, is the act of terminating the company's life and winding up its business.

1 Administration

Section overview

- Administration is relevant where a company is in financial difficulties but not necessarily insolvent or close to insolvency.

- Administration results in a moratorium on actions against the company.

- An administration order is an order of the court which puts an insolvency practitioner in control of the company, principally to insulate the company from its creditors and with a view to rescuing the company as a going concern.

1.1 The purpose of administration

The purpose of administration, originally set out in the Insolvency Act 1986 ('IA '86') was substantially revised by the Enterprise Act 2002. The law governing administration can be found in the new schedule B1 to the IA '86. The role of the administrator is now to carry out the following, in the order set out:

- To rescue the company as a going concern.

- If this is not reasonably practicable, to achieve a better result for the company's creditors as a whole than would be likely with a winding-up.

- If neither is reasonably practicable, and provided the administrator does not unnecessarily harm the interests of the creditors as a whole, then to realise the company's assets to make a distribution to one or more preferential or secured creditors.

  (The term 'unnecessarily harm' is not defined and will no doubt be tested in the courts before its meaning is made clear.) Where there are no funds available for the unsecured creditors, the administrator will realise the company's assets and make payments to preferential creditors, and fixed and floating chargeholders, and will arrange for the company to be placed into creditors' voluntary liquidation.

1.2 Appointment of an administrator

An administrator is appointed either by the court or out of court according to the following requirements.

A court must be satisfied that the company is, or is likely to become, unable to pay its debts and that the order is reasonably likely to achieve the purpose of the administration.

Applicant		Appointment by court	Appointment out of court
Company	Ordinary resolution	Apply to the court and show that	Cannot appoint in specified circumstances, including where the company is already in liquidation or administration or where applications are pending.
Directors (this is the most usual type of appointment)	Majority decision	• The company is or is likely to be unable to pay its debts and • An administration order is reasonably likely to achieve the purpose of administration Must give notice of application to QFCH (below) who may intervene	Otherwise must give five days' prior notice to any QFCH. Must file at the court • Notice of the intended appointment and actual appointment

Applicant	Appointment by court	Appointment out of court
		• Statutory declarations that the company is likely to become unable to pay its debts and as to the appointment being lawfully and properly made • Statement from administrator that purpose of administration reasonably likely to be achieved and that he consents to the appointment.
One or more creditors		Not applicable.
Qualifying Floating Charge Holder (QFCH) (ie at least one floating charge which on its own or together with other fixed or floating charges amounts to a charge over the whole or substantially the whole of the company's property. The floating charge must contain power to appoint an administrator (or administrative receiver)).	Must show that • The floating charge is a qualifying floating charge and • It is enforceable A QFCH may apply even if the company is in liquidation Must notify any other QFCH	Must give two days' prior notice to any prior QFCH before any appointment is made. Must file in court • Notice of appointment • Statutory declaration as to lawfulness of appointment and enforceability of the charge • Statement by administrator that purpose of administration likely to be achieved and that he consents to the appointment No appointment can be made out of court if the company is in liquidation or administration (or administrative receivership)

Worked example: Petition for administration order

A has sold goods worth £29,567 to B Ltd on credit. B Ltd has exceeded the credit terms extended. A has discovered that the management of B Ltd is experiencing difficulties, but believes that the business is sound and that the debt could be paid if the business was managed properly. A is also aware that B Ltd has a loan from the bank which is secured by a floating charge.

A suspects that the bank might seek to wind up the company and fears that this might mean that the unsecured debts may not be paid. A therefore applies to the court for an administration order so that debt collection will be frozen while an action plan is implemented to ensure that debts can be paid.

1.3 The duties of the administrator

As soon as he takes office, the administrator must take control of the company's property and use his powers to manage the company in accordance with any proposals that have been approved by a creditors' meeting or according to any directions given by the court. In particular, he must take a number of steps including the following:

Timescale	Event
Within 7 days	File notice of his appointment with the Registrar of Companies
	Require any of the company's officers and employees to provide a statement of affairs (who have 11 days to comply with any such request)

Timescale	Event
Within 8 weeks	Submit a statement of his proposals for achieving the aim of administration to • The Registrar • The company's creditors • The company's members
Within 10 weeks	Hold a creditors' meeting (unless he considers there to be insufficient property to make a distribution to unsecured creditors over and above the 'ring-fenced asset distribution' set out in the Act and ≥ 10% creditors do not require one regardless). The creditors may either accept the proposals or reject them (in which case the court may make any order it sees fit, including the termination of the administrator's appointment).
One year after appointment	The administrator's appointment is terminated unless extended by the court or (once only) by a prescribed majority of the creditors.

1.4 The consequences of administration

The administrator takes on the powers previously enjoyed by the directors and generally 'may do anything necessarily expedient for the management of the affairs, business and property of the company' (s 59 (1) IA '86). The administrator's powers are set out in Schedule 1 IA'86. Specifically, he may

• Remove or appoint a director

• Call a meeting of members or creditors

• Apply to court for directions regarding the carrying out of his functions

• Make payments to secured or preferential creditors

• Make payments to unsecured creditors, if the administrator feels that to pay the unsecured creditor will assist the achievement of the administration (for example, if the company has been denied further supplies by a major supplier unless payment is tendered), and otherwise with the permission of the court

• Present or defend a petition for the winding up of the company

Any creditor or member of the company may apply to the court if they feel that the administrator has acted or will act in a way that has harmed or will harm his interest. The court may take various actions against the administrator.

During the period of administration and from the presenting of a petition for an administration order, the following consequences take effect:

Moratorium	There can be • No resolution or court order to wind up the company • No enforcement of fixed charges or other security over the company's property (except with the consent of the administrator or the court) • No recovery of property which the company has on a HP or leasing arrangement or enforcement of retention clauses (without the consent of the administrator or the court) • No other legal proceedings (including forfeiture of a lease) can be commenced against the company (except with the consent of the administrator or the court)
Assets subject to a floating charge	The administrator can sell property which is subject to a floating charge and use the proceeds for the business without obtaining the chargee's consent (§ 70 Sch B1 IA'86)

Assets on HP or subject to fixed charge	The administrator can sell such assets with approval of the court and proceeds must be used to pay off the owner or chargee (§ 72 Sch B1 IA'86)
Directors	Directors' powers are suspended and the administrator may remove or appoint directors
Employees	Employees are not automatically dismissed (since the administrator is the agent of the company which continues to be the employer) but the administrator may terminate contracts of employment
Transactions at an undervalue and preferences	These may be avoided. See section 4.5 below

1.5 Advantages of administration

Administration may be preferable to liquidation for the following reasons:

- For the **company**, it does not necessarily cease to exist at the end of the process and it also provides temporary relief from creditors to allow breathing space to formulate rescue plans.

- For the **members**, as they will continue to have shares in the company. If the administration is successful, regenerating the business should enhance share value and will restore any income from the business.

- For the **creditors**, who should obtain a return in relation to their past debts. Any creditor may apply to the court for an administration order and qualifying floating chargeholders may appoint an administrator without reference to the court. It may also be in the interests of the creditors to have a continued business relationship with the company once the business has been turned around.

2 Receivership

Section overview

- A secured creditor with a charge over land usually has the power to appoint a receiver in the event of the borrower's default.

- A receiver will realise the charged asset in order to pay off the chargeholder's debt.

- With some exceptions, administrative receivers can no longer be appointed by floating chargeholders.

The term 'receiver' has, somewhat confusingly, come to be used to denote two types of office, one of which was virtually abolished by changes made to the Insolvency Act 1986 by the Enterprise Act 2002, whilst the other remains.

2.1 Administrative receiver

An 'administrative receiver' is appointed by a floating chargeholder and is essentially a manager with control over the whole, or substantial part, of the company's property and wide powers over its business. Subject to any conflicting provision contained in the charge document, his powers are extensive and include the power to borrow, to take legal proceedings, to appoint professional advisers and to pay off creditors with preferential rights (Sch 1 IA '86). However, with some exceptions, administrative receivers can no longer be appointed by holders of floating charges created on or after 15 September 2003. As a result, administration and company voluntary arrangements are much more likely to be adopted in the case of company insolvency, as alternatives to liquidation.

2.2 Fixed charge receiver

The term 'receiver' may also indicate a 'non-administrative receiver' or 'LPA receiver' (so-called because such receivers were traditionally appointed under the Law of Property Act 1925). The scope for these receivers was not curtailed by the Enterprise Act 2002 and, on the contrary, some commentators report rising activity in the receivership market.

A receiver may be appointed by the holder of a fixed charge over land in the event of the borrower's default. His role is to collect rent and/or sell the property. Unlike liquidators, administrators and trustees in bankruptcy, a receiver does not need to be a qualified insolvency practitioner and, in practice, will often be a surveyor or other property specialist. Although his main concern is to realise the property for the benefit of the lender, he also owes a duty of care to the borrower to act prudently and to have regard to his interests (but not to go to extensive lengths to enhance the value of the property before selling it, by pursuing planning applications or renewing leases, for example).

The appointment of a receiver may provide a relatively quick and inexpensive remedy for a lender and may be attractive where a straightforward exercise of his power of sale is not appropriate. Although the appointment of a receiver is often followed by liquidation, it is quite possible for the company to remain solvent and to continue in business once the receiver has performed his duties and vacated office. The appointment of a receiver will normally cause floating charges to crystallise and become fixed charges (although they are ranked as floating charges on a winding up, since they were created as such).

2.3 Relationship between administration, administrative receivership and receivership

Where a company is in administrative receivership, an administrator can only be appointed by the court and only in specific circumstances. The appointment of an administrator automatically dismisses the administrative receiver and prevents any future appointment of an administrative receiver.

Where a LPA receiver has been appointed, an administrator can still be appointed. In such cases, the administrator is entitled to require the LPA receiver to vacate office. Once a company is in administration, fixed chargeholders cannot enforce their security, except with the consent of the administrator or the court.

3 Company Voluntary Arrangements

Section overview

- Company Voluntary Arrangements (CVAs) were introduced by the Insolvency Act 1986 and are intended to avoid a company being wound up.

- A CVA is an agreement between the company and its creditors, which sets out how the company's debts are to be paid and in what proportions.

- A company is entitled to continue trading for the duration of the CVA.

A CVA may comprise either one or both of a 'composition of debts' (where the company agrees to pay a limited proportion of its total debt, eg 60p in the pound) or a 'scheme of arrangement' (where the company agrees to pay its debts over a defined period, typically 3–5 years). A CVA may result in one or more creditors taking an interest in the company by way of a debt-equity swap.

3.1 The procedure

In practice, a CVA is often part of the administration process but it need not be. A company may appoint a nominee, who will be a qualified insolvency practitioner, to consider its proposals for a CVA. This may be at any time, whether the company is solvent or not, and the nominee will be required to report to the court as to whether he considers the proposed CVA has a reasonable prospect of being approved and implemented. If insolvency proceedings have already commenced, however, the procedure may be initiated by an administrator or liquidator, who will then act as nominee.

Meetings of the company's creditors, of whose claim the nominee has notice, and its members must then be called to consider the proposed CVA. Approval is required as follows:

- A simple majority in value of the members voting in person or by proxy or by written resolution

- A majority of more than 75% in value of creditors voting in person or proxy (provided that not more than half in value of the creditors not connected with the company vote against it)

If the members' and creditors' meetings arrive at different results, the resolution of the creditors will prevail, although any member may apply to the court to challenge approval of a CVA.

If approved, the CVA becomes binding on all unsecured creditors who were entitled to vote, whether or not they received notice (including unknown creditors). Preferred creditors, however, retain their priority, and secured creditors remain entitled to enforce their security against the company (unless they agree otherwise). Approval of the CVA must be reported to the court and the court may discharge any administration or winding up order previously made.

Any creditor entitled to vote may also challenge the approval of a CVA within 28 days of the court being notified of the results of the creditors' and members' meetings. Such a challenge must be on the grounds:

- That the CVA unfairly prejudices his interests and/or

- That there has been some material irregularity at or in relation to the meetings at which the proposed CVA was considered

In the event of a successful challenge, the court may revoke or suspend the approval of the CVA and/or give directions regarding further meetings to consider a revised proposal or to reconsider the original proposal.

Once approved (and if not successfully challenged), the nominee acts as the supervisor and implements the CVA.

3.2 Moratorium

By important changes introduced by the Insolvency Act 2000, where the directors of a small company wish to propose a CVA, they may apply for a short moratorium, during which they can prepare and submit a proposal to their creditors. (This gave small companies the significant advantage of a 'breathing space' which, otherwise, was only available by entering into administration.)

Prescribed documents must be submitted to the court, including the proposed CVA, a statement of the company's affairs and confirmation that the nominee believes the proposal to have a reasonable prospect of being approved and implemented. Once these documents are filed, a moratorium of 28 days will come into effect, subject to extension of up to two months with the agreement of both the members and creditors' meetings. The existence of the moratorium must be advertised and stated on all business documents. It should also be notified to the Registrar of Companies.

Generally speaking, no winding up or other insolvency proceedings can be commenced during the moratorium period. Nor can security over the company's property be enforced, or any legal process undertaken. Any winding up petitions presented prior to the moratorium will be stayed and a floating charge cannot crystallise during the moratorium. The company cannot requisition or hold any meeting without the consent of the nominee or court and it can only sell property (other than in the ordinary course of its business), or pay off pre-moratorium debts, with the approval of the nominee or creditors' committee (if there is one) and, if the property is charged, the consent of the charge-holder or court. The nominee must monitor the company's affairs during the moratorium and the moratorium will be terminated if the nominee withdraws his consent to act, provided he does so properly and on specified grounds.

3.3 Ability to continue trading

The company may continue trading during the life of a CVA, although existing creditors are likely to renegotiate the terms of their dealings with the company and seek greater protection, for example by obtaining directors' personal guarantees of new liabilities and including retention of title clauses in contracts for the sale of goods.

4 Liquidation

Section overview

- Winding up, or liquidation, is the process of terminating the life of a company and is carried out by a liquidator.

- A company is most likely to be wound up where it has become insolvent.

- Liquidation may proceed as a members' voluntary winding up (where the company is solvent) or as a creditors' voluntary winding up.

- Alternatively, liquidation may be imposed compulsorily on the company by the court.

- The liquidator is bound to realise the company's assets and apply the proceeds in a particular order, including distributing any surplus to contributories once creditors have been satisfied.

4.1 Members' voluntary liquidation

Subject to the requirement for a declaration of solvency (see below), the members may resolve to wind up the company either:

- By **ordinary resolution** where the articles provide for dissolution on the expiry of a fixed term or the happening of a specified event (this is rare) or

- By **special resolution** for any reason whatsoever

The winding up is deemed to commence when the resolution is passed and notice must be given in the *Gazette* within 14 days.

A voluntary winding up is a members' voluntary winding up only if the directors make and deliver to the registrar a **declaration of solvency** (s 89 IA '86).

This is a statutory declaration that the directors have made full enquiry into the affairs of the company and are of the opinion that it will be able to pay its debts in full, together with interest (at the applicable rate), within a specified period not exceeding 12 months. It is a **criminal offence** punishable by fine or imprisonment for a director to make a declaration of solvency without having reasonable grounds for it. The declaration must

- Be made by all the directors or, if there are more than two, by a majority of them

- Include a statement of the company's assets and liabilities as at the latest practicable date before the declaration is made.

The declaration must be:

- Made not more than five weeks before the resolution to wind up is passed and
- Delivered to the registrar within 15 days after the meeting (s 89 IA '86).

The company may appoint a liquidator by passing an ordinary resolution to that effect. If the liquidator later concludes that the company will be unable to pay its debts, he must call a meeting of creditors and lay before them a statement of assets and liabilities (s 95 IA '86).

In a members' voluntary winding up the creditors play no part, since the assumption is that their debts will be paid in full. However, a members' voluntary liquidation may become a creditors' voluntary liquidation where the liquidation process is not progressing to the satisfaction of the company's creditors.

4.2 Creditors' voluntary liquidation

Where a company intends to wind up voluntarily (and passes an ordinary or special resolution to that effect as the case may be) but the directors are unable to make a declaration of solvency, the liquidation proceeds as a creditors' voluntary winding up, even if in the end the company pays its debts in full (s 96 IA '86). Despite its label, this type of liquidation is not initiated by the creditors.

The company must convene a meeting of creditors within 14 days of the proposed members' resolution to wind up the company, giving at least seven days' written notice of this meeting. The notice must be advertised in the *Gazette* and two local newspapers. The notice must either

- Give the name and address of a qualified insolvency practitioner to whom the creditors can apply before the meeting for information about the company, *or*

- State where a list of creditors can be inspected.

One of the directors presides at the creditors' meeting and lays before it a full statement of the company's affairs and a list of creditors with the amounts owing to them. The members and the creditors are entitled to nominate a liquidator. If the creditors nominate a different person to be liquidator, their choice prevails over the nomination by the members. If they do not appoint one, it will be the members' nominee who will take office. The creditors may also appoint a liquidation committee to act with the liquidator.

It may be the case that the members' nominee takes office as liquidator pending the creditors' meeting. During this period the powers of the members' nominee as liquidator are restricted to

- Taking control of the company's property

- Disposing of perishable or other goods which might diminish in value if not disposed of immediately, and

- Doing all other things necessary for the protection of the company's assets.

This prevents an obliging liquidator selling assets to a new company formed by the members of the insolvent company, in order to defeat the claims of the creditors at minimum cost and enable the same people to continue in business until the next insolvency supervenes. Such a transaction is referred to as 'centrebinding' following *Re Centrebind Ltd 1966*.

> *Re Centrebind Ltd 1966*
>
> *The facts:* The directors convened a general meeting, without making a statutory declaration of solvency, but failed to call a creditors' meeting for the same or the next day, for which they were liable to pay a small fine. The liquidator chosen by the members had disposed of the assets before the creditors could appoint a liquidator. The creditors' liquidator challenged the sale of the assets (at a low price) as invalid.
>
> *Decision:* The first liquidator had been in office when he made the sale and so it was a valid exercise of the normal power of sale.

As a result of the restrictions introduced to prevent centrebinding (mentioned above), the members' liquidator is now required to apply to the court for leave if he wishes to perform any other act.

4.3 Compulsory liquidation

A company may be obliged to wind up by the court on the petition of, usually, a creditor or member. It tends to be a less straightforward and more time-consuming and expensive process than a voluntary winding-up. Around 90% of all compulsory liquidations follow a creditor's petition and most of these are on the grounds of the company's insolvency.

A petition may be brought for a compulsory winding up on one of seven statutory grounds (s 122 IA '86), the most significant of which are:

Ground	Explanation
That the company is unable to pay its debts (s 122 (1)(f))	A creditor must (in petitioning on the grounds that the company is unable to pay its debts) show either • That he is owed more than £750 and has served on the company at its registered office a written demand for payment and the company has neglected, either to pay the debt or to offer reasonable security for it within 21 days, *or* • That he has attempted to enforce a judgment against the company by execution on the company's property but it has failed to satisfy the debt, *or*

Ground	Explanation
	• That, taking into account the contingent and prospective liabilities of the company, it is unable to pay its debts as they fall due or that its assets are less than its liabilities.
That it is just and equitable to wind up the company (s 122(1)(g))	This ground is usually relied on by a member who is dissatisfied with the directors or controlling shareholders over the management of the company (for example, where there is management deadlock or where relations within a quasi-partnership break down). It must be shown that **no** other remedy is available. (This provision was discussed in Chapter 6.)

A member's petition to wind up the company on the grounds that it is just and equitable to do so, will only be considered if the company is solvent (otherwise he has nothing to gain from it) and he has been a registered shareholder for at least six of the last 18 months prior to the petition (subject to some exceptions).

The **BIS** (Department for Business, Innovation and Skills) may petition for the compulsory winding up of a company

- If a public company has not obtained a trading certificate within one year of incorporation

- Following a report by BIS inspectors that it is in the public interest and just and equitable for the company to be wound up.

On a compulsory winding up, the court will usually appoint the Official Receiver (an officer of the court) as liquidator, although he may be replaced by an insolvency practitioner at a later date. The Official Receiver **must investigate** (s 132) the causes of the failure of the company, and generally, its promotion, formation, business dealings and affairs.

The liquidation is deemed to have commenced at the time (possibly several months earlier) when the petition was first presented, with the following consequences:

- Any disposition of the company's property and any transfer of its shares subsequent to the commencement of liquidation is void unless the court orders otherwise.

- Any legal proceedings in progress against the company are halted (and none may be commenced) unless the court gives leave.

- Any seizure of the company's assets after commencement of liquidation is void.

- The employees of the company are automatically dismissed and the liquidator assumes the powers of management previously held by the directors.

- Any floating charge crystallises.

- The assets of the company may remain the company's legal property but under the liquidator's control, unless the court orders the assets to be vested in the liquidator.

- The business of the company may continue, but it is the liquidator's duty to continue it with a view only to realisation, for instance by sale as a going concern.

Worked example: Petition for compulsory liquidation

A has sold goods worth £29,567 to B on credit. B Ltd has exceeded the credit terms extended and A has presented B Ltd with a written demand to their registered office, which B Ltd has not responded to after a month. B Ltd have sold on the goods which they purchased from A and do not dispute the value of the invoice.

What action can A take?

A can petition the court for the compulsory winding up of the company because the company has failed to satisfy its demand for a debt of over £750 within 21 days. He will petition on the ground that the company is unable to pay its debts.

Interactive question 1: Insolvency [Difficulty level: Exam standard]

Zorro Ltd incorporated 15 years ago and is in the business of supplying pet foods and products to small retailers. After 13 successful years it borrowed £150,000 to expand its premises and the loan was secured by a fixed charge on those premises. Due to a nearby out-of town retail park completed 18 months ago, Zorro Ltd has suffered a significant downturn in its business. One of its regular suppliers of Bunny Mix, who often extended credit terms over short periods and who was also suffering due to the new retail park, has recently tried to recover a debt of £1,725 against the company but he has received no reply to his latest written demand 25 days ago. He is seriously concerned that he will never see his £1,725 again but he would rather see Zorro Ltd recover its fortunes in spite of the retail park.

1   Can he petition the court for a compulsory winding up?
2   Can he appoint an administrator in the hope that the company can be rescued?

See **Answer** at the end of this chapter.

4.4 The role of the liquidator

Once a liquidator is appointed, whether in a voluntary or a compulsory winding up, his role is to:

* Settle the list of contributories (ie members who have a liability to contribute in the event of a winding up)

* Collect and realise the company's assets

* Discharge the company's debts

* Redistribute any surplus to the contributories according to the entitlement rights attached to their shares.

On his appointment, the powers of the directors cease save to the extent that they are permitted to continue by the liquidator or (in a voluntary winding up) by the company or creditors as appropriate.

Once the liquidation is complete, the liquidator must act as follows:

* In a **voluntary winding up**, he must prepare an account showing how the winding up has been dealt with and lay it before a meeting of the members and/or creditors. Within the following week he should then file details with the Registrar who will enter the details on the company's file and the company will be deemed to be dissolved three months thereafter.

* In a **compulsory winding up**, the liquidator must go back to the court which then makes an order dissolving the company. He then files the order and the Registrar records on the company file that the company is dissolved as from the date of the order.

4.5 Avoidance of charges

In certain cases, charges or transactions entered into or debts incurred by the company may be invalidated, as follows:

Transaction	Explanation	
Charges	Charges not registered within 21 days are void against the liquidator and creditors (and the chargee becomes an unsecured creditor)	
Transactions at an undervalue	A transaction '**at an undervalue**' is a gift or a transaction in the **two years** prior to liquidation (or administration), by which the company gives consideration of greater value than it receives, for instance a sale at less than full market price (s 238 IA '86), **unless** the company enters into it	If at the time of the undervalue or preference the company was unable to pay its debts, or became so by reason of the transaction (save in the case of a

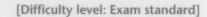

	• In **good faith** • For the **purpose of carrying on its business** • **Believing on reasonable grounds** that it will benefit the company
Preferences	A company '**gives preference**' to a creditor or guarantor of its debts if it does anything • By which his position will be benefited if the company goes into insolvent liquidation • And with the intention of producing that result • **Six months** before the commencement of liquidation with a person **unconnected** with the company or two years in the case of a connected person ('connected' generally means a director, shadow director or associate) (s 239 IA '86)
Floating charge	A floating charge created within 12 months prior to winding up (or 2 years if given to a connected person) may be void or voidable

preference with a connected person), and the company later goes into liquidation or administration, the liquidator or the administrator can apply to the court for an order to restore the position to what it would have been if no such transaction had taken place, for example by ordering the return of property or discharging any security.

You will recall that if the liquidator can show that the directors are guilty of wrongful or fraudulent trading the court may order that they be personally liable for some or all of the company's debts (ss 213, 214 IA '86).

Interactive question 2: Avoidance of charges [Difficulty level: Exam standard]

Trading Ltd has recently begun a process of liquidation (in February 2007) following resolutions by the members and creditors to wind up the company. Archibold and Duke, the two directors, have been researching insolvency on the internet and it has led them to be concerned over a number of transactions entered into by Trading Ltd over the past few years. They advise you that Trading Ltd has actually been unable to pay its debts since April 2006.

They ask for your advice as to whether the following transactions might be avoided by the liquidator.

A	A floating charge in favour of Adam plc for £100,000 created in March 2005	☐ Yes ☐ No
B	A sale of 10 cars in March 2005 for £80,000. Archibold and Duke knew that they were probably worth over £90,000 but they honestly believed that the sale would be in the best interest of keeping the company afloat	☐ Yes ☐ No
C	A purchase in August 2006 of some car spares for £10,000 which Archibold made as a bit of a favour for the vendor. He suspected that they were only worth £7,500	☐ Yes ☐ No
D	A loan that Duke made to the company a few years previously was paid off in June 2006	☐ Yes ☐ No

See **Answer** at the end of this chapter.

4.6 Priorities on liquidation

A liquidator in a compulsory winding up **must**, and in a voluntary winding up is **likely to**, adhere to the following prescribed order for distributing the company's assets:

	Priority	Explanation
1	Costs	Including the costs of getting in the assets, liquidator's remuneration and all costs incidental to the liquidation procedure
2	Preferential debts	• Employees' wages (for a prescribed period and subject to a prescribed maximum) • Accrued holiday pay • Contributions to an occupational pension fund These rank equally
3	Floating charges	Subject to ring-fencing (see below)
4	Unsecured ordinary creditors	A certain percentage of assets is 'ring-fenced' for unsecured creditors where there is a minimum fund for distribution of £10,000, namely 50% of the first £10,000 of floating charge realisations and 20% of the floating charge realisations thereafter (subject to a prescribed maximum)
5	Deferred debts	For example dividends declared but not paid and interest accrued on debts since liquidation
6	Members	Any surplus (meaning that the company is in fact solvent) is distributed to members according to their rights under the articles or the terms of issue of their shares

Note that secured creditors with fixed charges (and indeed floating charges) may appoint a receiver to sell the charged asset, passing any surplus to the liquidator. In the event of a shortfall they must prove for the balance as unsecured creditors. Note, however, that a floating charge holder who faces a shortfall on his secured debt (which is therefore treated as unsecured) cannot share in the ring fenced part available to unsecured creditors.

Interactive question 3: Priorities on liquidation

[Difficulty level: Exam standard]

Buffers Ltd has an issued share capital of 5,000 × £1 shares and is in compulsory liquidation. The liquidator has a fund of £8,500 available for distribution and needs to distribute the fund to settle the following claims so far as possible:

- The directors declared a dividend of 10p, six months ago but it has not been paid.

- The liquidation costs, including remuneration, amount to £2,500

- Moneylender plc had a floating charge over the company's stock in trade which has now crystallised and the value is £4,000

- The company's employees have been paid, with the exception of some accrued holiday pay worth £1,200

- Mr Staples, the local stationery supplier is an unsecured creditor and is owed £830.

It is clear that there will not be a surplus for distribution to the members.

A   Which debt will be discharged first?
B   Will Mr Staples receive all of the money owed to him?
C   Will the members receive the dividend?
D   Do the ring-fenced provisions apply?

See **Answer** at the end of this chapter.

Following dissolution of a company (by whatever means) its property vests in the Crown as *bona vacantia* (s 1012 CA '06), which means that there is no known person entitled to it. However the Crown has the power to disclaim it, in which case any interested person may apply to the court to have the property vested in them on such terms as the court sees fit.

5 Individual voluntary arrangements

Section overview

- An individual voluntary arrangement ('IVA') is an arrangement available to an individual (including sole traders and partners) to reach a compromise with his creditors, with the aim of avoiding bankruptcy.

- IVAs are governed by the Insolvency Act 1986 and supervised by licensed insolvency practitioners.

Sole traders and partners may well wish to pursue the option of an IVA in order to protect the survival of their business. An IVA normally provides for the debtor to pay reduced amounts towards his total debt over a period of, usually, five years. Once approved, an IVA binds *all* of the debtor's creditors and none may pay petition for bankruptcy.

5.1 The procedure

An individual may apply to the court for an interim order where he intends to submit a proposed arrangement to his creditors. This application need not include details of the proposed arrangement in full although it often will. Such an interim order effectively imposes a moratorium on actions against the debtor and creditors cannot take any action against him (although a secured creditor may continue to enforce his security against the debtor). The individual's nominee (who must be a licensed insolvency practitioner) is required to submit his comments on the proposal's chances of success.). The nominee must call a creditors' meeting (which need not be held in person), giving notice of:

- The proposals and the nominee's comments thereon
- A list of creditors
- A statement of affairs, ie a list of the debtor's assets and liabilities
- Details of the meeting including a form of proxy.

The creditors may reject the proposals or accept them (with or without modification) by a majority of 75% in value of those creditors who vote, either in person or proxy. Once approved, a **supervisor** is appointed (who is usually the nominee) to be responsible for supervising the scheme and distributing sums to the creditors. Upon completion of the IVA, assuming all its terms are complied with, the debtor is fully discharged from all liabilities contained in it.

Application may be made to the court on the basis that the terms of the IVA are unfairly prejudicial to a creditor or that there has been some material irregularity in relation to a meeting of the creditors. In addition, a creditor may petition the court for bankruptcy in exceptional circumstances, for example where the debtor fails to comply with the terms of the IVA.

(Note that an IVA can be made without the added protection of an interim court order and that there is also an alternative 'fast track' procedure available to post-bankruptcy IVAs where the Official Receiver is the proposed nominee. In such cases, the creditors receive the proposal on a 'take it or leave it' basis.)

5.2 Advantages and disadvantages of an IVA

The advantages of an IVA are as follows:

Advantages	
For the individual	• The sole trader is permitted to continue in business and to operate a normal bank account (but without an overdraft facility)
	• There is flexibility in drawing up the proposals to suit his personal and financial circumstances
	• He does not suffer the restrictions that would be imposed by bankruptcy, for example not being able to act as a director of a limited company
	• Details of IVAs are not published in the press as details of bankruptcy are
For the creditor	• It is essential that an IVA is considered as it is likely to give greater satisfaction to creditors than bankruptcy would
	• The costs of administering an IVA are significantly less than bankruptcy, thus enabling a higher return to creditors

However, there are some disadvantages, namely:

- The period of an IVA is usually five years, which is longer than the three years applicable in bankruptcy

- There is no opportunity for a trustee in bankruptcy to investigate the debtor's actions or the possibility of hidden assets.

Note that the debtor's home and assets are still at risk unless excluded from the IVA and that if the terms of the IVA are not complied with, he may still be made bankrupt.

6 Bankruptcy

Section overview

- A person may become bankrupt either by petitioning the court himself or by his creditor petitioning the court for bankruptcy.

- Bankruptcy is effectively the equivalent for a sole trader or partnership (or other individual) of a compulsory winding up in the case of a company.

- It should be considered as a last resort after IVAs.

6.1 The procedure

A petition is presented to the court either

- By the individual or
- By an unsecured creditor who is owed £750 or more (at the time the petition is presented) or
- By the supervisor of, or any person bound by, an approved IVA

The court hearing will normally take place at least 14 days after the service of the petition to give time for the debtor to file objections and for creditors to attend. If the court is satisfied that the debtor is unable to pay his debts as and when they fall due, it will make a bankruptcy order.

Where the debtor himself petitions for bankruptcy, the court will not make a bankruptcy order where

- The total unsecured bankruptcy debts would be less than £40,000

- The estate would be at least £4,000

- The debtor has not, in the previous five years either been made bankrupt or entered into a composition or scheme with his creditors, and

- It would be appropriate to appoint someone to make a report which may lead to approval of an IVA (s 273 IA '86).

The reason for this provision (which does not apply where a creditor petitions for bankruptcy) is to discourage bankruptcy, in favour of an IVA, where there is this level of value in the estate as against the total debt.

Where a creditor petitions for bankruptcy, he will be able to show that the debtor is unable to pay his debts, if he can show that

- He has served a statutory demand on the debtor that has not been satisfied or set aside within 21 days or

- His attempts to enforce a judgment order have not been satisfied.

The creditor may present a petition within the three week period following service of a statutory demand where the value of the property is likely to be diminished significantly during that period. In such cases an interim receiver is appointed, rather like a provisional liquidator. However, if a bankruptcy order is made, the debtor becomes an **undischarged bankrupt** and the order is advertised in the *Gazette* and in a local and/or national newspaper.

Also from the date of the order, the Official Receiver is appointed to administer the bankruptcy and to act as trustee of the bankrupt's estate, unless an insolvency practitioner is appointed to act as trustee (which is likely where the estate is sufficient to pay his fees and the creditors). The Official Receiver must investigate the debtor's financial affairs and must report to his creditors, and may report to the court. He will also give notice of the bankruptcy order to local authorities, utility suppliers, the land registry and any other relevant bodies or organisations. He must act to maximise the funds available to satisfy the creditors and then pay creditors with provable debts in a prescribed order, similar to the compulsory winding up of a company. If there is insufficient money available to pay all unsecured creditors, the trustee in bankruptcy will declare a dividend, ie so many pence in the pound, so that the creditors receive part-payment of their debts.

6.2 The effect of bankruptcy

Regardless of who petitions the court, once a bankruptcy order is made, the debtor becomes an undischarged bankrupt and is subject to a number of personal restrictions, for example

- He cannot act as a director of a company or an insolvency practitioner

- He faces criminal liability for failure to provide information or co-operate with the Official Receiver by handing over his property, for example

- Under ICAEW rules, he may not practise as a chartered accountant

The court may stay any action against the debtor from the date of the petition and, generally speaking, the bankrupt can no longer be sued by his creditors once the order is made. There are exceptions however, for example a secured creditor can still enforce his security.

The bankrupt's estate automatically vests in the trustee in bankruptcy (subject to the rights of secured creditors) and does not need any written contract or transfer of rights or property. The trustee in bankruptcy has extensive powers, although some are subject to the court's approval.

Note that the bankrupt's 'estate' is defined to **exclude**

- Such tools of the trade and other items as are necessary for use personally in his employment, business or vocation

- Such clothing and household provisions as are necessary to satisfy the basic domestic needs of the bankrupt and his family

- Property held by the bankrupt on trust for another person

- Certain tenancies protected in some way by legislation

6.3 Distribution to creditors

The trustee in bankruptcy must require the creditors to prove their debts (which they do by completing **proof forms**) and he will then rank them according to the prescribed order and make payments accordingly. The order is as follows:

	Debt	Explanation
1	Costs	The costs of realising the estate, the remuneration of the trustee and incidental expenses
2	Pre-preferential debts	As provided by certain statutory provisions, for example funeral expenses where the bankrupt is deceased
3	Preferential debts	Remuneration of employees (for a prescribed period and subject to a prescribed maximum) Sums payable in connection with occupational pension schemes Accrued holiday pay
4	Ordinary debts	Where the fund is insufficient to pay all unsecured creditors they rank equally
5	Interest	Creditors may prove for interest up to the date of bankruptcy (and therefore only if all preferential and ordinary creditors have been paid in full)
6	Postponed debts	For example a debt owed to the bankrupt's spouse
7	Surplus	Any surplus is returned to the bankrupt (this is of course unlikely)

Once the trustee has completed the distributions, he reports to the creditors who will usually release him from his trusteeship.

6.4 Discharge of bankruptcy

One year after the bankruptcy order, a bankruptcy is discharged (although he may be made subject to a **bankruptcy restrictions order or undertaking** for between 2 and 15 years where he was culpable to some extent for his insolvency). This means that all his debts are treated as discharged, all personal restrictions are lifted and effectively his slate has been wiped clean. However, there may remain a certain stigma attached to a discharged bankrupt and his credit history will have been damaged.

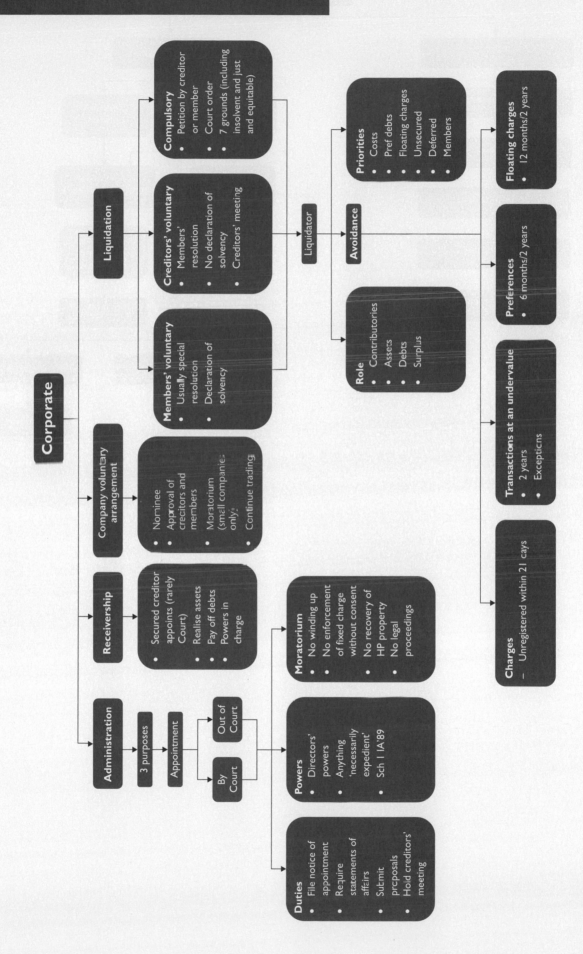

Corporate

Liquidation

Compulsory
- Petition by creditor or member
- Court order
- 7 grounds (including insolvent and just and equitable)

Creditors' voluntary
- Members' resolution
- No declaration of solvency
- Creditors' meeting

Members' voluntary
- Usually special resolution
- Declaration of solvency

Company voluntary arrangement
- Nominee
- Approval of creditors and members
- Moratorium (small companies only)
- Continue trading

Receivership
- Secured creditor appoints (rarely Court)
- Realise assets
- Pay off debts
- Powers in charge

Administration
- 3 purposes
- Appointment
  - Out of Court
  - By Court

Powers
- Directors' powers
- Anything 'necessarily expedient'
- Sch I IA'89

Moratorium
- No winding up
- No enforcement of fixed charge without consent
- No recovery of HP property
- No legal proceedings

Duties
- File notice of appointment
- Require statements of affairs
- Submit proposals
- Hold creditors' meeting

Liquidator

Role
- Contributories
- Assets
- Debts
- Surplus

Priorities
- Costs
- Pref debts
- Floating charges
- Unsecured
- Deferred
- Members

Avoidance

Floating charges
- 12 months/2 years

Preferences
- 6 months/2 years

Transactions at an undervalue
- 2 years
- Exceptions

Charges
- Unregistered within 21 days

CHAPTER 8

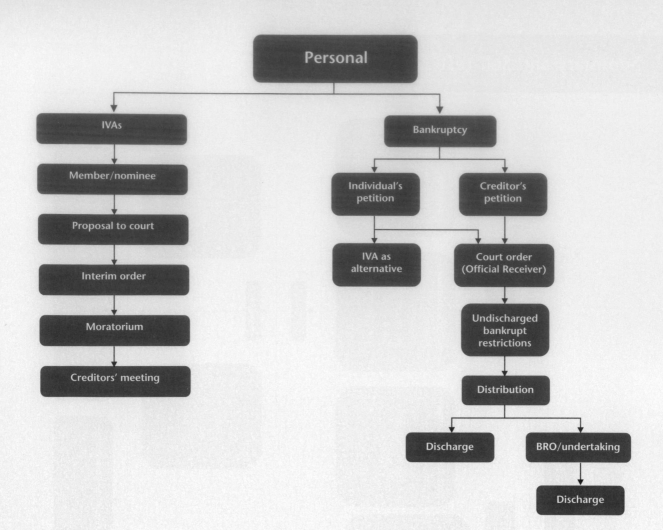

ICAEW

Self-test

Answer the following questions.

1   Who may apply to the court for an administration order but cannot appoint an administrator out of court?

2   What must an administrator do

    A   Within 7 days?

    B   Within 8 weeks?

    C   Within 10 weeks?

3   What does CVA stand for?

4   The normal duration of a CVA is

    ☐   Up to 12 months

    ☐   3-5 years

    ☐   5-10 years

5   What are the two most important grounds for **compulsory liquidation?**

    (1)   ....

    (2)   ....

6   A members' voluntary winding up is where the members decide to dissolve a solvent company.

    ☐   True

    ☐   False

7   In what way are the powers of the members' nominee liquidator restricted pending the creditors' meeting?

8   A creditor must satisfy one of three criteria in order to petition for a compulsory winding up.
    What are they?

    •   ....

    •   ....

    •   ....

9   Who will the court appoint as liquidator in a compulsory winding up?

10 Certain transactions may be avoided if they occur within a certain time period of insolvency. Match the time period with the transaction.

    A   Floating charge in favour of an unconnected person   (i)   6 months

    B   Transaction at an undervalue   (ii)   1 year

    C   Preference in favour of an unconnected person   (iii)   2 years

11 Put the following in order to represent the correct priority in a distribution of assets on a compulsory winding up:

    A   Floating charges

    B   Deferred debts

    C   Preferential debts

    D   Members

    E   Costs

    F   Unsecured ordinary creditors

C
H
A
P
T
E
R

8

12   Name four effects of a compulsory liquidation order:

•   ....

•   ....

•   ....

•   ....

13   Can an individual who is subject to an IVA still act as a director of a company?

Now go back to the Learning Objectives in the Introduction. If you are satisfied you have achieved these objectives, please tick them off.

Answers to Interactive questions

Answer to Interactive question 1

1   Yes. As a creditor who is owed more than £750 and whose written demand has not been satisfied in 21 days, he can petition the court on the grounds that the company is unable to pay its debts.

2   No. He is an unsecured creditor with no floating charge, so appointing an administrator is not an option open to him. He may, however, apply to the court to appoint an administrator.

Answer to Interactive question 2

A   No. Floating charges created within the previous 12 months can be avoided.

B   No. It is a transaction at an undervalue within the past two years but it will not be avoided where the company entered into it in good faith for the purposes of carrying on the business and believing it to be in the company's best interests.

C   Yes. This is a transaction at an undervalue within the previous two years.

D   Yes. This is a preference given to a connected person and within the two years prior to liquidation.

Answer to Interactive question 3

A   The costs of the liquidation, including the liquidator's remuneration.

B   He will receive £800 of the £830 owed, after payment of the costs, holiday pay (being a preferential debt) and floating charge.

C   No. This is a deferred debt which ranks after unsecured creditors and the fund is insufficient to pay the debt.

D   No, as the fund available for distribution is below £10,000.

1   A creditor with no minimum value of debt (if he is not also a qualifying floating charge holder)

2   A   File notice of his appointment with the Registrar

       B   Submit a statement of his proposals to the Registrar and the company's members and creditors

       C   Hold a creditors' meeting

3   Company voluntary arrangement

4   3–5 years

5   (1)   Company is unable to pay its debts

       (2)   It is just and equitable to wind up the company

6   True

7   He may only

- Take control of the company's property
- Dispose of goods which are perishable or which would otherwise diminish in value very quickly
- Do things necessary for the protection of the company's assets

    (except with leave of the court).

8
- He is owed more than £750 and the company has failed to satisfy his written demand for payment within 21 days
- His attempts to enforce a judgment order by execution have failed
- The company is unable to pay its debts

9   The Official Receiver

10   Floating charge in favour of an unconnected person *1 year*

       Transaction at an undervalue *2 years*

       Preference in favour of an unconnected person *6 months*

11   E, C, A, F, B, D

12
- Official Receiver appointed as liquidator
- Liquidation deemed to have commenced at time when petition first presented
- Disposition of company property since commencement of liquidation deemed void
- Legal proceedings against the company are halted
- Employees are dismissed
- Any floating charge crystallises

13   Yes

CHAPTER 9

Partnership

Introduction

Examination context

Topic List

Summary and Self-test

Answers to Interactive questions

Answers to Self-test

Learning objectives

- To define partnership

- To understand and apply the rules of agency as they apply to partnership

- To identify the differences between companies and partnerships

- To understand the concept and characteristics of a limited liability partnership

- To know the procedure for the formation of a limited liability partnership and the administrative consequences thereof

Specific syllabus references for this chapter are: 1e, 2a, b, c and i.

Syllabus links

The practical effects of partnership will be relevant when looking in detail at audit firms and their liability in the Audit and Assurance paper.

Examination context

Partners' authority will be examined in the context of agency law, commonly in a scenario question. The law on partnerships may also be examined by requiring a comparison with companies.

In the assessment, candidates may be required to:

- Identify the differences between partnerships and companies

- Recognise the authority a partner has to enter into contracts on behalf of the partnership

- Identify the procedure required to form a limited liability partnership and the administrative consequences

- Identify the rights and duties which a member of a limited liability partnership possesses

1 Ordinary partnerships

Section overview

- A partnership is 'the relation which subsists between persons carrying on a business in common with a view of profit'.

- A partnership can be an informal arrangement or it can be formalised and regulated by a written partnership agreement.

- A partnership can be termed an 'ordinary' (or traditional) partnership in order to distinguish it from a limited liability partnership (see section 3 below).

- The Partnership Act 1890 governs ordinary partnerships.

Partnership is a common form of business association. It is **flexible**, because it can be either a **formal** or **informal** arrangement, thus suiting both large organisations and small operations.

Some professions prohibit their members from carrying on practice through limited companies and therefore operate as partnerships. However some permit their members to trade as 'limited liability partnerships' which share many characteristics with companies (and which are described in section 3 of this chapter). Businessmen are not so restricted and generally prefer to trade through a limited company for the advantages this can bring.

1.1 Definition

A **partnership** is 'the relation which subsists between persons carrying on a business in common with a view of profit' (s 1 Partnership Act 1890). This definition can be further explained as follows:

Relation which subsists	A partnership does not have a separate legal personality, it is merely a relationship between persons.
Between persons	'Person' includes companies. There must be at least two partners.
Carrying on a business	• Business includes 'every trade, occupation or profession'.
	• It can be a single transaction (often referred to as a 'joint venture').
	• The business must involve some activity, so if two or more persons are merely the passive joint owners of revenue producing property, such as investments or rented houses, that fact of itself does not make them partners.
	• A partnership begins when the partners agree to conduct their **business activity** together which may well be before the business actually begins to trade. Thus in *Khan v Miah 2001* the parties to a proposed venture (running a restaurant) were partners even before the restaurant opened because, on the facts, they were clearly carrying on the business (by leasing premises, hiring equipment and opening a bank account).
In common	ie as joint proprietors (normally evidenced by the sharing of profits). For example, where a shop owner employs a shop assistant, they are both concerned with running a business at a profit but they cannot be said to be partners.
With a view of profit	The test is one of intention, so if partners plan to make a profit but actually make a loss, that does not stop the arrangement being a partnership. However if the purpose of the common endeavour is actually to gain business experience, for example, there is no partnership (*Davies v Newman 2000*).

The word **'firm'** is correctly used to denote a partnership. It is **not** correct to apply it to a registered company (though newspapers often do so). The word **'company'** may form part of the name of a partnership (for example, 'Smith and Company') but the words 'limited company' and 'registered company' can **only** be applied to a registered company.

Interactive question 1: Partnerships   [Difficulty level: Exam standard]

Interactive question text.

Identify whether the following three statements are true or false in relation to an ordinary partnership.

		True	False
A	In England and Wales, an unlimited partnership has no existence distinct from the partners	☐	☐
B	Partners share equally in the venture's profits	☐	☐

See **Answer** at the end of this chapter.

1.2 Formation and regulation of a partnership

A partnership can be a very informal arrangement with no written formality at all; people simply agree to run a business together and then do so.

On the other hand, it may be appropriate to formalise the arrangement with a written partnership agreement, particularly where the partnership is a vast organisation with substantial revenue and expenditure, such as many accountancy firms. The advantages of an agreement are that it sets out details which are not otherwise implied by law (such as the nature of its business) and that it can expressly override provisions which might otherwise be implied by law and which are not appropriate (for example the proportions in which profits are to be shared).

In addition, partnerships are governed by the Partnership Act 1890, which sets out basic rights and duties of partners, such as the rights to share profits, to take part in business decisions and to veto new partners and the duty to share losses and indemnify other partners. These **rights and duties in most cases can be expressly overruled** in a partnership agreement but will be assumed **in the absence of any express provision**. The key provisions of the Act are set out below:

Provisions of the Partnership Act	Description
Profits and losses	These are shared equally in the absence of contrary agreement. If the partnership agreement states that profits are to be shared in certain proportions but is silent as to losses, then losses are to be shared in the same proportions.
Management	Every partner is entitled to take part in managing the firm's business; ordinary management decisions can be made by a majority of partners.
Change in business	Any decision on changing the nature of the partnership's business must be unanimous.
Indemnity	The firm must indemnify any partner against liabilities incurred in the ordinary and proper conduct of the partnership business or in doing anything necessarily done for the preservation of the partnership property or business.
Remuneration	No partner is entitled to remuneration for acting in the partnership business.
Variation	The partnership agreement may be varied with the consent of all the partners.
Records and accounts	These must be kept at the main place of business and must be open to inspection by all partners.
Interest on capital	None is paid on capital except by agreement. However, a partner is entitled to 5% interest on **advances** beyond his original capital.
New partners	New partners must only be introduced with the unanimous consent of existing partners.

Provisions of the Partnership Act	Description
Expulsion	A partner may only be expelled by a majority of votes when the partnership agreement allows; even then, the power must only be used in good faith and for good reason.
Dissolution	The authority of the partners after dissolution continues so far as is necessary to wind up the partnership affairs and complete transactions already begun. On dissolution, any partner can insist on realisation of the firm's assets, payment of the firm's debts and distribution of the surplus.
Capital deficiency	The remaining partners share a capital deficiency (what a partner owes but cannot pay back) not as a loss but in ratio to the amounts of capital which they originally contributed to the firm.

In addition to the rights and duties set out in the Partnership Act, partners also owe fiduciary duties to the partnership by reason of being fiduciaries (in the same way that some directors' duties are fiduciary in nature). These duties arise out of general principles of equity. For example, it is a breach of the duty to act in good faith, to exercise a legal right (eg to expel a partner) for an improper motive. The fiduciary nature of their relationship also prohibits partners from keeping profits derived from the partnership without the consent of the other partners and requires them to avoid conflicts of interest without full disclosure. Breach of these fiduciary duties may render the partner responsible liable to account to the partnership for any monies received or to make good any other loss suffered.

Interactive question 2: Partnership regulation   [Difficulty level: Exam standard]

Dolittle Solicitors has four partners, Ahmed, Bridget, Charles and Don. Ahmed, Bridget and Don want to invite Edith to be a partner. Charles does not want to invite Edith to be a partner because he does not feel that she has sufficient experience in a senior position in the firm yet. Ahmed, Bridget and Don decide to expel Charles from the partnership and invite Edith to take his place. Ahmed also wants to be paid a salary as he carries out many of the administrative functions of the partnership. There is no provision for new partners in the partnership agreement, but the agreement does allow partners to remove partners by majority decision. Are the following statements true or false?

		True	False
A	Ahmed, Bridget and Don may invite Edith to be a partner without Charles' consent	☐	☐
B	Ahmed, Bridget and Don may not expel Charles from the partnership on these grounds	☐	☐
C	Ahmed is not entitled to a salary for acting in the partnership business	☐	☐

See **Answer** at the end of this chapter.

1.3 Partners' liability and authority

Partners are jointly and severally liable for the acts of their fellow partners in so far as they bind the firm. Thus it is necessary to consider the authority of partners to bind the firm. This is based on the principles of agency (which you studied in Chapter 3). The Partnership Act 1890 provides that each partner is the agent of the partnership and his fellow partners for the purpose of the business of the partnership. A partner's authority may be actual (express or implied) or apparent.

The Act also provides that the firm and the partners will be bound by all partners' acts for carrying on in the usual way business of the kind carried on by the firm unless

- He has no authority to act for the firm in the particular matter **and**

- The person with whom he is dealing **either** knows that he has no authority **or** does not know or believe him to be a partner.

The courts have interpreted this provision to mean that the binding act should be done in the firm's name for the purpose of the firm's business, and by a person who purports to act as a partner.

Worked example: Partners' authority

Faith, George, Harbajan and Ingrid are partners in an animal hospital. They are all authorised to carry out the business of being a vet on behalf of the practice. The partners have assigned Faith the position of hospital manager with authority to purchase medicines and other supplies that the hospital needs. The hospital has approved suppliers who have been informed that the only person with authority to buy goods on behalf of the practice is Faith.

One day Faith was perusing the catalogue from a supplier and saw an advert for a new drug. One of the hospital's approved suppliers was advertising for hospitals to participate in a drugs trial in respect of this drug in return for a number of free drugs. Faith rang the supplier and volunteered the hospital for the drugs trial. George, Harbajan and Ingrid are very unhappy that Faith made this commitment without consulting them and are wondering if they can avoid the commitment on the grounds that Faith was not authorised to bind them in a contract involving drugs which have not yet been subject to clinical trials.

In addition, Ingrid has recently placed a large order on behalf of the partnership with a non-approved supplier because it was offering a good deal on a drug which the hospital uses regularly. The supplier was aware that she was a partner in the hospital and therefore entered into the contract. Faith is very annoyed and wishes to cancel the contract because she is concerned that the hospital will not have sufficient need of the drug and that too many will go to waste.

- **Faith's commitment to the drugs trial**. Participating in a drugs trial, while not the direct business of the partnership, is sufficiently connected with the business of the partnership to be considered the business of the partnership. In addition, Faith was acting in the normal course of her duties, dealing with drug companies to obtain drugs for the partnership. This being the case, Faith has authority to bind the partners in this way, in the absence of any express agreement that partners will not commit the partnership to participation in drugs trials. Even if there were such a restriction on her authority, the supplier would have had to have been aware of it in order for her contract not to bind the firm.

- **Ingrid's purchase of the drug**. Although approved suppliers of the hospital are aware that only Faith is authorised to buy drugs, a non-approved supplier, who has not been told this, is entitled to assume that a partner has the power to bind the other partners when buying drugs connected with the partnership business. Therefore the partnership will be bound by this contract.

The Act specifically provides that where a partner pledges the credit of the firm for a purpose which has no apparent connection with the firm's ordinary business, the firm will not be bound unless he has actual express authority to do so.

If any **restriction** is placed on a partner's authority to bind the firm, **no act** done in contravention of that restriction is **binding** on the firm where the third party has **notice of the restriction**.

Note that (except where a partner has actual authority) his authority often **depends on the perception of the third party**. Generally speaking, if the third party genuinely believes that the partner has authority, it is highly likely that the acts of the partner will bind the firm.

Note that a **new partner** admitted to an existing firm is liable for debts incurred only after he becomes a partner. He is not liable for debts incurred before he was a partner unless he agrees otherwise.

Where a partner retires, he remains liable for any outstanding debts incurred while he was a partner, unless the creditor has agreed to release him from liability. He is also liable for debts of the firm incurred **after** his retirement if the creditor knew him to be a partner (before retirement) and has not had notice of his retirement. Therefore, it is **vital** on retirement that a partner **gives notice** to all the creditors of the firm. He may also consider entering into an agreement with the continuing partners that they will indemnify him against any liability for post-retirement debts.

The liability of the partnership for a partner's acts before he retired is not affected by that partner's retirement.

Interactive question 3: Authority of partners   [Difficulty level: Exam standard]

Smith & Co has two partners, Alice and Ben, following Colway's retirement last month. Alice and Ben decide to allocate £10,000 for the purposes of upgrading their IT system and Ben agrees that Alice should go ahead and purchase the necessary hardware and software that they need. Alice gets carried away and orders supplies worth £18,500 from the firm's usual office supplier Solution Ltd. The new letterhead without Colway's name has not arrived from the printers and so she uses a piece from the old supply for making the order.

Which of the following best describes the legal position?

A   The contract is not binding because Alice acted beyond her authority

B   The contract is enforceable against Alice only because she acted beyond her authority and cannot therefore bind her fellow partners

C   The contract is binding on Alice and Ben because her acts bind existing partners only and she had implied authority as a partner of a firm

D   The contract is binding on Alice, Ben and Colway because the letterhead led Solutions Ltd to believe that Colway was still a partner and it did not know about the £10,000 limit.

See **Answer** at the end of this chapter.

1.4   Dissolution and insolvency of a partnership

In the absence of any express provision to the contrary contained in the partnership agreement, the Partnership Act 1890 provides that a partnership is dissolved in the following instances:

- The **death or bankruptcy** of a partner
- **Expiry** of a fixed term partnership
- **Completion** or termination of a single joint venture, if applicable
- **Subsequent illegality**
- **Notice** given by a partner if it is a partnership of indefinite duration
- **Order of the court**, for example where it is deemed just and equitable to do so.

A partnership agreement may include other circumstances in which a partnership will be dissolved. More commonly, it will provide that the partnership business shall continue on the death, retirement or bankruptcy of any partner so that dissolution is merely a technicality. It may also provide that the partnership shall only be dissolved by mutual consent of all the partners.

Where a partnership is in default on any secured loan, its creditors may take action against the partners individually or sue them in the name of the partnership. If the partnership is insolvent, bankruptcy proceedings may be brought in respect of individual partners and/or the partnership may be wound up in the same way as an unregistered company (under Part V Insolvency Act 1986).

2 Comparison between ordinary partnerships and companies

> **Section overview**
>
> - The key difference between a company and an ordinary partnership is that a company has a separate legal personality, distinct from its members, whereas an ordinary partnership does not.
>
> - There are many other differences, some incidental to this key difference and some arising from specific statutory provisions.

The principal differences between a registered company and an ordinary partnership are given in the tables below, the first noting the differences which are commonly seen as advantages of incorporating a business, the second noting those commonly seen as disadvantages, or conversely, advantages of running a business as a partnership.

2.1 Advantages of incorporation

Factor	Company	Ordinary partnership
Legal entity	Separate legal entity distinct from its members	Has no independent existence
Liability	Company liable on its contracts	Partners (personally) are jointly and severally liable on partnership contracts
Limit on liability	Members' liability can be limited by shares or guarantee	Partners' liability unlimited
Ownership	Company owns assets and ownership not affected by change of members	Partners own assets jointly
Finance	In addition to fixed charges, a company can raise finance by creating a floating charge over its undertaking or assets, allowing it to deal with them without the lender's consent prior to any crystallisation	An ordinary partnership cannot do so
Change of membership	Company has perpetual succession (ie it is unaffected by a change in its members)	The death, retirement or bankruptcy of a partner dissolves the partnership (subject to the terms of any partnership agreement)
Transferability of ownership	Members' shares freely transferable (subject to articles)	A partner may assign his interest but the assignee does not become a partner as a result
Limit on membership	No maximum, minimum one	No maximum, minimum two

2.2 Disadvantages of incorporation

Factor	Company	Ordinary partnership
Formation	A company must be registered under the Companies Act	No particular formality is required for a partnership to exist
Administrative consequences	A company must file accounts and documents with the Registrar of Companies	A partnership does not have to comply with such formalities

Factor	Company	Ordinary partnership
Cost	A company faces the cost of compliance with administrative requirements and an annual audit	A partnership has no such cost
Privacy	A number of the company accounts and documents must be open to public inspection	Only partners have a right of access to the partnership accounts
Management	A company member cannot be directly involved in the management of the company unless he is also a director	Every partner has a right to participate in the management of the partnership (subject to the terms of any partnership agreement)
Withdrawal of capital	A company is subject to strict rules concerning repayment of capital	It is more straightforward for a partner to withdraw capital

Interactive question 4: Company vs partnership [Difficulty level: Exam standard]

Indicate whether or not each of the following statements is true or false.

		True	False
A	A benefit for the participants of a partnership over a company is that because it has separate legal personality, they have limited liability	☐	☐
B	A benefit for the members of a company over a partnership is that it continues in existence even if its participants change	☐	☐
C	A benefit of a limited company over a partnership is that a company's liability is limited	☐	☐
D	A benefit of a partnership over a company is that a partnership is not subject to any legislative regulation	☐	☐

See **Answer** at the end of this chapter.

3 Limited liability partnerships

Section overview

- A limited liability partnership (LLP) is a corporate body, which combines the features of an ordinary partnership with limited liability.

- It is governed by the Limited Liability Partnerships Act 2000.

- Its members are agents of the LLP.

- An LLP is wound up like a company, rather than being dissolved on a change of membership.

- Particular documents must be sent to the Registrar of Companies on and subsequent to incorporation.

The limited liability partnership was introduced by the **Limited Liability Partnerships Act 2000**. Essentially an LLP is an incorporated partnership that has a legal personality separate from that of its members (whose liability is limited) and which is subject to regulation similar to that applicable to a registered company. An LLP is not liable to tax in the same way as a company, rather the partners ('members') are taxed as individuals on partnership profits, just as in an ordinary partnership. It is often an attractive way forward for firms of professionals because it preserves the partnership ethos in the context of limited liability.

An LLP should not be confused with a **limited partnership** registered under the Limited Partnership Act 1907. Such partnerships are extremely rare and they are only mentioned here to avoid potential confusion with LLPs. Briefly, a limited partnership requires at least one general partner who has control of the management of the business and whose liability must be unlimited. The other partners are not entitled to participate in management and cannot bind the partnership and their liability is limited to the amount of capital they invested in the business.

3.1 Formation of an LLP

An LLP is created by the registration with the Registrar of Companies of a lawful business carried on by two or more persons with a view to profit. The incorporation document must be signed by at least two subscribers and must state the following:

- The **name** of the LLP (which must end with the words Limited Liability Partnership or the abbreviation LLP)

- The **location** of its **registered office** (England and Wales or Wales)

- The **address** of its registered office

- The names and addresses of all the **members** of the LLP

- The names of the two **designated members** who are to be responsible for signing notices and accounts and delivering them to the registrar

There is also a registration fee.

3.2 Regulation and administration

An LLP is not required to have (but normally will have) a formal partnership agreement dealing with matters of internal regulation and duties owed by the partners to each other. Any such agreement does not have to be filed with the Registrar. In the absence of any express agreement to the contrary, the provisions of the Act and the Limited Liability Partnerships Regulations 2001 (as amended) will apply. Broadly speaking, these regulations apply the provisions of companies legislation to LLPs (with necessary modifications) and also default provisions in line with the Partnership Act 1890, dealing with profit share, remuneration, inspection of books and expulsion.

There is no maximum limit on the number of members in an LLP. New members (apart from the original subscribers) are admitted by agreement of the existing members. A person ceases to be a member by giving reasonable notice to the other members or by following any other agreed procedure. Changes in membership do not affect the existence of the LLP but must be notified to the Registrar within 14 days.

Subject to any partnership agreement, every member may take part in the management of the LLP, essentially taking on the duties and responsibilities of directors. The obligations to keep and retain accounting records, to prepare and publish annual accounts (and to have them audited) apply to an LLP as they do to a company. Similarly, special rules for small- and medium-sized LLPs and audit exemption rules apply as they do to companies. There is no requirement to provide the equivalent of a directors' report.

Note that an LLP is required to comply with the following:

- To maintain a register of charges and to register charges with the Registrar
- To notify the Registrar of any change to membership, designated members or registered office
- To provide the name of the LLP on correspondence and outside its place of business
- To deliver an annual return to the Registrar

As in the case of companies, the members of an LLP may apply to the court in cases of unfair prejudice, although this right can be excluded with unanimous consent for an agreed period.

Interactive question 5: Regulation of LLPs   [Difficulty level: Easy]

Are the following statements true or false in relation to LLPs?

		True	False
A	There is a maximum limit on the number of members in an LLP of 50	☐	☐
B	There must be at least one general partner who has unlimited liability and control of the management of the LLP	☐	☐
C	An LLP is normally subject to a requirement to have its accounts audited annually just like a company	☐	☐
D	The members of an LLP are required to prepare a report along the same lines as a directors' report	☐	☐

See **Answer** at the end of this chapter.

3.3   Authority and liability of LLP members

The LLP, as a separate legal entity, is primarily liable for the debts and obligations of the firm's business. Generally speaking, the members of the LLP will not face personal liability. There is an exception which may apply to an LLP of professionals, where each member owes a duty of care. If a member in this case is in breach of that duty (for example an accountant who negligently prepares incorrect accounts), he may be personally liable in respect of an award of damages against the firm. However, it is likely that the claimant will be unable to show that the negligent member accepted personal liability. If it is considered that he was acting only for the LLP, then it will be for the LLP to meet the liability for damages.

A member may be found guilty of fraudulent or wrongful trading or liable to disqualification in the same way as a director of a company.

The Act provides that each member is an agent of the LLP and therefore has the power to bind the LLP by his acts. However, the LLP will **not** be bound where

- The member does not have authority and
- The third party is aware that he does not have authority or does not know or believe him to be a member of the LLP.

3.4   Termination and insolvency of an LLP

An LLP, unlike an ordinary partnership, is not dissolved by one of its members leaving. It can be dissolved, or terminated, by agreement of the members unanimously (or otherwise in accordance with any agreement).

Where the LLP becomes insolvent, members of the LLP may propose a voluntary arrangement, apply to put the business into administration or resolve to go into voluntary or compulsory liquidation.

Basically the law relating to companies' insolvency applies to LLPs, with two notable modifications:

- Withdrawals made by members within two years prior to winding-up may be clawed back if it can be shown that the member (at the time of the withdrawal) knew or had reasonable grounds to believe that the LLP was or would become insolvent.

- On a winding up, past and present members may be required to contribute to the assets of the LLP to the extent that they have agreed to do so in any LLP agreement. Note that in the absence of any relevant provision in an LLP agreement (which is not obligatory) the legal liability of members on liquidation is not clear.

Interactive question 6: Formation of LLP

[Difficulty level: Easy]

Under the Limited Liability Partnerships Act 2000, certain requirements must be met in order for an LLP to be legitimately formed. Indicate whether each of the following is a necessity of incorporation.

		Yes	No
A	An incorporation document signed by at least two subscribers must be sent to the Registrar of Companies	☐	☐
B	The name and address of at least one designated member must be given	☐	☐
C	Details of the assets of the LLP must be given on registration	☐	☐
D	A statement detailing the level of contribution that will be required from past and present members in the event of a winding-up must be included	☐	☐

See **Answer** at the end of this chapter.

Summary and Self-test

Summary

```
┌──────────────────────┐      ┌──────────────────────────────┐
│ All partners agents   │      │ Formal partnership agreement  │
│ of partnership and    │◄─────┤                               │──┐
│ co-partners           │   ┌──┤ Ordinary    │──►               │  │    ┌───────────┐     ┌──────────────────────┐
└──────────────────────┘   │  │ Partnership │  ┌──────────────────────────────┐  │  │ Fiduciary │     │ Partnership Act. 1890 │
                            │  └─────────────┘  │ Formal partnership agreement  │──┴──┤ duties    │     └──────────────────────┘
                            │                   └──────────────────────────────┘     └───────────┘
                            ▼
```

Acts binding unless	Relation which subsists between persons carrying on a business in common with a view of profit	Indemnity Share in losses	Share in profit Right to participate Right to see account No right to renumeration	Share in profit Right to participate Right to see account No right to renumeration

Acts binding unless
- No authority and
- Third person knows no authority **or** does not know/believe him to be a partner

Company		Partnership
Yes	Minimum 2	No
Company unlimited	Minimum 2	Partners: joint and several liability
Members: limited		Unlimited
Company owns	Minimum 2	Partners own
Floating charge		No
Minimum 1	Minimum 2	Minimum 2
Perpetual succession		Change = dissolution
Freedom to transfer		Assignee not partner
Registration	Minimum 2	Formality unecessary
Administrative burden		No
Cost		No
Publicity		Privacy
Directors	Minimum 2	Partners

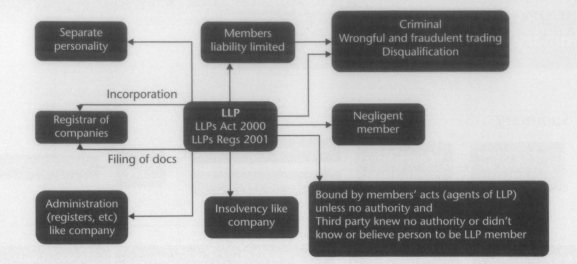

Self-test

Answer the following questions.

1   What is the statutory definition of 'partnership'?

2   A partnership can exist when parties enter into a single transaction rather than a series of transactions.

    True [ ]
    False [ ]

3   Name five rights of partners.

    • ....
    • ....
    • ....
    • ....
    • ....

4   Complete the following definition.

    Partnership .... is assets beneficially ....
    by the partners (the firm). It does not have to be in ....shares.

5   Which of the following completes a correct sentence?

    A partner is an agent of the firm and therefore binds the partnership by his acts in the partnership business

    A   Provided he has actual authority

    B   Provided the third party knows he is a partner

    C   Provided the third party doesn't know that he has no actual authority

    D   Provided the third party doesn't know that he lacks actual authority **and** knows or believes him to be a partner

6   Name four differences between companies and ordinary partnerships which make incorporation advantageous.

    • ....
    • ....
    • ....
    • ....

7   Name five differences between companies and ordinary partnerships which make partnership advantageous.

    • ....
    • ....
    • ....
    • ....
    • ....

8   An LLP has a separate legal personality.

    [ ]   True
    [ ]   False

9   Which of the following must be included on the incorporation form?

    A   Name of LLP
    B   Location of registered office
    C   Addresses of all branches
    D   Names of all members of the LLP
    E   Tax status of each member of the LLP
    F   Names of designated members

10   Members of LLPs are agents of the LLP and of each other.

    ☐   True
    ☐   False

11   Which of the following **must** an LLP deliver to the Registrar annually?

    A   Incorporation documents
    B   Audited accounts
    C   Annual return
    D   Tax returns

12   Can the members of an insolvent LLP propose a voluntary arrangement?

    ☐   Yes
    ☐   No

Now, go back to the Learning Objectives in the Introduction. If you are satisfied you have achieved these objectives, please tick them off.

Answer to Interactive question 1

A   True

B   True (subject to any contrary agreement)

Answer to Interactive question 2

A   False. All existing partners must consent to new partners being admitted.

B   True. Even where the partnership agreement allows for the expulsion of a partner, it must be in good faith and for a good reason, not just because he doesn't agree with a policy of the other partners, apparently on reasonable grounds.

C   True. The partners could agree to pay him a salary but he has no right to one.

Answer to Interactive question 3

D

Answer to Interactive question 4

A   False. Partnerships do not have separate legal personality but companies do, so it is a benefit of companies that members may have limited liability.

B   True.

C   False. The company's liability is unlimited (it is the members' liability that may be limited).

D   False. Although nothing like as extensive as the companies legislation, the Partnership Act 1890 does lay down some rules for partnerships, although most may be varied or overridden by a partnership agreement.

Answer to Interactive question 5

A   False. There is no maximum limit.

B   False. This is the case with a limited partnership under the 1907 Act.

C   True (but note that exemptions may apply).

D   False. There is no such requirement, notwithstanding that in most respects the administrative consequences of incorporation are the same for an LLP as for a company.

Answer to Interactive question 6

A   Yes

B   No. Two designated members are required.

C   No

D   No

Answers to Self-test

1   Partnership is the relation which subsists between persons carrying on a business in common with a view of profit.

2   True

3   • To be involved in decision-making
    • To share in profits
    • To examine accounts
    • To insist on openness and honesty
    • To veto new partners
    • To be indemnified by fellow partners

4   Property
    Owned
    Equal

5   D

6   • Separate entity
    • Members' liability can be limited
    • Company owns property and is liable on contracts
    • Company can create floating charge
    • Company has perpetual succession

7   • No formality required on creation

    • Partnership need not register accounts and other documents

    • Partnership has greater freedom and privacy and less cost through not having to comply with requirements of companies legislation

    • All partners can participate in management

    • Withdrawal of capital is generally easier

8   True

9   A, B, D, F

10 False. Members of an LLP are agents of the LLP but not of each other

11 B and C

12 Yes

CHAPTER 10

Criminal law

Learning objectives

*   To identify circumstances where an accountant will be protected from dismissal and victimisation if he raises concerns about malpractice in the workplace

*   To identify instances of fraud, bribery, corruption and money laundering and to know the consequences of each

*   To be able to select appropriate courses of action in the event of money laundering, in accordance with national and international regulations

*   To recognise interaction between case law, legislation, ethics and ethical codes in relation to these offences

Specific syllabus references for this chapter are: 3a, b, c, d, e.

Syllabus links

There are links with directors' duties, which we have already considered, since directors can be in a position to carry on fraudulent trading for example. Your Assurance and Audit and Assurance studies will also address professional ethics generally and, in particular, the obligation and authority of an auditor or assurance provider to make a protected disclosure.

Examination context

In the sample paper there were five questions on criminal law (out of 50).

In the assessment, candidates may be required to

*   Identify circumstances where an accountant is protected from dismissal and victimisation if he raises concerns ('whistleblows') about malpractice in the workplace

*   Identify instances and consequences of fraud and money laundering

*   Advise on appropriate courses of action for an accountant faced with a money laundering scenario

*   Identify instances and consequences of bribery and corruption

*   Recognise the role of ethics and ethical codes and their interaction with law

1 Whistleblowing

Section overview

- UK law gives people at work protection when they raise genuine concerns about criminal or civil offences, danger to health and safety or the environment, a miscarriage of justice or the cover up of any of these.

- A disclosure must be a qualifying disclosure, made in good faith to the appropriate person in the appropriate manner, and the person making it must have a reasonable belief that the information is valid.

'Whistleblowing' is the name commonly given to workers making a disclosure of wrongdoing (usually) by their employer. That wrongdoing is often, though not necessarily, of a criminal nature. The relevant legislation is the Public Interest Disclosure Act 1998, which inserts a number of new provisions in the Employment Rights Act 1996. Note that the legislation does not impose an *obligation* to whistleblow, rather it protects individuals who choose to do so, whether as a matter of conscience or ethics or because they are following internal rules and procedures.

This protection is afforded to workers generally (and not just to 'employees') and there is no requirement as to age or length of service. It therefore includes agency and home workers, but self-employed people and volunteers are not included. The protection means that any worker who is victimised or sacked in breach of the Act can present a complaint to an employment tribunal that he has been subjected to a detriment in contravention of the statutory provisions. He may seek an interim order to keep his job and/or compensation. Awards of compensation are uncapped and based on the losses suffered.

In order to receive protection, the disclosure made by a worker must be

- A qualifying disclosure of information
- Made in the public interest
- Made to the appropriate person

1.1 Qualifying disclosure

A disclosure is a qualifying disclosure if, in the **reasonable belief** of the worker making it, the information disclosed tends to show one or more of the following:

- That a **criminal offence** has been committed, is being committed or is likely to be committed.

- That a person has **failed**, is failing or is likely to fail with any **legal obligation** to which he is subject.

- That a **miscarriage of justice** has occurred, is occurring or is likely to occur.

- That the **health and safety** of an individual has been, is being or is likely to be endangered.

- That the **environment** has been, is being or is likely to be damaged.

- That **information** tending to show any matter falling within these categories has been, is being or is likely to be deliberately **concealed**.

The wrongdoing disclosed is commonly a wrongdoing committed by the employer, but a disclosure could also be made about the acts of fellow workers. In *BP Plc v Elstone 2010*, it was held that a worker was entitled to pursue a claim where he had suffered detriment caused by his current employer in respect of protected disclosures that he had made during his previous employment. A provision in the Enterprise and Regulatory Reform Act 2013 (ERRA 2013) provides for the employer to be vicariously liable for acts of co-workers, subject to a defence if the employer takes all reasonable steps to prevent the co-worker's wrongdoing. It is not known when this provision will come into force.

The test of reasonable belief is subjective in that it is specific to the worker making the disclosure. However, the fact that the belief has to be reasonable implies that rumour or unfounded suspicions will not be sufficient. Thus, in *Bill v D Morgan plc* 2000, an accountancy assistant was held not to have a 'reasonable belief' for these purposes, where he could not point to any documentation to back up his allegations of financial and accounting irregularities.

Where the disclosure is of something 'likely to occur' the worker should tread very carefully. It is likely that an employment tribunal determining whether the disclosure is protected or not would want to see evidence that there were objective and verifiable grounds for his belief that the event would occur. A disclosure which amounts to a mere expression of opinion rather than fact is not a qualifying disclosure (*Goode v Marks & Spencer Plc 2010*).

1.2 Public interest

The requirement that a disclosure must be made in the public interest was introduced by ERRA 2013 and comes into force at the end of June 2013. The term 'public interest' is not defined.

A previous requirement for a disclosure to have been made 'in good faith' in order to be protected was repealed by ERRA 2013. Where a disclosure is not made in good faith, however, the court or tribunal may reduce the amount of compensation by up to 25%. The term 'good faith' is not defined in the legislation, but generally can be taken to mean that the intention is honest, and not the result of a grudge, antagonism towards the employer or some ulterior personal motive.

1.3 Made to appropriate person

The spirit of the Act is to encourage workers to raise concerns internally in the first instance but it does make provision for the disclosures to be made otherwise. In order to be a **protected disclosure**, the disclosure must be to one of the persons specified by the Act.

Type of disclosure	Requirements
Internal	To the employer or other responsible person
Legal adviser	In the course of obtaining legal advice
Minister	To a minister of the Crown (where the worker is in a public body such as the NHS)
Prescribed person/ regulator	To bodies prescribed by the Secretary of State (and in respect of subject categories also prescribed), such as the Health and Safety Executive, HM Revenue and Customs or the Financial Services Authority. Normally the matter disclosed will need to be something in which there is a serious public interest.
Wider	To other persons, such as the media, police, MPs or non-prescribed regulators, provided it is reasonable in all the circumstances and the disclosure is not made for personal gain **and** provided the worker • Reasonably believed he would be victimised if he raised the matter internally or with a prescribed person **or** • Reasonably believed a cover up was likely and there was no prescribed person **or** • Had already raised the matter internally or with a prescribed regulator. Whether it is reasonable in all the circumstances will depend on a number of factors, including the seriousness of the matter and whether it is continuing, the identity of the person to whom disclosure is made, whether there has been a breach of confidentiality and whether the worker complied with relevant procedures.

1.4 Protection

A worker has the right not to be subjected to 'any detriment by any act, or any deliberate failure to act' by his employer as a result of having made a protected disclosure. The right not to suffer a detriment covers a number of issues, such as lack of promotion, lack of training or opportunity, unjustified disciplinary action, pay issues or failure to renew contracts as a result of having made a protected disclosure. In addition, an 'employee' who is dismissed or selected for redundancy principally for having made a protected disclosure shall be regarded as having been automatically unfairly dismissed. A worker who is not an 'employee' and is dismissed may rely on the general right not to suffer a detriment.

An employment tribunal may award compensation to any worker who has been victimised for making a protected disclosure. The amount of such compensation will be whatever the tribunal considers to be just and equitable, having regard to the loss suffered and the nature of the complaint.

Compensation may include an amount for injury to feelings and it is not subject to a maximum limit. (In January 2009, for example, a railworker was awarded £200,000 for whistleblowing after he was pressurised to lie about an accident he witnessed.)

Worked example: Whistleblowing

Jazmin is an accountant at Calibrations Ltd. She has recently come across documents that show that the company is illegally dumping waste into a local river. She raised this issue with the managing director who ignored her. She spoke to the managing director again and threatened to tell the external auditors, so he fired her.

Jazmin has a substantiated (and therefore reasonable) belief that the company is breaking the law. She has correctly raised this with the managing director.

Jazmin's disclosure to the managing director therefore qualifies as a protected disclosure. She is therefore given employment protection. She can make a claim for unfair dismissal which is likely to be found in her favour (since dismissal for making a protected disclosure is automatically unfair) unless the MD can prove she was dismissed for another reason. If the tribunal confirms she has been unfairly dismissed, she can claim compensation from Calibrations Ltd.

1.5 Gagging clauses

Any confidentiality clause or 'gagging clause' in an employment contract or severance agreement which seeks to limit a worker's right to make disclosures or is, in any other way, in conflict with the Act, will be void to the extent of any such conflict.

2 Fraud

Section overview

- We shall address fraud as a basic criminal offence as well as in the context of fraudulent trading and insider dealing.

- Fraud can be committed by an abuse of position or failing to disclose information as much as by deliberately making false representations.

- Directors and others can be guilty of fraudulent trading where they carry on a business with an intent to defraud creditors or for any fraudulent purpose.

- Insider dealing is the criminal offence of dealing in securities while in possession of sensitive information as an insider.

2.1 Fraud

Historically, prosecutions for fraud were made under various common law and statutory offences relating to defrauding and deception. The Fraud Act 2006 has now established a single statutory offence of fraud, which offence can be committed in three ways:

Fraud by false representation	**Dishonestly** making a **false representation** of fact or law, **intending** thereby to make a **gain** for himself or another or to cause another party **loss** or expose that party to the risk of making loss.

Fraud by failing to disclose information	**Dishonestly failing to disclose** to another person **information** which he is under a legal **duty to disclose** thereby **intending** to make a **gain** for himself or another or to cause another party **loss** or expose that party to the risk of making loss.
Fraud by abuse of position	**Occupying a position** in which he is **expected to safeguard**, or not to act against, the **financial interest of another person**, and **dishonestly abusing** that position, thereby **intending** to make a **gain** for himself or an other, or to cause another party **loss** or expose that party to the risk of suffering loss. It is likely that 'abuse' will be widely construed.

The maximum penalty for fraud under the Act is 10 years' imprisonment and an unlimited fine.

2.2 Fraudulent trading

Fraudulent trading is both a criminal and civil offence which may be committed where a business is carried on with **intent to defraud creditors** of the company or creditors of any other person or for **any fraudulent purpose**.

The criminal offence, punishable by an unlimited fine and/or imprisonment for up to 10 years, arises under s 993 Companies Act 2006 regardless of whether or not the company is in liquidation (which means that the offence can be committed even while the company is operating as a going concern). Fraudulent trading is generally associated with directors but it may be committed by any person who is knowingly a party to the fraudulent manner of trading, for example a company secretary or financial adviser. The offence may also be committed by non-corporate traders, under parallel provisions contained in the Fraud Act 2006.

It is difficult to extract from cases involving fraudulent trading a clear definition of the phrase but it seems that some positive act is needed and not just neglect. Furthermore, there must be some element of dishonesty and the test for intent to defraud is essentially subjective, concerned with the defendant's state of mind or intentions at the time of the alleged fraudulent trading. 'Any fraudulent purpose' is widely defined and has been said to cover frauds against future creditors as well as existing ones.

Where a court considers that a person (usually, but not necessarily, a director) has been guilty of fraudulent trading, it may disqualify that person for up to 15 years from acting as a director or being involved in the management of companies, under the Company Directors Disqualification Act 1986.

Fraudulent trading also carries civil liability for any persons who were knowingly parties to it. Any such person may be held liable for some or all of the debts of the company, as the court may decide. This civil liability only arises where the company is in liquidation and only the liquidator can apply to court for a declaration of civil liability (s 213 IA).

Worked example: Fraudulent trading

Arnold, a director of Five-a-Day Ltd is aware that the company has a number of debts outstanding and the finance director has advised him that he can see no way of the company recovering its profitability sufficiently to settle its debts in the foreseeable future. However, when the sales director of Sunshine Fruits Ltd offers Arnold a consignment of pineapples for £800 with 50% to be paid on delivery and 50% three months later, he accepts, optimistic that it might aid the recovery of the company.

There is a possibility that Arnold may be guilty of fraudulent trading and liable to criminal sanctions (as well as civil remedies) and, if the finance director is party to the transaction in any way (although this seems unlikely), he may also be liable. However, it is necessary for the prosecution to show an intent to defraud creditors or the carrying on of business for any fraudulent purpose. Knowing full well that a company has no hope of paying its debts *may* be sufficient in certain circumstances, although case law on this offence is not very extensive or clear and it is arguable that more is required, for example, deliberately moving assets out of a company and into another company (especially where that other company is also controlled by the director). Often the offence of **wrongful trading** (which imposes civil liability where a company is in liquidation and a director knew or should have known that there was no reasonable prospect of avoiding insolvent liquidation) is more easily proved and is likely to be more appropriate in this case. (Unlike fraudulent trading, the offence of wrongful trading is limited to directors.)

2.3 Insider dealing

Insider dealing is governed by the Criminal Justice Act 1993.

The principal offence of **insider dealing** is dealing in securities while in possession of inside information as an insider, the securities being price-affected by the information. It is also an offence to

- **Encourage another** to **deal** in them, or to

- **Disclose** the **information** other than in the proper performance of one's employment, office or profession.

Some of these terms need explanation:

Dealing	Dealing is **acquiring or disposing** of, or agreeing to acquire or dispose of, relevant securities whether directly or through an agent or nominee or a person acting according to direction
Encouraging another to deal	Where a person, having information as an insider, encourages another person to deal in price-affected securities in relation to that information, **knowing** or having reasonable cause to believe that dealing would take place. It is irrelevant whether: • The person encouraged realises that the securities are price-affected securities • The inside information is actually given to that person (so, a simple recommendation to the effect that 'I cannot tell you why but now would be a good time to buy shares in Bloggs plc' would infringe the law) • Any dealing actually takes place.
Securities	Securities include shares, debt securities and warranties and must be regulated on a regulated market such as the Stock Exchange. Unlisted securities or face-to-face transactions are not included.
Inside information	Inside information is '**price sensitive information**' relating to a particular issuer of securities that are price-affected and not to securities generally. The information must not have been made public but must be information which, in the event that it were made public, would be likely to have a significant effect on the price of the securities. It must be specific or precise (for example, information that a takeover bid would be made for a specific company or details of how much would be offered for shares).
Insider	A person has information as an insider if it is (and he knows it is) inside information, and if he has (and knows he has) it from an inside source, that is • Through being a director, employee or shareholder of a company or by having access to it because of his employment, office or profession (eg as auditor), or • Through a source within either category.

Defences

The individual has a defence regarding **dealing** and **encouraging** others to deal if he can show that:

- He did not expect there to be a profit or avoidance of loss, or
- He had reasonable grounds to believe that the information had been disclosed widely, or
- He would have done what he did even if he did not have the information.

Note that where information is disclosed **in the course of one's employment** or profession, **no offence** is committed. Thus where an auditor passes on information to the partner responsible for the audit he is not guilty of an offence. If the partner then deals, he may potentially be liable but the auditor will not be.

Penalties

Maximum penalties given by the statute are **seven years' imprisonment** and/or an **unlimited fine**. Contracts remain valid and enforceable in civil law.

3 Bribery

Section overview

- Bribery is an extremely serious offence which undermines public confidence in administrative, professional and judicial affairs.

- Bribery is involved primarily with the offering or receiving of gifts or payments.

The Bribery Act 2010 ('the Act') came into force on 1 July 2011. The Act is intended to simplify the previous law on bribery and corruption, which was to be found in common law and a number of statutes.

3.1 Bribery offences

The Act creates four main offences:

- Bribing another person
- Being bribed
- Bribing a foreign public official
- Corporate failure to prevent bribery

The **offence of bribing another person** is committed where a person offers, promises or gives a financial or other advantage to another person, intending the advantage either to induce that person to perform improperly a relevant function or activity or to reward him for such improper performance. It is irrelevant whether the person offered is the same person as the one who performs the function. It is also an offence if the person knows that the acceptance of the advantage would itself constitute improper performance of a relevant function or activity. It does not matter in either case whether the offer is made directly or through a third party.

The **offence of being bribed** is committed where a person requests or accepts or agrees to receive a financial or other advantage improperly or as a reward for improper performance or intending that improper performance should result. It does not matter whether the advantage is received or to be received through a third party nor whether the advantage is for the benefit of the receiving party or another person.

In both of these offences, a 'relevant function or activity' includes any function of a public nature or any activity connected with business or carried out in the course of employment and applies where the person performing that function or activity is in a position of trust or is otherwise expected to perform it in good faith or impartially. The function or activity is relevant even if it has no connection with the UK and is performed outside the UK. 'Improper' performance means performance which does not meet the standard that a reasonable person in the UK would expect.

The **offence of bribing a foreign public official** is committed where a person offers, promises or gives any financial or other advantage to the official or a third party with the official's consent or acquiescence or at his request and that official is not permitted or required by the written law applicable to him to be so influenced. This must be done with the intention of influencing the official in that capacity and to obtain or retain business or an advantage in the conduct of business.

The Act also provides a new **offence of failing to prevent bribery**. This is committed by a commercial organisation that fails to prevent an offence being committed by a person who performs services for or on behalf of the organisation in any capacity, including as agent, employee or subsidiary. Commercial organisations for these purposes include companies and partnerships based in the UK or doing business in the UK. The organisation does have a defence, however, if it can prove that it had in place 'adequate procedures' designed to prevent persons associated with it from committing bribery.

'Adequate procedures' is not a defined term but the Secretary of State has recently published guidance about procedures that a relevant commercial organisation may put in place to prevent its employees and others from committing bribery, in order to avail itself of this defence. The size of an organisation and the extent of its exposure to risk will be taken into account in considering the steps which it is expected to take. However, senior management is expected to take responsibility for an organisation's anti-corruption programme and the organisation's staff must be trained in its procedures, which must be kept under review. The guidance makes it clear that the extension of hospitality and gifts is permitted where the purpose is to establish or encourage good business relations, but will fall foul of the Act where the purpose is to persuade the other party improperly to award business or favours to the organisation.

3.2 General defence and penalties

A person charged with a bribery offence may have a defence if he can prove that his conduct was necessary for the proper exercise of any function of an intelligence service or the proper exercise of any function of the armed forces when engaged on active service.

Proceedings for an offence under the Act may only be instituted by or with the consent of either the Director of Public Prosecutions, the Director of the Serious Fraud Office or the Director of Revenue and Customs Prosecutions.

The maximum penalty under the Act is ten years' imprisonment and/or an unlimited fine.

Interactive question 1: Bribery   [Difficulty level: Exam standard]

Indicate whether an offence of bribery is committed in the following instances:

1	Financial Wizards LLP extends an invitation to 20 senior partners in three local accountancy firms to be wined and dined at the England v Wales Six-Nations rugby match, in the hope of securing new business	☐	Yes	☐	No
2	Jack offers a HM Customs and Revenue inspector a sum of money to turn a blind eye to a minor irregularity in his financial records, but the inspector refuses to accept it.	☐	Yes	☐	No

See **Answer** at the end of this chapter.

4 Money laundering

Section overview

- Money laundering is the process by which the proceeds of crime (either cash or other property) are converted into assets which appear to have a legitimate (rather than illegal) origin.

- 'Relevant persons', including accountants in practice, are required by law to report any knowledge or suspicion of money laundering to the authorities (currently the Serious Organised Crime Agency ('SOCA')

- The primary legislation on money laundering is the Proceeds of Crime Act 2002 ('POCA 2002'), supplemented by the Money Laundering Regulations 2007 ('the Regulations').

The term 'money laundering' covers any activity by which the apparent source and ownership of the proceeds of crime are changed, in such a way that the cash or other assets appear to have been obtained legitimately.

'Proceeds of crime', termed 'criminal property' in POCA 2002, means any assets which have been procured by means of a criminal act. A criminal act is one which constitutes an offence against the state, punishable by fines and/or imprisonment.

4.1 Examples of money laundering

Although money laundering is an international problem, and can involve transfers of funds between many different countries, it is also widespread within individual countries in small- and large-scale operations.

Examples of money laundering include:

- Illegal arms sales
- Smuggling
- Drug trafficking
- Prostitution
- Tax evasion
- Bribery
- Other financial fraud

Methods which criminals might use to launder money include:

- Buying and selling luxury goods, for example cars – thereby obtaining a seemingly respectable payment from the subsequent buyer

- Buying investments and cashing them in

- Overpayment of tax

- Depositing money with a solicitor or accountant, then requesting the return of funds

- Feeding cash into cash-based businesses

- Buying chips in a casino and then cashing in unspent chips

Many such transactions take place through the Internet and are generally known as 'cyberlaundering'.

4.2 Proceeds of Crime Act 2002 - The offences

The POCA 2002 sets out the offences described in the table below:

Offence	Description	Defences	Penalty
Money laundering	1 **Concealing** criminal property, ie concealing or disguising its nature, source, location, ownership etc, or removing it from UK	A report was made to MLRO or SOCA It was intended to make a report to MLRO/SOCA but there was a reasonable excuse for not having done so	14 years' imprisonment Unlimited fine
	2 **Arranging** ie being concerned in an arrangement, knowing or suspecting that it will facilitate the acquisition, use or control of criminal property by or on behalf of an other person		
	3 **Acquiring**, using or possessing criminal property	(3 only) If the person acquired used or possessed the property for 'adequate consideration' and did not know that such payment might facilitate criminal conduct.	
	4 Knowingly **inciting** or **assisting** another person to commit or attempting to commit any of the above offences		

Offence	Description	Defences	Penalty
Failure to report	Failure to inform MLRO or SOCA as soon as practicable, of any knowledge or suspicion that another person is engaged in money laundering Failure to inform MLRO/SOCA of any information which raises reasonable grounds for suspicion (ie an offence can be committed if a person **should have been** suspicious in the circumstances)	There was a reasonable excuse for not making a report The person does not know or suspect money laundering and his employer has not provided him with appropriate training	5 years' imprisonment Unlimited fine
Tipping off	Disclosing to a third person that a disclosure or report has been made to the SOCA or other appropriate person, where that disclosure is likely to prejudice any investigation that might be carried out as a result of the report Disclosing that an investigation is being contemplated or carried out, where that disclosure is likely to prejudice such an investigation	The person did not know or suspect that the disclosure was likely to prejudice the investigation The person had lawful authority or reasonable excuse to make the disclosure	2 years' imprisonment Unlimited fine

Note that the reasonable excuse defences have been interpreted narrowly by the courts but fear of physical violence or other menaces would almost certainly be sufficient.

4.3 The Money Laundering Regulations 2007

The Regulations came into effect in December 2007 (superseding the 2003 Regulations and subsequently amended by further regulations in 2012). They apply to 'relevant persons', namely:

- Credit and financial institutions

- Accountants in practice including auditors, insolvency practitioners, external accountants and tax advisers

- Independent legal professionals, including solicitors and barristers

- Estate agents

- Casinos

- 'High value dealers' (i.e. those who sell goods for cash for 15,000 Euros or more (and 'cash' in this context means coins, notes and travellers' cheques only))

The Regulations are designed to achieve two purposes:

- To enable suspicious transactions to be recognised and reported to the law enforcement agencies, and

- To ensure that if a client comes under investigation in the future, a relevant person can provide part of the audit trail

The Regulations cover the following:

- Customer due diligence
- Record-keeping, procedures and training
- Supervision and registration
- Enforcement

The expression 'customer due diligence' (or 'CDD') replaces the expression 'knowing your client' from the 2003 Regulations and includes:

- Identifying customers and verifying their identity
- Identifying any beneficial owners
- Obtaining information on the purpose and nature of the business relationship

Relevant persons must carry out CDD measures when they:

(a) Establish a business relationship
(b) Carry out an occasional transaction
(c) Suspect money laundering or terrorist financing
(d) Doubt the veracity or accuracy of information obtained

This is to be done on a risk-sensitive basis. There are detailed exceptions where CDD measures need not be carried out. In other cases, extra measures may be required (in particular, where a potential new client is not physically present and a face-to-face meeting with the practitioner is not possible).

For potential clients which are companies and partnerships, in order to carry out CDD measures effectively, the professional bodies advise that relevant persons should identify who has ultimate control or significant influence, for example:

- Executive directors
- Senior financial managers
- Significant shareholders
- Substantial loan creditors

The importance of **record-keeping** is that if an investigation is mounted into suspected money laundering, and information is lacking from the client, the investigators may require information from the practitioner. Records must be kept for a minimum of five years.

These internal systems have been outlined in your Assurance study manual and will be discussed more fully at the application stage in Audit and Assurance.

Non-compliance with any of the Regulations is a criminal offence in itself, regardless of whether money laundering has taken place. The maximum sentence is two years' imprisonment or an unlimited fine, or both.

4.4 Duty to report

Generally speaking, accountants working in practice or other 'relevant persons' must report **knowledge or suspicion** of money laundering to a nominated officer within their workplace (usually called the Money Laundering Reporting Officer, or 'MLRO'). The MLRO has a duty to consider the facts and, if appropriate, to report the matter to the Serious Organised Crime Agency, usually by submitting a Suspicious Activities Report. Sole traders are not required to nominate an officer and, therefore, report direct to the SOCA. Failure to comply with the duty to report will mean a potential criminal liability, but making an authorised disclosure (eg to a MLRO or SOCA) may provide a defence against a charge of money laundering.

By way of example, a report should be made in the following circumstances:

- Where a new customer is reluctant to provide proof of his identity or there appears to be no genuine reason for him to use the business's services

- Where the customer's transaction is not of the type or size normally conducted by that customer

- Where a cash transaction is unusually large or

- Where the customer requires a payment to be made to a third party who appears to have no connection with the transaction.

4.5 Knowledge and suspicion

If a relevant person has knowledge, or virtual certainty, that money laundering has taken place, this must be reported to the SOCA. Belief or probability (ie more than 50% likelihood) that such an offence has been committed should also be reported.

'Suspicion' is more difficult to define. The courts have interpreted it as being something less than knowledge or belief but more than speculation. Although suspicion is by nature personal and subjective, it should still be built on some objective foundation. There should be some degree of consistency in the way that a firm's MLRO treats possible causes of suspicion.

If there are reasonable grounds for suspicion, the activity concerned should be reported. But this should not necessarily be taken to include higher-than-normal risk factors which may affect certain types of business or certain areas of a business's operation.

For example, the fact that a client, or a client's supplier, demands payment in cash is not in itself suspicious, unless there are grounds for suspicion that the objective of this is tax evasion or some other criminal activity. Some of the questions that should be asked might be as follows:

- Is the transaction or activity normal for this customer?
- Does the transaction or business make sense from a business/personal point of view?
- Has the pattern of transactions changed?
- Where the transaction is with an entity in another country is there a good business reason for this?

Firms must ensure that all staff are properly trained in, know and understand the procedure for dealing with suspicions, including the identity of the MLRO.

It is also essential that firms follow the Regulations on awareness and training so that staff are able to identify, and therefore report, suspicious transactions.

Note that suspicious activities include anything as described above which has come to a relevant person's attention during the course of his or her business. This need not be the activity of a client itself.

4.6 Confidentiality and privileged circumstances

Generally speaking, the need to make a report takes precedence over considerations of client confidentiality. The Act offers protection where information rightly disclosed under the Act results in a breach of confidentiality. Accountants should take care not to disclose information that is not relevant to the offence known or suspected.

However, the Act does provide that where a relevant professional adviser receives information in privileged circumstances, it shall be a defence to a charge of failing to report, provided there is no intention of furthering a criminal purpose. Thus, if a client asks for advice on tax law and the purpose of seeking that advice is to evade paying taxes, the tax adviser would not be bound or excused by legal privilege and should make a report of suspicion of money laundering. If a client feared that tax evasion had mistakenly taken place and was seeking clarification with the intention of ceasing to evade taxes, then legal privilege applies, and no report should be made.

Privileged circumstances are **limited to the provision of legal advice and acting in respect of litigation**. Relevant professional advisers are accountants, auditors and tax advisers who are members of a relevant professional body, such as the ICAEW.

Worked example: Professional privilege

Rita is an accountant working in the forensic department of her firm. She has been asked to be an expert witness in a personal injury case. During the course of an interview with the claimant, Bob, in which Rita is seeking to ascertain the lost earnings for the relevant period, Bob tells her that he has not always reported all his earnings to HM Customs and Revenue in recent years.

This constitutes a money laundering offence, as he has been retaining the proceeds of criminal conduct (failing to declare his proper income to HMRC). However, the information is received in privileged circumstances and Rita is not required to report this knowledge.

This exemption is a potentially difficult area for accountants as they may be involved in giving advice on legal issues as part of a portfolio of services and therefore will need to exercise judgement as to when a suspicion has been formed in privileged circumstances.

You should note that this is a specific legislative provision which means that certain information received by an accountant in specific circumstances need not be disclosed. It is not the same as the broader 'legal professional privilege' which, as a matter of law, attaches to all communications between a person and a solicitor or barrister where those communications are in respect of litigation or the giving of legal advice. That general privilege does not extend to accountants, even where accountants give advice on tax or other legal matters.

R (on the application of Prudential plc) v Special Commissioner of Income Tax 2013

The facts: The Prudential was served with notices during a tax investigation by the HMRC, requiring it to disclose documents concerning its tax liability. The Prudential argued that the documents contained tax advice from accountants and were therefore protected by legal advice privilege.

Decision: The Supreme Court held that legal advice is privileged only where it is given by solicitors, barristers and appropriately qualified overseas lawyers, unless specific legislation provided otherwise.

Worked example: Money laundering

Joe is an audit manager who is reviewing the audit of White Group Ltd. The White Group is a large group of companies, of which White Group Ltd (WGL) is the ultimate parent company. WGL's subsidiaries are all trading companies which operate in a variety of industries. This is as a result of diversification from the original company which manufactured machine parts. There seems to be little business justification for the nature of the diversification, and although the various subsidiary companies of WGL carry out very different businesses, there seem to be a high number of transactions and transfers between them. WGL also has a subsidiary overseas in a country well known to be a tax haven. Joe discovers that small but regular transfers of cash from each of the other subsidiaries have been made to this overseas subsidiary.

Joe has begun to suspect that the White Group is being used to launder the proceeds of criminal money. In addition to the existence of the overseas subsidiary which is receiving repeated small transfers from all the businesses, many of the businesses are cash-rich despite not having very good trading records, and recent investigation of some transfers between the fancy goods retail outlet and the metal parts manufacturing company caused him to be suspicious, as there appeared to be no real business purpose for them.

As Joe has reasonable suspicion that the group may be carrying on money laundering, he should make a report to the MLRO (if the company has one) or the SOCA, because if he does not do so he is committing the crime of failing to report. In carrying out a number of transactions for the group, he may be committing the crime of assisting money laundering to take place. If he makes a report, he must then take care not to commit the offence of tipping off, by making any other party aware of the fact that he has suspicions and has raised them with the authorities.

Interactive question 2: Money laundering [Difficulty level: Exam standard]

Angela is an auditor working at Frazzle Ltd. She has been auditing the journals put through after the trial balance had been extracted which therefore affect the financial statements. There is one round sum journal relating to cash which appears to have no justification, for which the description reads 'Transfer per CB' and which the accountant cannot explain. CB is the managing director. During the course of the audit, Angela has also noticed a distinct change in the lifestyle of CB from previous years. He is driving an expensive car and his address as noted in the company records has changed to an address in a much more lavish part of town. None of this is explained by payroll transactions in respect of CB.

Angela should:

A   Do nothing. She has no grounds for reasonable suspicion of criminal activity, as the change in the managing director's lifestyle might be explained by a legacy or a lottery win.

B   Ask the managing director about what the transfer relates to. If the answer causes her to be suspicious that illegal activity might be taking place, given the other factors causing suspicion, she should make a report to her MLRO.

C   Make a report to the MLRO without delay and not query the transaction with the managing director, as that might constitute the offence of tipping off

D   Make a report to the MLRO without delay and let the company accountant know that such a report has been made as a professional courtesy

See **Answer** at the end of this chapter.

Interactive question 3: Money laundering

One of your clients, a builder, always requires payment in cash. You have no evidence that he is evading income tax, only the knowledge that he is paid in cash.

Should your MLRO report this as a suspicion to SOCA?

☐ Yes

☐ No

Interactive question 4: Money laundering

A client tells you over a business lunch that he is having a swimming pool installed at his home. The contractors have asked for payment in cash, which he suspects is because they will not be declaring it to HM Revenue and Customs.

Do you have a duty to disclose this to SOCA?

☐ Yes

☐ No

5 Law and ethics

Section overview

- Chartered accountants accept the responsibility of acting in the public interest and also the role of being at the forefront of the fight against domestic and international corruption in all its forms.

- Accountants must have regard to ethical codes from the ICAEW and other relevant bodies in addition to the legal requirements of statute and regulations already discussed in this chapter.

The commission of the criminal offences which you have just studied causes a major distortion of trade, undermines the development of emerging markets and impacts upon a company's reputation and ability to secure investment.

Of course, accountants should conduct themselves at all times with the utmost integrity in providing their services, but over and above this, they are encouraged to play a role proactively in upholding ethical standards for tackling corruption on a domestic and international level. It goes without saying that acts of bribery, fraud and insider dealing are unethical as well as criminal acts.

You will be aware that many issues of corporate governance have arisen in response to high profile corporate and accounting scandals and a significant influence in such matters is the profound effect that allegations and investigations of criminal activity can have on companies and executives. It is the criminal law, as well as the regulatory law, that is responsible for introducing and formulating governance requirements and criminal sanctions provide an effective means of achieving sound corporate governance.

If you come across anything which points to any of the criminal activities discussed in this chapter, then you will need to consider whether the information you have discovered and may wish to disclose is confidential or whether there is a duty to disclose it in the public interest or as required by law, thus overriding the duty of confidentiality. It goes without saying that you should investigate the matter first, to check your understanding of the relevant act and the circumstances in which it took place, as you will be aware that not all suspicions turn out to be well founded and an unwise disclosure could be extremely detrimental to many, including you.

In summary, you will need to consider

1   Consulting with or reporting to any person in accordance with any legal requirement (for example, the MLRO or SOCA in relation to money laundering, a prescribed body in relation to whistleblowing or the police in the event of fraud).

2   Referring to guidance from ICAEW or other relevant body (for example, the ICAEW code of ethics and the CCAB (Consultative Committee of Accountancy Bodies) guidance on money laundering procedures).

3   Obtaining legal advice from a solicitor or in-house lawyer.

4   Having preliminary discussions with your senior work colleague responsible for the work you are doing.

5   Seeking advice from the ICA Ethics Advisory Service.

Summary

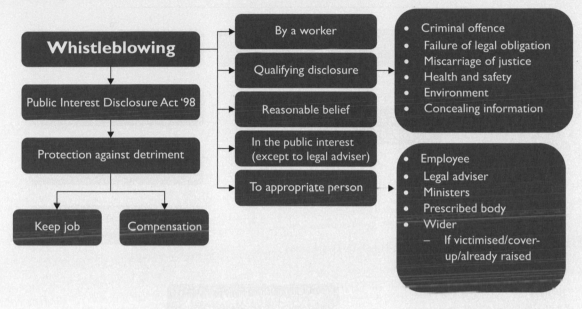

Whistleblowing

Public Interest Disclosure Act '98

Protection against detriment

- Keep job
- Compensation

- By a worker
- Qualifying disclosure
- Reasonable belief
- In the public interest (except to legal adviser)
- To appropriate person

- Criminal offence
- Failure of legal obligation
- Miscarriage of justice
- Health and safety
- Environment
- Concealing information

- Employee
- Legal adviser
- Ministers
- Prescribed body
- Wider
  - If victimised/cover-up/already raised

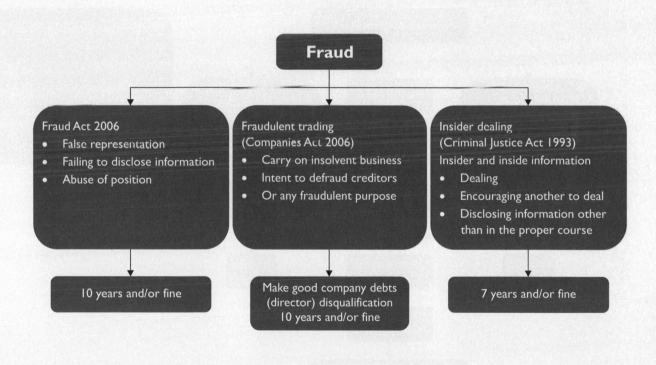

Fraud

Fraud Act 2006
- False representation
- Failing to disclose information
- Abuse of position

Fraudulent trading (Companies Act 2006)
- Carry on insolvent business
- Intent to defraud creditors
- Or any fraudulent purpose

Insider dealing (Criminal Justice Act 1993)
Insider and inside information
- Dealing
- Encouraging another to deal
- Disclosing information other than in the proper course

10 years and/or fine

Make good company debts (director) disqualification 10 years and/or fine

7 years and/or fine

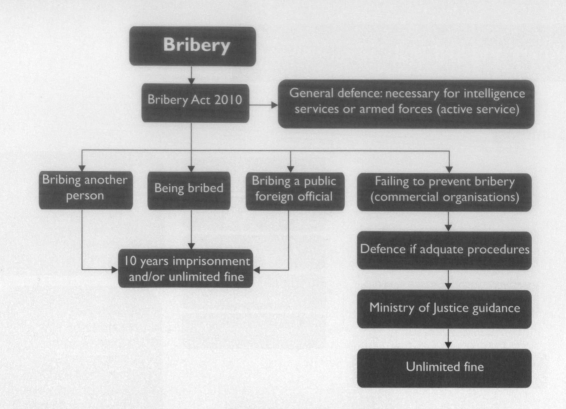

Bribery

Bribery Act 2010 → General defence: necessary for intelligence services or armed forces (active service)

- Bribing another person
- Being bribed
- Bribing a public foreign official
- Failing to prevent bribery (commercial organisations)

10 years imprisonment and/or unlimited fine

Defence if adquate procedures

Ministry of Justice guidance

Unlimited fine

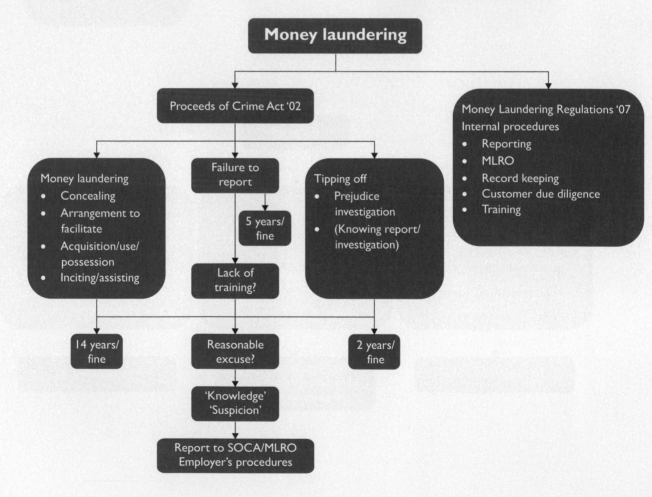

Money laundering

Proceeds of Crime Act '02

Money Laundering Regulations '07
Internal procedures
- Reporting
- MLRO
- Record keeping
- Customer due diligence
- Training

Money laundering
- Concealing
- Arrangement to facilitate
- Acquisition/use/ possession
- Inciting/assisting

Failure to report

Tipping off
- Prejudice investigation
- (Knowing report/ investigation)

5 years/ fine

Lack of training?

14 years/ fine

Reasonable excuse?

2 years/ fine

'Knowledge' 'Suspicion'

Report to SOCA/MLRO
Employer's procedures

Self-test

Answer the following questions.

1   Which Act governs the law on whistleblowing?

2   A person making a qualifying disclosure must be able to show, on the balance of probabilities, that the matters alleged are true.

☐ True

☐ False

3   A worker must make a disclosure to his employer in the first instance.

☐ Yes

☐ No

4   Which of the following applies in the event of a valid whistleblowing?

A   The worker is entitled to keep his job
B   The employer is liable to a fine
C   The worker may claim damages
D   The employer must make a written apology to the worker

5   Fill in the blanks.

The Fraud Act 2006 makes the following criminal offences:

* Fraud by false ....

* Fraud by .... information

* Fraud by .... position

6   Can a person be found guilty of fraudulent trading only once the company is in liquidation?

☐ Yes

☐ No

7   Dealing in securities while possessing inside information as an insider is an offence. What are the other two principal offences of insider dealing?

8   Would the following statement constitute an offence under the Criminal Justice Act 1993? If so, which offence?

'I can't tell you why, but now would be a good time to buy shares in Bloggs plc'.

9   What is the maximum penalty for insider dealing?

10   Complete the blanks:

Insider information is '.. ....
.... 'relating to a .... of securities that are .... and not to securities generally. It must, if .... , be likely to have a significant effect on .... and it must be specific or ....

11   A person who accepts a bribe is guilty of an offence as well as the person who pays it.

☐ True

☐ False

12   Define money laundering.

13 Identify which of the following statements are true and which are false.

A	It is a defence to the offence of failing to report a suspicion of money laundering that a person had not had sufficient training to understand the legal requirement on him	☐ True	☐ False
B	It is a defence to the offence of failing to report a suspicion of money laundering that a person formed the suspicion in privileged circumstances	☐ True	☐ False
C	It is a defence to the offence of failing to report a suspicion of money laundering that a person disclosed his suspicion to the relevant MLRO at his firm	☐ True	☐ False

14 Indicate which of the following statements are true and which are false.

A	The maximum prison sentence for an accountant assisting in money laundering is five years	☐ True	☐ False
B	The maximum prison sentence for an accountant failing to make a report of a suspicion of money laundering is five years	☐ True	☐ False
C	There is no prison sentence for the offence of tipping off, this is punished by fine only	☐ True	☐ False

15 Where an accountant gives advice on matters of revenue law, his advice is said to be protected by legal professional privilege and need not be disclosed under any circumstances.

☐ True

☐ False

Now, go back to the Learning Objectives in the Introduction. If you are satisfied you have achieved these objectives, please tick them off.

ICAEW

Answer to Interactive question 1

1   No. Such corporate hospitality is likely to be regarded as entirely proper and will not constitute an offence under the Bribery Act 2010.

2   Yes. The offer of a financial advantage constitutes an offence of bribery, regardless of whether or not it is accepted.

Answer to Interactive question 2

C   If Angela did nothing, she might be committing the offence of failing to report a reasonable suspicion. On the basis of the cash transfer, coupled with the other observations Angela has made, this appears to be a case of reasonable suspicion rather than mere speculation and, whilst it might be reasonable not to make further enquiries (although making normal audit enquiries does not necessarily constitute tipping off), she should not do nothing at all.

It would be best if Angela reported her suspicion to the MLRO. If Angela were also to inform the company accountant of her report, she would be committing the offence of tipping off. Despite any personal or professional regard Angela has for the company accountant and any potential trouble he might be in, Angela should not inform him about the report. Nor should she discuss her concerns with the managing director, since he is himself the object of the suspicion and to do so would also constitute tipping off.

Answer to Interactive question 3

No   It is common for builders and similar small businesses to require payment in cash, and this fact alone need not excite suspicion. However if any other aspect of the client's business appears abnormal (e.g. a lifestyle more lavish than his declared income might suggest), then suspicion of tax evasion should be reported to SOCA.

Answer to Interactive question 4

Yes   If the information comes to you during the course of your business this must be reported. Although the possibility of tax evasion is not an issue between you and your client, the suspicion of the criminal act has been communicated to you at a lunch which you have attended because of your business.

The intention to commit a crime (in this case tax evasion) can itself be a crime, and although you do not know for a fact that the contractor intends to evade tax, it seems probable that he does.

You should not inform the client of your action, as this could constitute 'tipping off' under s.333 POCA 2002. Your report to the SOCA can name only your client: if the SOCA decides to investigate, it can ask for the information from your client.

(Note that if the information came to you through a friend, you would not need to make a report, although your friend might be advised either to refuse to deal with the contractor or at least not to talk about it to anyone.)

1   The Public Interest Disclosure Act 1998

2   False. The disclosure must be made in the reasonable belief that it is true.

3   No. This is generally desirable but not compulsory.

4   C   A: This is in the discretion of the court.

    B + D: The Act affords protection to the worker rather than imposing sanctions on the employer.

5   False representation

    Failing to disclose information

    Abuse of position

6   No. Civil liability (IA 1986) depends upon the company being in liquidation but the criminal offence (CA 2006) can be committed regardless of whether or not the company is in liquidation.

7   Encouraging another to deal

    Disclosing inside information other than in the proper performance of one's employment, office or profession

8   Yes. The offence of encouraging another to deal. It is immaterial whether the person actually deals.

9   Seven years' imprisonment and/or an unlimited fine

10 Inside information is '**price-sensitive information**' relating to a **particular issuer** of securities that are **price-affected** and not to securities generally. It must, if **made public**, be likely to have a significant effect on **price** and it must be specific or **precise**.

11 True. The Bribery Act 2010 contains an offence of being bribed.

12 Money laundering is the term given to attempts to make the proceeds of crime appear respectable.

    It covers any activity by which the apparent source and ownership of money representing the proceeds of crime are changed so that the money appears to have been obtained legitimately.

13 A   True
    B   True
    C   True

14 A   False (14 years)
    B   True
    C   False (2 years)

15 False. Although an accountant may not be required to report information concerning the commission of a money laundering offence by his client, which he receives in such circumstances, the more general 'legal professional privilege' extends only to solicitors, barristers and suitably qualified foreign lawyers and not to accountants, even if they advise on tax laws.

CHAPTER 11

Employment and data protection law

Introduction

Examination context

Topic List

Summary and Self-test

Answers to Interactive questions

Answers to Self-test

Learning objectives

- To be able to distinguish between an employee and an independent contractor ☐

- To understand the legal consequences of being an employee ☐

- To understand that an employment contract includes terms implied by law and to know what they are ☐

- To identify the circumstances in which an employee is unfairly dismissed and appreciate the consequences ☐

- To identify circumstances in which an employee is wrongfully dismissed and appreciate the consequences ☐

- To recognise whether an employee is entitled to claim a statutory redundancy payment ☐

- To understand the content and significance of the Data Protection Act 1998 ☐

Specific syllabus references for this chapter are: 4a, b, c, d and e.

Syllabus links

The practical effects of accounting for employees are looked at in Accounting and auditing payroll systems are addressed in Assurance.

You dealt with information processing and security in Business and Finance. The Data Protection Act is one of the reasons information must be kept secure.

Examination context

You may expect several questions on employee status and the contents of an employment contract. Redundancy, wrongful dismissal and unfair dismissal are particularly important exam topics. Although data protection is a relatively minor area of the syllabus, you should be prepared for questions on its practical application.

In the assessment, candidates may be required to:

- Identify who is an employee and the main legal consequences of employment status

- Identify the key features of employment contracts

- Recognise circumstances in which an employment contract may be terminated and the consequences of termination

- Identify when a dismissal constitutes a wrongful dismissal or an unfair dismissal

- Identify the circumstances where an employee can claim a statutory redundancy payment

- Identify the key requirements of the Data Protection Act 1998 on the use of personal information and how the Act can affect the manner in which information systems are used by businesses

1 'Employee' status and its significance

Section overview

- An 'employee' can be distinguished from an 'independent contractor' or self-employed person.

- An employee is treated quite differently from an independent contractor in a number of respects, including taxation, social security, health and safety, employment protection and liability in tort.

An employee is someone who is employed under a '**contract of service**', ie a contract of employment, which can be express or implied and oral or in writing. An independent contractor is someone who works under a **contract for services** and is also described as 'self-employed'. A traditional equity partner with a capital stake in the firm, involvement in management decisions and a share in profits and losses is not an employee. Nor is a fixed share equity partner (*Tiffin v Lester Aldridge LLP 2012*). Whether so-called 'partners' are employees will depend on the facts of each case. A salaried partner, for example, is likely to be an employee for employment law purposes.

The courts are often faced with determining whether someone is an employee or an independent contractor. In doing so, the wording of any contract will not be conclusive (but may be relevant) and, instead, the courts will apply **a multiple test**, taking into account a number of factors described below. None of these factors is conclusive and the weight attached to each may vary. This multiple test looks at the economic reality underpinning the employment relationship and asks whether, on balance, the person can be said to be working 'on his own account' or is better described as an 'employee'.

There are three essential elements, or conditions, that **must** be present in order for the contract of service (and thus the employer/ employee relationship) to exist, namely:

Condition	Explanation
Personal service	The employee must have agreed to provide his own work and skill in the performance of a service for his employer. However, the fact that an employee is able to delegate that performance in limited circumstances (for example when he is sick or only with permission) will not mean that this condition is not met.
Control	There must be some element of control exercisable by the employer over the employee.
Mutuality of obligations	There must be an obligation on the employer to provide work and an obligation on the employee to do that work. Thus a 'casual worker' who works as and when required, even if in preference to others, cannot be an employee because there is no 'mutuality of obligations'.

If these factors are not present there can be no contract of service. The fact that they are present, however, does not mean that there *will* be a contract of service. The level of service and degree of control will be taken into account along with the other factors listed below:

Factors taken into account	Explanation	Significance of factor
Personal performance	Can he delegate or subcontract the task to another person if he so chooses and, if so, to what extent?	The greater the freedom to delegate, the less likely someone will be considered to be an employee (and **total freedom** will mean that the condition of personal service is not satisfied).
Degree of control	ie if and to what extent the employer can tell the employee not only what to do but also how and when to do it. Are there any restrictions on where he works or for how long he works, for example?	The greater the degree of control, the more likely someone will be considered to be an employee.

Factors taken into account	Explanation	Significance of factor
Mutuality of obligations	ie whether there is an obligation on the employer to provide work and an obligation on the employee to perform that work.	The existence of a mutuality of obligations is consistent with a contract of employment
Contractual provisions	The courts will consider the terms of any contract between the parties.	Contractual terms may not be conclusive but, for example, including provisions as to holiday and sick pay will make it more likely that the contract will be treated as a contract of service.
Tools and equipment	Who provides and maintains the tools and equipment needed for the job?	To the extent that such matters are the responsibility of the employer, the more likely someone will be considered to be an employee.
Uniform	Does he wear any uniform or display any logo belonging to the 'employer'?	If so, he is more likely to be considered to be an employee.
Employer's support staff	Can he utilise the employer's support staff?	If so, he is more likely to be considered to be an employee.
Payment of tax, NI	Is he paid gross or is tax deducted at source?	Deduction of tax and national insurance by the employer suggest a contract of employment.
Financial responsibility	Does he undertake any financial responsibility for investment or risk (for example as a result of delays in the performance of services he has agreed). Likewise, to what extent can he profit from sound management in the performance of his task?	The more he assumes responsibility for such matters (and profits from good performance) the less likely he will be considered to be an employee.
Sole 'employer'	Does he work for more than one person?	To the extent that the person is able to work for more than one employer, he is less likely to be considered as an employee.
Length of service	For how long has there been a working relationship between the parties?	The longer the relationship, the more likely he will be considered to be an employee.

It is fair to say that the **nature of the claim** brought before the court may influence its deliberations. For example, if the claim relates to a breach of health and safety obligations, there will be a real public interest in recognising an employer/employee relationship because of the statutory and common law duties owed by an employer to an employee. Similarly, an employment tribunal might conclude that someone is an employee, notwithstanding that the tax authorities treat him as a self-employed person.

Worked example: Employee or independent contractor?

A builder's labourer is paid his wages without deduction of income tax or National Insurance contributions and calls himself a self-employed contractor providing services. The person for whom he works can dismiss him, decide on which site he works and direct him as to the work he does, and also provides the tools that he uses. He is injured in an accident and sues on the basis that his 'employer 'owes him a legal duty of ensuring his safety.

Notwithstanding that he is paid gross and calls himself self-employed, it is likely that the other factors will tip the balance and he will be regarded as an employee working under a contract of employment.

Interactive question 1: Employee or independent contractor?

[Difficulty level: Exam standard]

Charles saw a sign advertising vacancies at a local building site. He contacted the foreman and was told that he would be required but that, because work depended on the weather conditions, he would work as and when required and would not be given an employment contract. He was also told that he would be accountable for his own income tax and national insurance. The foreman added that, like all of his employees, he would be provided with tools and that at the beginning of each day he would be told whether he would be needed and, if so, which site he would be working on that day. Lateness or theft of materials would lead to his dismissal. Which of the following best describes his legal status?

A   Charles is an employee because the provision of tools and control over his work, plus the fact that he is told that he could be dismissed for lateness or theft indicate that he is an employee.

B   Charles is not an employee due to the fact that he has to account for his own tax and national insurance.

C   Charles is an employee because he has responded to a job advertisement and the foreman referred to the contractors as employees.

D   Charles is not an employee because the fact that work is dependent on weather conditions means that there is no mutuality of obligations.

See **Answer** at the end of this chapter.

However, there are several other **practical reasons** why the distinction between a contract of service (employed) and a contract for services (self-employed) is important.

Significance of the distinction		
	Employee	**Self-employed**
Wrongful dismissal	Can claim wrongful dismissal	Cannot claim wrongful dismissal
Employment protection	There is legislation that confers protection and benefits upon employees under a contract of service, including • Minimum periods of notice • Entitlement to statutory redundancy payment • Remedies for unfair dismissal • Health and safety protection (Sometimes the protection is subject to the employee having completed a certain amount of continuous service.)	Note that increasingly, employment protection is given to 'workers' rather than 'employees'. 'Workers' is more widely defined and will often include those normally regarded as independent contractors as well as employees. It is important that you know to which term the legislation applies, for example, statutory protection against unfair dismissal applies to 'employees', but working time protection applies to 'workers'. Note too that statutory health and safety obligations on employers often relate to both employees and independent contractors.
Insolvency	In liquidation, an employee has preferential rights as a creditor for payment of outstanding salary and redundancy payments, up to certain limits	
Implied terms	There are rights and duties implied in an employment contract by common law and statute, for example a mutual duty of trust and confidence	These implied rights and duties do not generally apply to a contract for services

Significance of the distinction		
	Employee	**Self-employed**
Tortious acts	Employer is generally vicariously liable for tortious acts of employees, committed in the course of employment	Liability of person hiring an independent contractor for contractor's acts severely limited unless there is strict liability
Taxation	Deductions for income tax must be made by an employer under PAYE (Schedule E) from salary paid to employee	The self-employed are taxed under Schedule D and are directly responsible to HM Revenue and Customs for tax due
VAT		An independent contractor may have to register for, and charge, VAT.
Social security	Employers must pay secondary Class 1 contributions on behalf of employees Employees make primary Class 1 contributions There are also differences in statutory sick pay and levies for industrial training purposes	Independent contractors pay Class 2 and 4 contributions

Interactive question 2: Importance of employment status   [Difficulty level: Easy]

Indicate whether or not each of the following statements represents the legal and economic consequences that would follow a finding that someone is employed under a contract of service as opposed to a contract for services.

	Yes	No
A The company for which he works is required to declare and administer his income tax under PAYE	☐	☐
B The company will not be vicariously liable for any tort committed by him	☐	☐
C If the company is liquidated, he will have preferential rights to payment of salary	☐	☐
D He may be entitled to claim unfair dismissal in the event of his dismissal	☐	☐

See **Answer** at the end of this chapter.

2   The employment contract

Section overview

- An employment contract is usually made in writing although it can be created orally.

- Where there is no written contract covering them, an employer must provide a written statement of prescribed particulars within 2 months of the commencement of the employment.

- Certain duties are implied into a contract of employment on the part of the employee and employer, by common law and by statute.

An employment contract needs agreement between the parties, consideration and an intention to create legal relations just like any other contract. It may be written or oral. A written contract is likely to contain a number of express terms as to pay, hours, place of work and any special agreements between employee and employer going beyond legally required employment rights (such as maternity pay offered in excess of the statutory minimum).

Generally speaking, a change in contract terms can only be made with the **consent** of both parties to the contract. Also a new piece of legislation may result in a change to a term in an employment contract. Sometimes, an **express term** in the contract can give rights of variation, for example where a **'mobility clause'** allows an employer to require an employee to work at a different location. In such cases, the employer must exercise the power reasonably since the courts will imply terms of trust and respect which have the effect of overriding a strict application of contractual obligations.

United Bank Ltd v Akhtar 1989

The facts: An employee had a mobility clause in his employment contract under which he could be required to work anywhere in Great Britain. His employer gave him notice on 5 June that he would be transferred from Leeds to Birmingham as from 8 June. The employer refused the employee's request for a three-month delay, based on his wife's ill-health and the need to sell his house. The employee's subsequent request for 24 days' leave in order to sort out his affairs and to commence work in Birmingham on 10 July was unanswered. When pay was stopped with effect from 5 June, the employee resigned and claimed that he had been constructively dismissed.

Decision: The employee's claim succeeded. It was an implied term that the employer should exercise his right under the express provision reasonably, including giving reasonable notice.

2.1 Requirement for written particulars

Within two months of the beginning of the employment the employer must give to an employee a **written statement of prescribed particulars** of his employment (s 1 Employment Rights Act 1996), namely:

- The names of **employer** and **employee**
- The **date** on which employment began
- Whether any service with a previous employer forms part of the employee's **continuous period** of employment
- The scale or rate of **pay** and the intervals at which it is to be paid
- **Hours** of work (including any specified 'normal working hours')
- The **title** of the job that the employee is employed to do (or a brief job description)
- Any **holiday** and **holiday pay** entitlement
- **Sick leave** and **sick pay** entitlement
- **Pensions** and pension **schemes**
- Length of **notice** of termination to be given on either side
- Details of disciplinary procedures (or reference to where they can be found).

The last four particulars may be given by way of separate documents. The written particulars **do not constitute an employment contract**, although they provide persuasive evidence of what the contract contains. If the employee has a **written contract of employment** covering these points and has been given a copy, it is not necessary to provide him with separate written particulars.

If the employer fails to comply with these requirements the employee may apply to an employment tribunal for a **declaration** of what the terms should be. The tribunal may award compensation to an employee claiming unfair dismissal if the particulars are incomplete.

2.2 Employee's implied duties

Common law implies a number of duties on the part of the employee into any contract of employment:

Duty of faithful service (fidelity)	The employee has a **fundamental duty of faithful service** or fidelity to his employer. Thus an employee who works for an employer's competitor in his spare time, or who frustrates the commercial objectives of his employer, is in breach of this duty. Similarly, where an employee accepted personal commissions from suppliers on orders that he placed with them for goods supplied to his employer, he was justifiably dismissed and liable to account to the employer for the commissions.
To obey lawful and reasonable orders	The employee must show **obedience** to the employer's instructions unless they require him • To do an unlawful act or • To expose himself to personal danger (not inherent in his work) or • To do something outside his contract.
Not to misuse confidential information	This duty will not necessarily cease when the employment ceases. (Note that when someone invents or writes something as part of his employment, the right to the patent or copyright will normally belong to his employer.)
To exercise reasonable care and skill	The employee must demonstrate **reasonable competence, care and skill** in the performance of his work, bearing in mind the degree of skill and experience that the employee professes to have.
Personal service	The contract of employment is a personal one and so the employee may not delegate his duties without the employer's express or implied consent.
Trust and confidence	This is a mutual obligation imposed on both parties and is based on respect and consideration for each other. An employee should not, for example, make unjustifiable complaints or false accusations about his employer.

2.3 Employer's implied duties

The employer owes the following duties at common law:

To pay reasonable remuneration	This duty is subject to any express provision, for example to pay a rate fixed by the parties, or to pay nothing during a lay-off.
To indemnify employees	To **indemnify the employee** against expenses and losses incurred in the course of employment.
Health and safety	This is normally expressed as a duty to protect the employee against reasonably foreseeable risks to his **health, safety** and welfare at work. Health and safety obligations are also imposed by statute. This common law duty is three-fold and incorporates the obligations to provide • Safe plant and appliances • A safe system of work • Reasonably competent fellow-employees.
To provide work	To **provide work**. Generally speaking, an employer will not be liable for failing to provide work as long as he continues to pay wages (so liability is more likely to arise where someone is paid on a commission basis).

To provide accurate reference (where one is provided)	An employer does not have a duty to provide a reference (but if he does provide one, he must exercise reasonable care and skill to ensure that the information contained in it is accurate and gives a fair impression of the employee. In particular, an employer cannot divulge information that is not known to the employee (for example customers' complaints against the employee).
Not to disclose confidential information	The employer must not divulge confidential information about the employee to a third party without the employee's consent.
To maintain mutual trust and confidence	The employer must treat the employee with due respect and consideration. He must not, for example, conduct his business in a disreputable fashion, thereby damaging the employee's reputation and future employment prospects.

There is no duty to protect an employee's property.

Breach of a legal duty, if it is important enough, may entitle the injured party to treat the contract as discharged and to claim damages for breach of contract at common law. In addition, a breach of an employer's duty might give rise to a claim for wrongful and/or unfair dismissal.

Interactive question 3: Duties   [Difficulty level: Exam standard]

Identify whether the following statements are true or false in relation to the duties of the employer and the employee.

	True	False
A There is a duty of mutual trust and confidence between the employer and the employee	☐	☐
B An employer has a duty to pay reasonable remuneration	☐	☐
C An employer does not owe a duty to provide a reference for his employee	☐	☐
D An employee must always obey his employer's instructions	☐	☐

See **Answer** at the end of this chapter.

Legislation also imposes a number of implied duties on employers, often implementing European Directives on employment law issues. Many of these duties are concerned with 'family-friendly' employment and the 'work-life balance', for example provisions regarding maternity and paternity rights, flexible working arrangements and time off work. The principal duties implied by statute are as follows:

Subject	Duty
Pay	Under legislation protecting equal pay, contractual employment terms such as sick pay, holiday pay and working hours should be as favourable as those given to an employee of the opposite sex who is performing equal work or work of equal value, unless a 'genuine material factor' exists that justifies the discrepancy (for example, employees in London receiving a higher hourly rate than employees in Aberystwyth).
Health and safety	The Health and Safety at Work Act 1974 imposes general duties on employers, including a duty to ensure the continuing good health, safety and welfare of his employees, as far as is practicable. This general duty includes the following obligations: • To provide and maintain plant and systems of work that are safe and without risk • To make arrangements to ensure safe use, handling, storage and transport of articles/substances

Subject	Duty
	• To provide adequate information, instruction, training and supervision
	• To maintain safe places of work and ensure that there is adequate access in and out
	• To provide a safe and healthy working environment
	Certain additional duties are imposed on employers in particular categories, for example designers and manufacturers who must ensure that the articles designed or manufactured are safe and that there is adequate testing and examination. There are also extensive health and safety regulations which may be generally applicable or specifically applicable to particular hazards or risks.
	Contravention of the Act is an offence punishable by an unlimited fine and/or up to two years' imprisonment. If an offence is committed by a company, any director or other officer who consented to or was responsible for commission of the offence will also be guilty and liable to the penalties mentioned.
Discrimination	Not to discriminate on grounds of race, sex, disability, religion or belief, sexual orientation or age.

2.4 Notice provisions

Notice may be given without specific reason for so doing, unless the contract requires otherwise. If the contract states that notice may only be given in specific circumstances then generally it may not be given for any other reason. The notice must specify the date of its expiry.

It is a matter of negotiation between the employer and the employee how much notice is to be given by either party in order to terminate the contract. In the absence of an express provision, common law requires that a party gives **reasonable** notice, depending on the employee's position, the nature of the job and so forth. Additionally, statute lays down certain minimum periods which apply. This notice period depends on the employee's length of continuous service with the employer:

Length of continuous employment	Statutory minimum notice
≥1 month but < 2 years	Not less than 1 week
≥2 years but < 12 years	Not less than 1 week per year of continuous employment
≥12 years	Not less than 12 weeks

Either party may waive his entitlement to notice or accept a sum in lieu of notice.

During the period of notice an employee is entitled to pay at a rate not less than the average of his earnings over the previous twelve weeks.

3 Unfair dismissal

Section overview

• Employees covered by the statutory provisions for unfair dismissal have the right not to be unfairly dismissed.

• Breach of this right allows an employee to bring a claim for unfair dismissal to an employment tribunal.

• Reasons for dismissal are considered to be either automatically unfair or potentially fair.

• Remedies include reinstatement, re-engagement and compensation.

Legislation has widened the scope of protection to employees and increased the range of remedies available in the event of dismissal. Unfair dismissal is governed by the Employment Rights Act 1996 as amended by the Employment Act 2008.

3.1 The claim for unfair dismissal

Certain categories of employee are **excluded** from the statutory unfair dismissal code, including (generally speaking) persons employed to work **outside Great Britain** and employees dismissed while taking **unofficial strike** or other industrial action.

Otherwise, in order to pursue a claim for unfair dismissal, the employee must have been **continuously employed for at least two years**, whether full-time or part-time, with the same (or an associated) employer. (Note that employees who began their employment before 6 April 2012 may bring an unfair dismissal claim after only one year.)

In calculating **continuous employment**, it is possible for certain weeks to be excluded without them breaking the continuity, for example time spent on strike or on service in the armed forces. Also, where a business or undertaking is transferred and the employee then works for the transferee of the business, that change will not constitute a break in the employee's length of continuous employment.

However, where the reason for dismissal is automatically unfair (see 3.3 below), for example where the employee is pregnant, then there is no continuous employment requirement. Nor does the requirement apply where the reason for dismissal is the employee's political opinion or affiliation.

The **employee** must make a claim to an employment tribunal within **three months** of the effective date of termination, that is to say:

- Where there is termination by notice, the date on which the **notice expires**
- Where there is termination without notice, the date on which the **termination takes effect**
- Where an employee's fixed term contract is not renewed, the **date on which that term expires**

The **employee** must **show**:

- That he is a qualifying **employee** and
- That he has in fact been **dismissed**.

3.2 Dismissal

Dismissal for the purposes of an unfair dismissal claim may occur in one of three situations:

- The non-renewal of a contract for a fixed term or specific task or
- A termination by the employer, with or without notice or
- A constructive dismissal

Constructive dismissal occurs where the employer repudiates some **essential term** of the contract, for example by the imposition of a complete change in the employee's duties, and the employee resigns.

To establish constructive dismissal, an employee must show that:

- His employer has committed a serious breach of contract
- He left because of the breach
- He has not 'waived' the breach, thereby affirming the contract.

If he fails to show that he is treating the contract as repudiated (for example by walking out) he cannot claim that he has been constructively dismissed. Examples of breaches of contract which have led to claims of constructive dismissal include the following:

- A reduction in pay
- A complete change in the nature of the job
- A failure to provide a suitable working environment

The breach must be a serious one. Thus, in one case, an employer's refusal to give an advance against holiday pay was not sufficient.

Whether or not a dismissal has occurred is a question of fact and will depend on all the circumstances. Where an employee is dismissed, with or without notice, or where a fixed term contract is not renewed, he is entitled to request a written statement of the reasons for his dismissal within 14 days (provided he has been continuously employed for at least one year).

Any statement giving the reasons for dismissal which was provided by the employer will be admissible evidence in this regard. The fact that notice was given does not mean that an employee cannot bring a claim for unfair dismissal.

The following means of termination **do not constitute dismissal** for the purpose of unfair dismissal:

- Where the employee resigns (unless it is a case of constructive dismissal) or
- Where the contract is frustrated or
- Where the parties come to a mutual agreement to terminate the employment.

3.3 Automatically unfair reasons for dismissal

Some reasons are **automatically unfair**. These include:

- **Pregnancy** or pregnancy-related illness

- A spent conviction under the **Rehabilitation of Offenders Act 1974**

- **Trade union** membership or activities

- Dismissal on **transfer of an undertaking** (unless there are 'economic, technical or organisational reasons' justifying the dismissal)

- Taking (or proposing to take) steps to protect himself or others where he believes there to be serious and imminent danger

- Seeking to enforce **statutory rights** (for example relating to the national minimum wage, working time regulations or Sunday working)

- Making a **protected disclosure** under the Public Interest Disclosure Act 1998 (see Chapter 10).

In these cases, the employee is not required to have one year's continuous employment.

3.4 Potentially fair reasons

Once the employee has shown that he was dismissed, it is then for the **employer** to show the principal reason for the dismissal and that it was one of the potentially fair reasons (listed in s 98).

If the employer cannot satisfy the tribunal in this way, the dismissal is unfair.

If the tribunal **is** satisfied that the reason was one justifying dismissal, then it must decide whether the employer acted **reasonably**. Both criteria must be satisfied in order for a dismissal to be fair.

There are six grounds on which a dismissal is capable of being fair:

Reason	
Capability or qualifications	If the employer dismisses for **want of capability** on the part of the employee, the employer has to establish that the lack of capability at the time of dismissal was of such a nature and degree as to justify a dismissal, taking into account: - What the contract requires - The general standard of performance of his employees in this trade - The previous standard of performance of the dismissed employee himself '**Capability**' is to be assessed by reference to skills, aptitude, health or any other physical or mental quality. '**Qualification**' means any academic or technical qualifications relevant to the position that the employee holds. There must be a contractual obligation (express or implied) to hold the relevant qualification in order that a dismissal for lack of it can be considered fair. The lack of capability or qualification must be sufficiently serious and it may arise from one particular incident or a series of incidents. Thus, for example, a shop manageress who left her shop dirty and untidy, who failed to maintain cash registers and who did not put stock away was fairly dismissed.

CHAPTER

11

In another case, an airline pilot who landed his plane negligently on one occasion was held to have been fairly dismissed. It was recognised that the degree of professional skill was so high in his case that even small departures from that standard could be sufficiently serious as to justify dismissal.

Employee's misconduct	It is not necessary to prove that the employee is guilty of the alleged misconduct, only that the employer genuinely and reasonably believes him to be. Various types of misconduct have been held to justify dismissal, including abusive language, drink and drug abuse, theft and dishonesty, violence, downloading pornography, racial and sexual harassment and persistent lateness or absenteeism.
Redundancy	If an employee is dismissed mainly or only on the ground of **redundancy** (see section 5.1), he may claim remedies for unfair dismissal if he can show one of the following. • There were one or more other employees in similar positions who might have been made redundant and that he was selected for redundancy in breach of a customary arrangement or agreed procedure. • He was selected for a reason connected with trade union membership. A redundancy selection procedure should be in conformity with **good industrial relations practice**, ie • The employer should give as much warning as possible of impending redundancies. • The employer should consult with the trade union as to the best means of achieving the desired management result. • It should be possible to check criteria for selection against such things as attendance records, efficiency at the job and length of service. • The employer should ensure that the selection is made fairly. • The employer should consider whether an offer of alternative employment can be made.
Statutory restriction	This applies where there is a legal prohibition or restriction on either the employer or the employee which prevents the employment from being continued lawfully (for example, if a doctor or a solicitor employed as such is struck off the relevant professional register, or an employee loses his driving licence, which he needs to be able to do his job).
Some other substantial reason	ie some **other substantial reason** that could justify the dismissal of an employee holding the position that the employee held. Thus dismissal has been considered fair where, for example: • The employee was married to one of his employer's competitors • The employee refused to accept a change of shift working, made in the interests of the business and with the agreement of a large majority of other employees • The employee's alleged paedophile activity substantially risked the reputation of his public sector employer (even though the employee was not convicted of any offence) Following the abolition of the default retirement age, an employer who wishes to dismiss an employee on retirement grounds will need to satisfy this ground of 'some other substantial reason'. He will need to show that the retirement age is proportionate and objectively justified and also that a fair procedure has been followed.

Interactive question 4: Unfair dismissal 1   [Difficulty level: Exam standard]

Indicate whether or not Asif and Beatrice are entitled to pursue a claim for unfair dismissal in the following situations:

	Yes	No
Asif has been employed for twelve months, having commenced employment in March 2012, and has been given three months' notice of dismissal.	☐	☐
Beatrice commenced employment in May 2012 and had been employed for four months when she was dismissed without notice because her employer discovered that she was pregnant.	☐	☐

See **Answer** at the end of this chapter.

3.5 Reasonableness

Once the employment tribunal is of the view that the dismissal occurred for a potentially fair reason, it is then required to review the circumstances and to decide whether 'on the basis of equity and the substantial merits of the case', the employer acted reasonably in dismissing the employee. Whether the employer has acted reasonably or unreasonably is a question of fact depending on all the circumstances, including the size and resources of the business. The tribunal will consider:

- Have relevant **procedures** been followed? These may include internal procedures, contractual provisions or a code of practice relevant to the employment. In particular, the tribunal will have regard to the Acas code of practice in this area (see 3.6 below) in deciding whether the employer behaved reasonably.

- Did the employer take all **circumstances** into consideration? For example if an inexperienced employee is struggling to do his work, the employer is expected to help by advice or supervision in the hope that he may improve.

- What would any **reasonable employer** have done?

Except in the most flagrant cases it is not reasonable for an employer to dismiss an employee without first **warning** him that if he continues or repeats what has happened at least once he is likely to be dismissed. The tribunal might conclude that demotion (or some other step short of dismissal) might have been fair where dismissal was not.

In the case of a dismissal for want of capability or qualifications, reasonableness by the employer can be demonstrated by, for example

- Consultation with the employee to determine areas of difficulty
- Allowing a reasonable time for improvement
- Providing training if necessary
- Considering all alternatives to dismissal.

If the employer relies on **ill health** as the grounds of incapability there must be **proper medical evidence**. The employer is entitled to consider his own business needs.

In *Coulson v Felixstowe Dock & Rly Co Ltd 1975*, an employee was off work for considerable periods of time due to ill health. He was given six months to prove his fitness and warned that he would be regraded if he could not do so. He became ill again and was dismissed. It was held that the employer had acted reasonably and could not be expected to keep a job open indefinitely. The tribunal had to consider the fairness to the business as well as to the employee.

Interactive question 5: Unfair dismissal 2 [Difficulty level: Exam standard]

Indicate whether or not each of the following statements is correct.

The dismissal of an employee will constitute an unfair dismissal if it:

		Yes	No	Maybe
A	Is on the grounds of pregnancy	☐	☐	☐
B	Relates to an employee seeking to enforce the minimum wage	☐	☐	☐
C	Is on the grounds of the employee's misconduct	☐	☐	☐
D	Is due to the employee taking part in unofficial industrial action	☐	☐	☐

See **Answer** at the end of this chapter.

3.6 The effect of procedural irregularity

A dismissal may be unfair if it is carried out in breach of a relevant procedure relating to workplace dispute resolution. In these circumstances the tribunal may increase any award by up to 25% as a result of the employer's unreasonable failure to comply with that procedure. The tribunal may also reduce an award by up to 25% as a result of any unreasonable failure by the employee (s 3 Employment Act 2008).

The relevant procedure for these purposes is the Code of Practice on disciplinary and grievance issues published by the Advisory, Conciliation and Arbitration Service ('Acas'). Broadly speaking, this provides for investigation before taking action, notification to the employee of the nature of the disciplinary measures, a meeting to be held and for the employee to be able to appeal against any decision made against him. The code does not lay down a mandatory or rigid set of rules and does not prescribe time limits in which steps must be taken. Rather it sets out a set of standards which should be adhered to in any internal policy or procedure drawn up by the employer and provides for steps to be taken promptly and without unreasonable delay. The code is designed to encourage informal resolution and the emphasis is very much on communication and conciliation, aimed at avoiding the need for proceedings at an employment tribunal. The code does not apply to redundancy dismissals and non-renewal of fixed term contracts.

Acas has a discretion to offer conciliation services in the event of any dispute before it is presented to the tribunal and a duty to conciliate during any tribunal proceedings.

Note that if disciplinary action had already been taken before 6 April 2009 (the date on which the relevant provisions of the Employment Act 2008 came into force), the previous law will apply. In these circumstances, it is likely that a 'statutory dismissal and disciplinary procedure' will govern the procedure that the employer must follow in dismissing or taking disciplinary action against an employee and a breach of that procedure, if applicable, will render any dismissal automatically unfair.

3.7 Remedies for unfair dismissal

The remedies for unfair dismissal are more wide-ranging and may well be more advantageous to an employee than the remedy for wrongful dismissal. They are as follows:

Remedy	Description
Reinstatement	An order that the employee may return to the same job without any break of continuity. In deciding whether to exercise these powers, the tribunal must take into account whether the complainant wishes to be reinstated and whether it is reasonably practicable and just for the employer to comply. Such orders are in fact very infrequent.
Re-engagement	An order that the employee is given new employment with the employer (or his successor or associate) on terms that are comparable with the old job or otherwise suitable. The Employment Appeal Tribunal has ruled that an order for re-engagement should not be made if there has been a breakdown in confidence between the parties. This was in a case where the employee was dismissed following allegations of drug dealing on company premises and time-keeping offences. Compensation may be ordered in three categories (in each case subject to statutory maximums that are updated from time to time): • A **basic award**, calculated by reference to the employee's length of service and age and which is subject to a prescribed maximum amount. It is liable to be reduced where the employee unreasonably refuses an offer of reinstatement or otherwise behaves unreasonably. The basic award is also reduced by the amount of any redundancy payment made. However, the basic award is made for unfair dismissal regardless of the loss suffered by the employee and there is no duty on the employee to mitigate any loss. • A **compensatory award**, being such amount as the tribunal considers to be 'just and equitable in all the circumstances, having regard to the loss sustained by the complainant in consequence of the dismissal in so far as that loss is attributable to action taken by the employer' (and taking account of the basic award). This will be in respect of any additional loss of earnings, expenses and benefits and will be assessed on common law principles of damages for breach of contract, including a duty on the employee to take reasonable steps to mitigate any loss. • An **additional award**, which can only be awarded if the employer does not comply with an order for reinstatement or re-engagement and does not show that it was impracticable to do so. It comprises between 26 and 52 weeks' pay (subject to a prescribed maximum, as with the basic award).

In addition, a tribunal may order the employer to pay consequential losses to the employee to reflect any financial loss suffered as a result of the employer making unauthorised deductions or failing to make redundancy payments (s 7 Employment Act 2008).

4 Wrongful dismissal

Section overview

- Wrongful dismissal is a common law action that applies where an employer dismisses an employee in breach of contract.

- Summary dismissal may be justified in exceptional circumstances.

- The usual remedy for wrongful dismissal is damages but an injunction or declaration may be awarded.

4.1 Unfair dismissal or wrongful dismissal?

Although claims are most commonly brought for unfair dismissal nowadays, an action for wrongful dismissal can be brought instead or at the same time (although this is very rare). It might even be more advisable in certain circumstances, for example:

- Where an award of damages would exceed the statutory maximum for compensation in an unfair dismissal case

- Where a claim for unfair dismissal has not been brought within three months of the effective date of termination (an action for wrongful dismissal can be brought within six years of the breach)

- A dismissal might be 'fair' but nonetheless wrongful, if insufficient notice is given

- An employee might not qualify to bring a claim for unfair dismissal, for example if he lacks the necessary period of continuous employment.

Cases are commonly brought in the county court or High Court although employment tribunals have a concurrent jurisdiction.

4.2 What constitutes wrongful dismissal?

Wrongful dismissal occurs where the employer dismisses the employee in breach of the contract of employment. By way of example, wrongful dismissal may occur in any of the following circumstances:

- Where the employer terminates the employment with no notice

- Where the employer terminates the employment with less notice than is required by the contract or the statutory minimum periods of notice (see section 2.4)

- Where the employer terminates a contract for a fixed term or specific task before the expiry of that fixed term or before completion of the specific task

- Where the employee is selected for redundancy in breach of a selection procedure incorporated in his contract

- Where the employer wrongfully repudiates the contract and the employee 'accepts' his breach by resigning (this is the common law counterpart of the statutory 'constructive dismissal' discussed in relation to unfair dismissal)

- Where the contract provides for dismissal on specific grounds and the employee is dismissed on some other ground not included in the contract.

If the contract provides for the employer to terminate the contract without notice but subject to payment of a sum of money in lieu of notice, any dismissal is not wrongful but the employee may sue for the agreed sum under the contract in the event that the payment is not forthcoming. He will not be under any duty to mitigate his loss in such circumstances. Even where notice is given, it may still be possible for an employee to show some other breach and that he was wrongfully dismissed.

4.3 Summary dismissal

The employer will be justified in dismissing an employee summarily (ie with no notice or insufficient notice) in certain circumstances, in which case he incurs no liability. The following are examples of conduct by an employee which could justify summary dismissal by his employer:

- The **wilful refusal to obey** a lawful and reasonable order.

- **Gross misconduct**, in connection with the business (or outside it if it is sufficiently grave), for example, acceptance of a secret commission, disclosure of confidential information or assault on a fellow employee.

- **Dishonesty**, where the employee is in a position of trust.

- **Gross or persistent negligence** (and a lesser degree of neglect may suffice for senior employees) for example where an airline pilot landed his plane in a way that caused alarm among passengers and crew.

- **Breach of an express term** of the contract or work rules where the employee has been made aware that such a contravention will not be tolerated (for example, airline pilots may be subject to instant dismissal if they are found to be drunk or taking drugs).

Whether a dismissal is justified will be a question of fact based on the standards of ordinary people and the standards prevailing at the time (and decisions from old cases may be distinguished on this basis).

Summary dismissal also occurs where an employer is unable to continue to employ the employee, for example where a personal employer dies, an employing firm of partners is dissolved, an employing company is compulsorily wound up, or the employee's place of employment is permanently closed.

Interactive question 6: Wrongful dismissal   [Difficulty level: Exam standard]

Indicate whether or not each of the following represents circumstances under which an employer is likely to incur liability for wrongful dismissal:

		Yes	No
A	The employee has resigned as a result of his employer's serious breach of contract	☐	☐
B	An employee who has worked for an employer for six years is given one month's notice of dismissal	☐	☐
C	The contract between employer and employee states that the employee cannot be dismissed during a three month training period and the employer dismisses the employee after two months	☐	☐
D	The employee is guilty of gross negligence	☐	☐

See **Answer** at the end of this chapter.

4.4 Remedies for wrongful dismissal

Generally, the only effective remedy available to a wrongfully dismissed employee is a claim for **damages** based on the loss of earnings. The measure of damages is usually the sum that would have been earned **if proper notice had been given**, together with any other actual or potential benefits to which the employee was entitled. The employee is under a duty to **mitigate** his loss by, say, seeking other employment. The 'reasonableness' (or otherwise) of the employer's conduct will not be relevant, nor will questions of contributory conduct by the employee. The only issue is whether or not the employer is in breach of the contract of employment.

In rare cases an application might be made for an injunction to restrain a breach of contract or declaration as to what the employee's rights are. Both of these remedies are equitable and therefore in the court's discretion. Of course in the event of a breach of contract by the employer that falls short of a wrongful dismissal, the employee may sue for any loss suffered.

5 Redundancy

Section overview

- Redundancy is a form of dismissal (and may be fair or unfair depending on the circumstances).

- Redundancy gives rise to a right to a statutory redundancy payment provided certain criteria are met.

5.1 What is redundancy?

A dismissal is treated as caused by **redundancy** if the only or main reason is that:

- The employer has ceased, or intends to cease, to carry on the business for the purposes for which the employee has been employed, or

- The employer has ceased, or intends to cease to carry on the business in the **place** where the employee was employed, or

- The requirements of that business for employees to carry out work of a **particular kind**, or for them to carry out the work in the place where they were so employed, have ceased or diminished.

If the employee's contract contains a **mobility clause**, enabling the employer to require him to work at other places than his present place of employment, then any such requirement (because there is no longer work at his present place of employment) will not constitute redundancy. However, the tribunal has held that the fact that there is a mobility clause does not mean that 'the place where the employee was employed' is extended to include every place where he **could** be employed.

The proper test for determining whether or not an employee is redundant is to see whether there has been a reduction of the employer's requirements for employees to work at the place where the person concerned is employed. This is a question of fact.

In *British Broadcasting Corporation v Farnworth 1998* a radio producer's fixed term contract was not renewed and the employer advertised for a radio producer with more experience. It was held by the EAT that the less experienced radio producer was indeed redundant as the requirement for her level of services had diminished.

5.2 The right to a redundancy payment

Redundancy pay is calculated on the same basis as the basic award for unfair dismissal (ie according to age and length of service).

A person may claim a redundancy payment, provided he

- Is an **'employee'** within the Employment Rights Act 1996 (self-employed and partners are not covered) and

- Has been **continuously employed** for at least **2 years** at the relevant date and

- Follows the **procedure** for making a claim set out in the Act.

He must show that he has been:

- **Dismissed** by reason of redundancy, or

- **Laid off** or **kept on short time** for 4 or more consecutive weeks or 6 weeks in a period of 13 weeks. (He is 'laid off' in any week in which he earns nothing due to lack of work. He is 'kept on short time' in any week in which he earns less than half a normal week's pay).

He must apply to the employment tribunal within **six months** from the relevant date of termination (although the tribunal has a discretion to allow a late claim within the following six months).

He will **not be entitled** to a redundancy payment if he

- Is guilty of misconduct which would justify dismissal or

- Refuses a reasonable offer to renew his contract or

- Unreasonably refuses an offer of suitable alternative employment in the same capacity, at the same place and on the same terms and conditions as his previous employment, not being perceived as lower in status.

When there is a difference between the terms and conditions of a new contract and the previous contract, the employee is entitled to a **four week trial** period in the new employment. If either party terminates the new contract during the trial period, it is treated as a case of dismissal for redundancy at the expiry date of the previous employment. The employee can also still bring a claim for unfair dismissal.

Worked example: Redundancy

Amy works for Sparkle Windows Ltd in its factory in Basingstoke where she has worked for 18 years. Her contract contains a mobility clause providing that she may need to work in Winchester or Bournemouth if required. When Sparkle Windows Ltd closed the factory in Basingstoke, Amy travelled to Bournemouth but after a few weeks she resigned, saying that the travelling was making her ill and claiming statutory redundancy payment. Her employer refused, relying on the mobility clause in the contract.

Solution

Amy is entitled to a statutory redundancy payment. She is an employee with more than 2 years' continuous employment and has been dismissed for reasons of redundancy, namely that Sparkle Windows Ltd no longer has need of employees at the place where Amy was employed. The fact that she could be required to work elsewhere in Bournemouth and Winchester did not mean that she was to be regarded as being employed in those places.

Interactive question 7: Non-renewal of fixed term contract

[Difficulty level: Exam standard]

Nick commences employment under a three-year contract with Equis Ltd. After two years, he is given notice that the contract is not to be renewed. Which of the following claims might he seek to bring against Equis Ltd?

☐ Wrongful dismissal
☐ Unfair dismissal
☐ Constructive dismissal
☐ Redundancy pay claim

See **Answer** at the end of this chapter.

6 The Data Protection Act 1998

Section overview

- The Act is concerned with personal data (subject to some exemptions) held on computer-based information systems and manual files.

- The purpose of the Act is to protect individuals from misuse of information about them.

- The Act requires all those who hold or process personal data to comply with eight data protection principles in relation to that data.

- Individuals are given rights in relation to their personal data, such as rights of access and the right to prevent processing which is likely to cause damage or distress.

Data controllers are individuals, partnerships or companies who hold data that is processed or intended to be processed for their own use.

Data subjects are individuals (not companies) to whom personal data relate.

You should be aware that a proposed European data protection regulation is likely to make significant changes to data protection law in member states, although changes are not expected before 2014.

6.1 Scope and purpose

This Act applies where personal data is held on computer-based information systems or manual files. **Personal data** means data relating to an individual who can be identified from the data with or without other information in the data controller's possession. Note that as well as covering the recording of **facts**, the Act includes any expression of **opinion** about the individual or **intentions** of the data controller in relation to the data subject. The Act is also concerned with any 'processing' of the data, including the collection, use, disclosure and destruction of it.

The purpose of the Act is to protect individuals from use of incorrect information or misuse of correct, but confidential, information.

6.2 Penalties for non-compliance

Non-compliance with the Act may result in

- Civil liability in proceedings brought by the data subject

- Criminal liability to a fine (or, in very rare cases, imprisonment)

- The court ordering that relevant databases be forfeited, destroyed or erased

- Cost of rectifications

- A fine of up to £500,000 imposed by the Information Commissioner (for serious contravention of the eight principles (below) in a way likely to cause substantial damage or distress)

A data controller must notify the Information Commissioner (who maintains a public register of data controllers in the UK) of its data processing operations. Failure to notify the Information Commissioner is a criminal offence.

For each data controller the register will show (among other things) the types of data, the purpose for which the data is held and who the data subjects are.

6.3 The eight data protection principles

The Act sets out eight data protection principles with which data controllers must comply when holding or processing personal data as follows:

	The principle
Lawful processing	Personal data shall be processed fairly and lawfully
Lawful purpose	Personal data shall be obtained only for one or more specified and lawful purposes, and shall not be further processed in any manner incompatible with that purpose or those purposes
Relevant, not excessive	Personal data shall be adequate, relevant and not excessive in relation to the purpose or purposes for which they are processed
Accurate	Personal data shall be accurate and, where necessary, kept up to date
Length of time	Personal data shall not be kept for longer than is necessary for the purpose for which it is processed
Rights	Personal data shall be processed in accordance with the rights of data subjects under the Act
Technical and organisational measures	Appropriate technical and organisational measures shall be taken against unauthorised or unlawful processing of personal data and against accidental loss, or damage to personal data
Transfer outside Europe	Personal data shall not be transferred to a country outside the European Economic Area unless that country or territory ensures an adequate level of protection for data subjects

6.4 The rights of data subjects

The rights of data subjects are as follows:

	The right
Access	Right of subjects to access data held about them (which must not be kept in an encoded form). Principally, a subject can obtain a copy of information held, including any in pictorial form
Avoidance of damage	Prevention of processing likely to cause damage or distress
Junk mail	Prevention of processing for direct-marketing (junk mail)
Automatic decisions	To request that no decision that materially affects you should be based solely on automatic processes (for example, automatic credit scoring)
Compensation	Right to compensation if damage is caused by contravention of the Act
Action against inaccurate data	Right to take action to rectify or destroy inaccurate data
Information Commissioner	Right to ask the Information Commissioner to assess whether the Act has been contravened

6.5 Exemptions from the Act

Certain data is exempt from the Act which means that the eight data protection principles and the data subject's rights will not apply to this data. The following are exempt from the Act either because of their routine nature or because of security implications.

- Payroll and accounts
- Examination scripts
- Personal data held by unincorporated members' clubs
- Domestic data, eg household affairs
- Research where data does not identify data subject and is not used for any other purpose
- Data relating to crime prevention (including tax evasion)
- Data relating to national security
- Confidential references given by data controllers

 Interactive question 8: Data Protection Act 1998 **[Difficulty level: Exam standard]**

Kylie is a data subject of Compliance Ltd. She has asked to see the information held about her by the company on its personnel files. In doing so, she has discovered that the data was inaccurate, as it had not been updated to reflect the fact that Kylie has remarried and changed her name. She is also cross that the company has refused to show her its payroll records, as she is convinced that she is being paid less than a colleague of hers.

Answer the following questions:

	Yes	No
A Does the company face a potential criminal liability for maintaining inaccurate data?	☐	☐
B Is the company bound to pay her compensation in respect of the inaccuracy?	☐	☐
C Can Kylie demand access to the company's payroll records?	☐	☐
D Can Kylie demand that the company correct the data?	☐	☐

See **Answer** at the end of this chapter.

Summary and Self-test

Summary

(Sections 1–2 of this chapter)

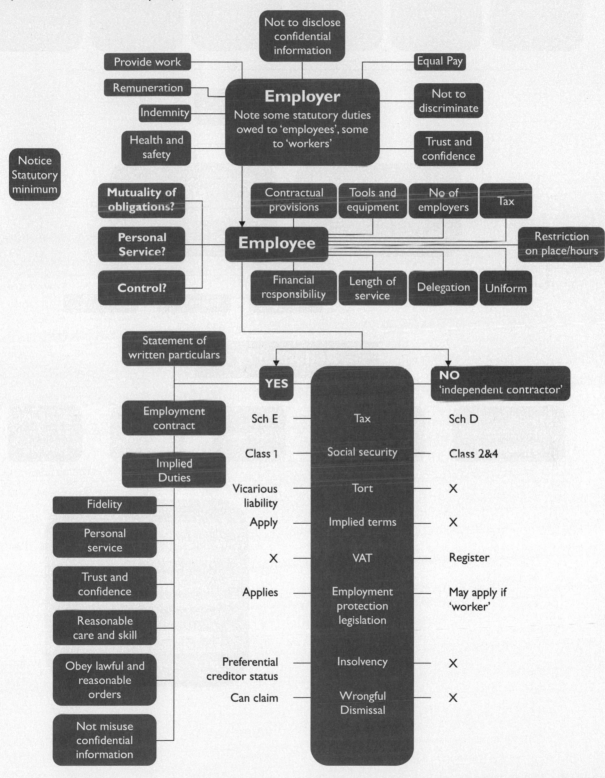

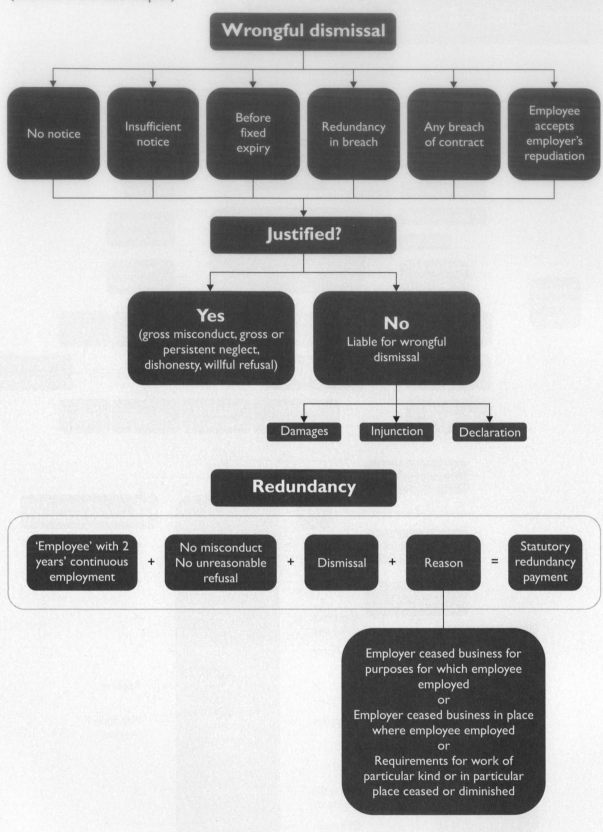

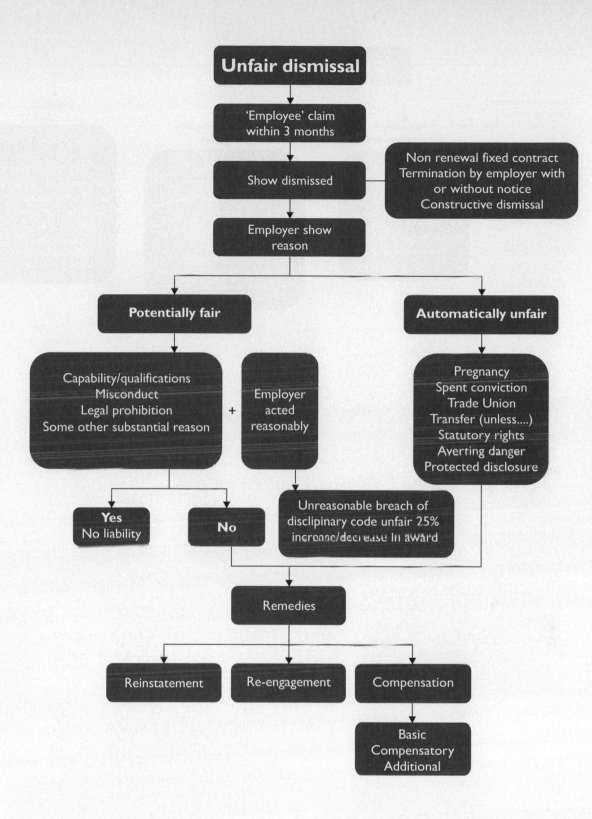

Unfair dismissal

'Employee' claim within 3 months

Show dismissed

Non renewal fixed contract
Termination by employer with or without notice
Constructive dismissal

Employer show reason

Potentially fair

Capability/qualifications
Misconduct
Legal prohibition
Some other substantial reason

+

Employer acted reasonably

Automatically unfair

Pregnancy
Spent conviction
Trade Union
Transfer (unless....)
Statutory rights
Averting danger
Protected disclosure

Yes
No liability

No

Unreasonable breach of disciplinary code unfair 25% increase/decrease in award

Remedies

Reinstatement

Re-engagement

Compensation

Basic
Compensatory
Additional

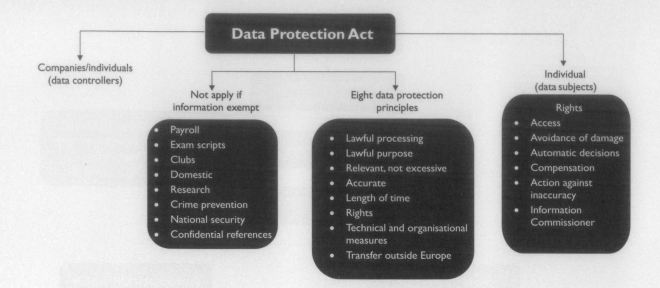

Self-test

Answer the following questions.

1 Identify six of the factors taken into account in determining whether or not someone is an independent contractor rather than an employee.

- ....
- ....
- ....
- ....
- ....
- ....

2 Working for more than one employer is an automatic sign of self-employment.

True ☐

False ☐

3 Are partners employees?

4 Unless there is a mutuality of obligations, to provide and to perform work, there cannot be a contract of employment and the person working cannot be an employee.

True ☐

False ☐

5 Name five matters in respect of which the distinction between employed and self-employed workers is important.

- ....
- ....
- ....
- ....
- ....

6 Within what period must an employer provide a written statement of employment particulars where no contract has been provided?

7 Which of the following are duties owed by the employer by health and safety legislation?

A To ensure adequate access to places of work

B To make provision for medical personnel at the place of work

C To ensure the safe-keeping of an employee's personal effects while he is engaged in his work duties

D To provide a healthy working environment

8 What is the statutory minimum period of notice to which an employee with 5 years' continuous service is entitled?

9 What is the necessary period of continuous employment for an unfair dismissal claim where dismissal is for the following reasons?

A Lack of qualification
B Making a protected disclosure
C Pregnancy

10   List the five potentially fair reasons for dismissal.

- ....

- ....

- ....

- ....

- ....

11   Name three automatically unfair reasons for dismissal.

- ....

- ....

- ....

12   By how much may an award be adjusted in order to take account of an unreasonable failure to comply with the Acas code of practice in a dismissal?

13   Which is the most frequent remedy awarded for unfair dismissal?

A   Compensation
B   Re-engagement
C   Reinstatement

14   Is summary dismissal ever justified? If so, when? Give two examples.

- ....

- ....

15   Name the 3 remedies available for wrongful dismissal.

- ....

- ....

- ....

16   What is the necessary period of continuous employment in a claim for a statutory redundancy payment?

17   The Data Protection Act applies to all companies in the UK.

☐ True

☐ False

18   Which of the following is not one of the eight data protection principles?

A   Personal data shall be accurate and, where necessary, kept up to date
B   Personal data shall not be kept for longer than six years
C   Personal data shall be adequate, relevant and not excessive

19   Is data relating to an employee's medical health including drug testing exempt from the Data Protection Act?

Now, go back to the Learning Objectives in the Introduction. If you are satisfied you have achieved these objectives, please tick them off.

Answers to Interactive questions

Answer to Interactive question 1

D   Assuming that there is no intention for Charles to be paid even when he is not required to work, then he is a casual worker and not an employee because there is no mutuality of obligations. If he were to be paid even in the absence of work, he would be an employee. In those circumstances, even though he does not receive an employment contract, the facts indicate a contract of service, since the employer provides the tools, controls when and where he works and reserves the right to dismiss him.

Answer to Interactive question 2

A   Yes.

B   No. An employer may be vicariously responsible for his employee's tortious acts.

C   Yes.

D   Yes.

Answer to Interactive question 3

A   True.

B   False. The duty is to pay the remuneration agreed between the parties (which, arguably, might not be 'reasonable'). However, in the absence of any express provision, the duty is then to pay reasonable remuneration.

C   True. However, if he does choose to provide one, he is obliged to ensure that it is accurate and fair.

D   False. He need not obey if obedience to the instruction would require him to do an unlawful act, expose himself to personal danger or do something outside his contract.

Answer to Interactive question 4

In both cases unfair dismissal may have taken place. Asif meets the continuous employment requirement (of one year, because he was employed prior to April 2012) and has been dismissed, so qualifies as a candidate for unfair dismissal if the circumstances surrounding the dismissal were unfair. Although Beatrice has not been employed continuously for two years, this is irrelevant as she has been dismissed for pregnancy.

Answer to Interactive question 5

A   Yes. Pregnancy-related dismissal is automatically unfair.

B   Yes. Dismissal as a result of the employee trying to enforce the national minimum wage is automatically unfair.

C   Maybe. The misconduct must be sufficiently serious.

D   No. An employee dismissed for this reason is not a qualifying employee within the Act.

Answer to Interactive question 6

The employer is likely to incur liability for wrongful dismissal in all cases except D, since gross negligence on the employee's part will justify summary dismissal.

Answer to Interactive question 7

Unfair dismissal or a claim for redundancy pay, provided he can prove the requisite facts. However, non-renewal cannot give rise to a claim for wrongful dismissal (although termination **before** the expiry of a fixed term contract would). Constructive dismissal is not relevant in this scenario.

Answer to Interactive question 8

A   Yes

B   No, only if Kylie could show loss

C   No, it is exempt from the Act

D   Yes

Answers to Self-test

1.
   - Who provides and maintains tools and equipment
   - Whether the person can delegate or subcontract
   - Whether the person wears the employer's uniform or displays its logo
   - Whether tax is deducted at source
   - Whether the person works for one or more parties
   - Whether there is any restriction on hours or place of work
   - Whether holiday and/or sick pay is provided for
   - The length of employment

2. False

3. Generally speaking, no (although a salaried partner, for example, may be).

4. True

5.
   - Social security
   - Taxation
   - Employment protection
   - Tortious acts
   - Health and safety
   - Implied terms
   - VAT
   - Rights on insolvency

6. Within two months after commencement of the employment

7. A and D

8. 5 weeks (1 week for each year's continuous service)

9.
   A 2 years
   B None
   C None

10.
    - Lack of capability or qualification
    - Employee's misconduct
    - Legal prohibition
    - Redundancy
    - Some other substantial reason

11.
    - Pregnancy
    - Spent conviction
    - Trade union membership or activities
    - Enforcement of statutory right
    - Protected disclosure
    - Taking steps to avert danger to health and safety at work

12. By up to 25% more (employer's failure) or less (employee's failure)

13. A Compensation

14. Yes, in cases of serious breach of contract by the employee (for example gross negligence or wilful refusal to obey lawful instructions).

15.
    - Damages
    - Injunction
    - Declaration

16. 2 years

17. True

18. B The principle is that data shall not be kept for longer than is necessary for the purpose for which it is processed.

19. No

Index

R

S

T

ICAEW

ICAEW

ICAEW

REVIEW FORM – LAW STUDY MANUAL

Your ratings, comments and suggestions would be appreciated on the following areas of this Study Manual.

	Very useful	Useful	Not useful
Chapter Introductions	☐	☐	☐
Examination context	☐	☐	☐
Worked examples	☐	☐	☐
Interactive questions	☐	☐	☐
Quality of explanations	☐	☐	☐
Technical references (where relevant)	☐	☐	☐
Self-test questions	☐	☐	☐
Self-test answers	☐	☐	☐
Index	☐	☐	☐

	Excellent	Good	Adequate	Poor
Overall opinion of this Study Manual	☐	☐	☐	☐

Please add further comments below:

Please return completed form to:
The Learning Team
Learning and Professional Department
ICAEW
Metropolitan House
321 Avebury Boulevard
Milton Keynes
MK9 2FZ
Elearning@icaew.com